Bruce Piloom
October 19 ♡ **W9-BOK-024**

546672

5418
H68
1982

JX
5418
H68
1982

HOROWITZ, IRVING

TAKING LIVES: GENOCIDE
AND STATE POWER

DISCARD

APR 0 8 1986
MAY - 9 1986
JUL 3  1989
JUL 1 7 1989

DEC 0 6 1995

APR 1 8 1997

# TAKING LIVES

## GENOCIDE AND STATE POWER

### Third Edition (Augmented)

Irving Louis Horowitz

CHAMPLAIN COLLEGE

Transaction Books
New Brunswick (U.S.A.) and London (U.K.)

Augmented third edition published 1982.

New material this edition copyright © 1982. Third edition copyright © 1980 by Transaction, Inc., New Brunswick, N.J. 08903.

All rights reserved under International and Pan-American Copyright Conventions. No part of this book may be reproduced or transmitted in any form or by any means, electronic or mechanical, including photography, recording, or any information storage and retrieval system, without prior permission in writing from the publisher. All inquiries should be addressed to Transaction Books, Rutgers—The State University, New Brunswick, New Jersey 08903.

Library of Congress Catalog Number: 79-66341
ISBN: 0-87855-882-9
Printed in the United States of America

**Library of Congress Cataloging in Publication Data**

Horowitz, Irving Louis.
    Taking lives.

    (Issues in contemporary civilization)
    Includes index.
    1. Genocide.  I.  Title.
JX5418.H68        301.5'92        79-66341
ISBN 0-87855-882-9 pbk.

# Contents

# Preface to the Augmented Third Edition

Any author must consider it good fortune when a work is still in demand after three editions. Still, this situation thrust upon me a small, but genuine problem: how to handle the "standard" third edition, which is only one year old, and the desire to add two more pieces to this puzzle without end.

It has become clear that my original treatment of genocide with respect to the Holocaust raised many problems, not least being the relationship between sociological and theological perspectives. Hence, I have decided to add, as an eleventh chapter, a discussion pinpointing the substance and range of the sensitive issues of definition.

I also felt compelled to add as an Appendix a demographic note detailing, indirectly to be sure, the extent and number of genocidal victims in the Soviet Union. It is a startling fact that other than the rather vague and off-handed remarks of a few politicians and writers, no scientific study of genocide within the Soviet Union has been undertaken. Hence, the need to make this data available seems sufficiently evident to justify publication in this ad hoc manner.

It should be added that no changes whatsoever were made to the Third Edition of *Taking Lives*. As a result, the present version is simply being called Third Edition (Augmented). In this way, readers and purchasers of the present edition need not feel compelled to seek out this new material, nor should they feel that the thesis of the book as such has in any way, either in general or in detail, been altered.

Irving Louis Horowitz
Princeton, New Jersey

# Foreword

In this remarkable, carefully reasoned but passionately argued book, Irving Louis Horowitz challenges our thinking on several of the most important contemporary issues—not merely those faced by social scientists, but those deeply significant for humans around the globe. Taking as his test-case issue the terrifying phenomenon of genocide, which he links in an entirely convincing argument with the rise of the nation-state, Horowitz challenges social scientists to grapple with both that all too prevalent phenomenon and that linkage with governments which now have the technological means to eradicate whole peoples within their own borders. I would agree with him that the major social science positions fail us badly in understanding those excruciatingly painful human issues.

The nation-state that gives us genocide ought to make us question the nation-state itself; this questioning is at the center of Horowitz's inquiry as he raises unforgettable questions about state power and collectivism, bureaucracy, terrorism (the best discussion of terrorism that I have seen), and the fate of human rights, individualism, and humanism.

Something of this basic position is suggested by a key sentence near the end of *Taking Lives* where he argues both against extreme statism and the social scientists who further it with schemes of "development," vulgar economism, manpower considerations, and other related intellectual concerns: "System building urges us not to worry about how many peoples' lives are taken, but to worry about the nature of the social system. I am arguing the reverse: that we worry less about the nature of the social system and more about how many lives are taken (whether by genocide, incarceration, war, or sacrifices demanded in the name of development) by each system, state or nation."

Horowitz's handling of the historical issues central to his argument owes much to traditions that knowledgeable readers will recognize, but the framing and range of questions and discussion are entirely his own. I would predict this book will long be read not in the hackneyed sense of "a social science classic," but because it will continue to state the case so brilliantly and persuasively for a human and creative democratic society, no matter how difficult it may be to attain such a society under late twentieth and twenty-first century conditions. Horowitz reminds us that social scientists have moral and possibly critical roles to play in the continuing political struggle.

Anselm L. Strauss
San Francisco, California
September 15, 1979

# Introduction

# Genocide and State Power

*One day in the afternoon of the world, glum death will come and sit in you, and when you get up to walk, you will be as glum as death, but if you're lucky, this will only make the fun better and the love greater.*

William Saroyan, ONE DAY IN THE AFTERNOON
OF THE WORLD

There is an old publishing adage, perhaps with as little standing as other hoary beliefs, to which I nonetheless subscribe: that one can modestly revise a second edition of a book, but to have a successful third edition, one must rethink a work in its entirety. I have done just that. First, in the light of changing circumstances; second, in terms of a deeper probing of the issues which I had initially raised; and third, as a response to commentaries received in reviews and correspondence from friends and colleagues.

The work has been so altered and expanded that rather than consider this a third edition, I prefer to think of it as a new work—which is why I took the liberty of giving it a new title. What began as a brief monograph, in the mode of a thoughtful essay, has now more than doubled in length, and hopefully deepened in scope. I have carefully researched the literature on the subject of genocide and,

ix

where appropriate, have added discussions of other works, while otherwise simply indicating an awareness of such efforts that have been made.

Given the ubiquitous nature of American publishing, I cannot say whether such an expansion makes this a "scholarly" or a "trade" book. This is hardly worth a ripple of thought—save for the fact that serious decisions about publishing, marketing, and format are at stake. My decision to change the title for this work indicates a concern to have the best of both the scholarly and trade worlds. These strategic considerations now accounted for, I should like to briefly address those areas of the work which have been expanded, added, and hopefully strengthened.

First, is the inclusion of a new chapter on the subject of individualism and state power, specifically on how taking life has become collectivized and transformed into an engineering feat. The tragic immolation which took place at Guyana should convince even the hard-headed communard that the loss of individual responsibility for one's own life and the corresponding failure to measure each case of arbitrary death in a singular manner, must lead us to pause and consider how the breakdown of individualism and its displacement with collectivism are profoundly related phenomena, adding a special dimension to the area of social structure and personality.

Second, is the addition of a section on "Revolution, Retribution, and Redemption." My concern is not simply to evaluate the *Gulag Archipelago* as the prototype of modern systems of incarceration and genocide, but to investigate how entire societies, and not just smaller total institutions, become absorbed in the genocidal process; how genocide is internalized as part of the experience labeled development, change, growth, revolution—all at the terrible expense of human life. This chapter is concerned with the justification of genocide by state power, as well as the forms of resistance to such justification engaged in by individuals capable of snapping the boundaries of the total institution.

Third, is the addition of what might for shorthand purposes be termed a chapter on the Amnesty International factor: the inclusion of new data on the treatment of political prisoners, minority groups, and deviant elements in a society, and how human rights become an element in policymaking. The incorporation of the typology herein first explored—one which understands the centrality of the experience of death in political regimes boasting stability and manifesting instability—whether they be Uganda, China, or Chile—enriches my effort. Beyond that, this volume provides the first evidence that genocide as a social indicator is a master factor in the human rights movement, however abortive, fragmented, and even hyprocritical that movement may have become in just a few years.

Fourth, the chapter on "Democracy and Terrorism" is related to the subject of genocide elliptically, since most acts of terror have a random quality—their increasingly organized aspects notwithstanding—whereas most acts of genocide are highly organized activities of the state. The relationship between the state and terrorism becomes itself an area of intense public debate, since in the effort to stamp out expressions of politically inspired homicide we frequently make appeals to the very organs of state authority which are the source of genocidal practice. This problem deserves treatment, if only to reveal the agonizing complexity of the issues.

Fifth, certain compressions and amalgamations from the original text have also been made. For example, the separate chapters on functional and existential visions of genocide have been collapsed into a single chapter. I have expanded discussion of alternative newer theories seeking to provide a social scientific explanation for genocide. The question and answer segment of the second edition has been revised and included in the appropriate places within the chapters as reorganized. This special postscript to the second edition came about because at the time (1976) I had decided not to make a thorough overhauling of the text. Now that such a decision has been made, the need for such a special supplement is obviated.

Sixth, the seriousness with which I view the phrase *state power* is also reflected in this volume. With the addition of a new chapter on bureaucracy and state power, and the amplification of the chapters on individualism and collectivism, the essential role of authority in *Taking Lives* is now more clearly etched. For genocide is neither capricious nor accidental. Neither does it follow any inexorable "laws" of economic development. Hence, making plain the essential nexus between genocide and statecraft became a central chore in the further reconsideration of this volume.

I have spent the better part of a quarter century—from *The Idea of War and Peace* to *Genocide and State Power*—on a subject that has a grimness on the face of it. Worse, it is the sort of subject that has few, if any, satisfactory answers, little operational utility, and one that just will not easily pass into the night. Things have, by all odds, become much worse. Comparisons between the fourteenth century and its "black plagues" and the twentieth century and its holocausts, nuclear explosions, and death-wish cults have become commonplace—much to the disadvantage of the present.

Yet I feel little sense of pessimism. The reason is the indefatigable spirit of human beings. Just when one thinks China is hopelessly mired in a totalitarian nightmare, voices of opposition are heard loud and clear; just as the Jewish communities of the Soviet Union seem to be passing into a quiet oblivion under a blueprint arranged by a Stalinist vision of the national question, massive opposition and emigration take place. Just as the Indians are said to have become a statistically insignificant demographic category in the American West, Indian consciousness, landholding claims, and political organization emerge out of the ashes. This, multiplied a hundred-fold, is a source of strength and realism.

To write the history of genocide as one long, uninterrupted nightmare is only a limited vision and a partial truth. The victims of genocide have often survived with integrity and even numbers quite intact; whereas oppressors have gone quietly into the long, still night of political oblivion. Any social analyst must be careful to avoid the twin errors of banality and sentimentality. A high price has been paid for social and political knowledge in our age—perhaps any age—although the obstacles to mature information have scarcely been greater. But that knowledge now exists at a level and among large numbers of people which, while not preventing an oppressive increase in genocide as an "ultimate weapon" of state power and its subordinates, has at least brought out into the open the fundamental struggle between individuals and states, persons and collectivities, justice and the law. Undue reification and polarization aside, a return to basics is long overdue. It alone makes possible the reconstruction of social science along lines more valuable and meaningful than the dross we have so painstakingly shed.

The most difficult decision I had to make was to change the title from *Genocide: State Power and Mass Murder* to a more succinct and yet more appropriate title — *Taking Lives*. But in order to express a sense of continuity with the earlier editions, I have kept as subtitle the phrase *Genocide and State Power*. It is the special relationship between the state and its monopoly on life-taking propensities that forms the essence of this work. The equation of state power and mass murder in the original subtitle does not accurately convey this special relationship of genocidal and state practice: this presumption of taking life as a unique capacity, morally and legally, of the authority system within a society. Beyond that, special pains have been taken to show genocide to be a singular type of mass murder, a historically distinct event that had its ultimate expression in the Holocaust.

It is impossible to write about genocide and state power and remain neutral to the notion of the state any more than one can be indifferent to the act of collective murder. I admit to a deepening sense of religiosity in my writings; hopefully, not at the expense of social science. In a century not just touched by, but saturated in such a terrible infliction as genocide, one must face the consequence, the lessons, of such a work. It is not just genocide which is evil, but the state which breeds such a monstrous total solution. It is not for nothing that Karl Marx spoke of "the withering away of the State" as a social goal.[1] Like in so many of his concepts, description is mixed with a good dose of prescription. But the Sovietization of the Marxist tradition, its infection with that terrible hybrid called Leninism-Stalinism converted the state from an evil to a good: the state, which began in Marx as a fundamental instrument of oppression, ended in Stalin and his successors as the instrument of all authority, the fountain of all wisdom, the source of all judgment.

To uphold the dignity of humanity, the original impulse behind Marx, means to oppose the state as the ultimate repository for all human goods. The words of Leo Baeck, writing from the inferno of the nazi concentration camps, carry forth the essential judgment on the state which animates my spirit, the spirit of this new edition.

The contemporary state "was to exist for its own sake. Its task and its function were not the good of the people whom it incorporated. The people existed for it, that it might have and strengthen its might. It did not demand its right from the imperium of belief, nor from the men from whom it took its existence; it carried its right within itself. It stood above morality, outside of conscience." Baeck knew too that behind the apparatus stands the degraded person doing its bidding remorselessly, without compassion. "Like the state, the servant of the state easily became something conceptual and mechanical—concepts can become machines. He ceased to be human as a 'servant of the state.' One is tempted to think of the legend of the 'Golem,' the untiring human shape without the essentials of a living human being."[2]

It is a sad truth that issues of great magnitude, like genocide, have passed from social theorists in the nineteenth century to theologians in the twentieth century. The impulse to know more about less has not simply invaded the social sciences, it is an impulse which offers guidance to such supposedly human sciences. If there is a higher purpose to this work, if one dare even to invoke teleological reasoning, it is to remind my brethren that the unity of social science, if it is to be more than a pious phrase, rests on the unity of human existence. The mobilization of our resources to attack a problem such as genocide is not a risky artifact demanding a suspension of scientific judgment, but quite the reverse, an issue which all people of this century are common witness to, and hence an area of investigation which demands the fullest utilization of scientific judgment.

Because the tendency to emotivism is so tempting it should not be permitted to preempt what is essentially an analytic examination. The hideous features of genocide are grave enough not to cheapen the phenomenon by pandering to oversimplified visions of good and evil. Yet one can hope that moral concerns will be strengthened by the explanations and evidence herein adduced. My work in this area has had a double mission: "externally" to examine the nature, history, and structure of genocide and its relations to organs of authority; and "internally" to examine the nature, history, and structure of social science and its relations to these same organs of authority—disguised as representatives of scientific information. The years that have passed in this area of my work convince me anew that the effort has been worthwhile and the goals, analytically at least, achievable.

Perhaps it is now clear why I chose to open this work with an apparently quixotic statement by William Saroyan, that genial giant of American literature and not incidentally, firm Armenian conscience. His special sense of human endurance well illustrates a master theme of this volume: the capacity of living and loving that goes on as long as the human species continues. Attempts to destroy social groups by states taking lives are rarely completely successful. Jews, Armenians, Ugandans, Vietnamese, Bantus, and untold other peoples share the strength of survival no less than the scars of genocide. This is why, in the pursuit of the sources of liquidation, I have tried to take into account the roots of human growth.

Irving Louis Horowitz
Princeton, New Jersey
March 15, 1979

# Notes to Introduction and Frontispiece Quotes

1.     Marx, Karl, and Friedrich Engels. "Manifesto of the Communist Party"; and Karl Marx, "Critique of the Gotha Program," *Basic Writings on Politics and Philosophy*, edited by Lewis S. Feuer. Garden City, New York: Doubleday/Anchor, 1959. pp. 1-41; pp. 112-132.

2.     Baeck, Leo. *This People Israel: The Meaning of Jewish Existence* (translated with an introduction by Albert H. Friedlander). Philadelphia: The Jewish Publication Society of America, 1964. pp. 314-315.

(Intro) Saroyan, William. *One Day in the Afternoon of the World*. New York: Harcourt, Brace, and World, 1964. p. ix.

(ch.1)  Merleau-Ponty, Maurice. *Humanism and Terror*. Boston: Beacon Press, 1969. p. 88.

(ch.2)  Arendt, Hannah. *Eichmann in Jerusalem: A Report on the Banality of Evil. Revised and enlarged edition. New York: Viking Press, 1964.*

(ch.3)  Böll, Heinrich. *Missing Persons and Other Essays*. New York: McGraw Hill Co., 1977. p. 223.

(ch.4)  Yeats, William Butler. *A Vision*. Quoted in *The Politics of Twentieth Century Novelists*, edited by George A. Panichas. New York: Thomas Y. Cromwell, 1974. p. xlix.

(ch.5)  Hersey, John. *The Wall*. New York: Alfred A. Knopf, 1950. p. 426.

(ch.6)  Djilas, Milovan. *Land Without Justice*. New York: Harcourt, Brace and Co., 1958. p. 166.

(ch.7)  Weber, Max. *Wirtschaft und Gesellschaft (Economy and Society*, part III, ch. 6) in *From Max Weber: Essays in Sociology*, edited by H. H. Gerth and C. Wright Mills. New York: Oxford University Press, 1946, pp. 240-44.

(ch.8)  Camus, Albert. *Resistance, Rebellion, and Death*. New York: Alfred A. Knopf, 1961. pp. 141-42.

(ch.9)  Rahv, Philip. *Essays on Literature and Politics: 1932-1972*. Boston: Houghton Mifflin Co., 1978. p. 147.

(ch.10) Wiesel, Elie. *Messengers of God: Biblical Portraits and Legends*. New York: Random House, 1976.

(ch.11) Dawidowicz, Lucy S.  *The War Against the Jews: 1933-1945*. New York: Holt, Rinehart & Winston, 1973. p. 342.

# Chapter 1

# Life, Death, and Sociology

*The ideas for which one lives and dies are by this very fact absolute, and one cannot at the same time treat them as relative truths which might be calmly compared with others and literally criticized.*

*Maurice Merleau-Ponty,* HUMANISM AND TERROR

The certainty of death is one of the few unchallenged facts of life. Hotly contested are the forms in which any individual will perish. This is a work on one such form: genocide. As such, it is not an exercise in the problem of death as such. An individual may hope for a natural end in old age. People may accept as equally natural, death as a consequence of sickness or disease. Accidental death, while hardly condoned, is not subject to social condemnation either. Death as a *social* problem in contrast to a *biographical* event begins when life is terminated as an arbitrary action by others.

First, there is death by capital punishment undertaken with the authority of law for specific crimes. Second, there is death brought about through participation in warfare, as a result of a defense of nation or assault upon another sovereign. This too carries with it the force of law, and is undertaken not with death as an end, but as a consequence of preserving or extending basic human values. Third, there is death by murder, taking life, often without official sanction, and not infrequently as an "act of passion" performed by one individual against another.

This volume is concerned with a special form of murder: state-sanctioned liquidation against a collective group, without regard to

1

whether an individual has committed any specific and punishable transgression. As the volume unfolds, a more detailed and richer definition of genocide will be offered, as well as formulas and models considered as less than noteworthy or satisfactory. But as an opening gambit, while issues of life and death are inextricably woven into the fabric of this volume, its specific focus is upon genocide. In a larger picture, genocide might be viewed as a special case of murder; but at the same time, genocide has come to define that larger picture by becoming an essential and unique expression of our century.

Mass murder and warfare among peoples is an ever-present truth of humankind. Genocide and its more intimate varieties like regicide, have been around for centuries. What makes genocide a particularly malevolent practice in this century, with wide-ranging consequences, is the role of modern technology in the systematic destruction of large numbers of innocents. Just as Hiroshima and Nagasaki moved us beyond the realm of warfare to annihilation, so too Auschwitz and other Nazi death camps moved us beyond the realm of sporadic assaults, to systematic dismemberment of populations. On this, Hannah Arendt spoke well and wisely, declaring that the current epoch in history is distinguished not by a desire to liquidate total populations, but the actual capacity to do so.[1] This gives the issue of genocide a cogency and urgency it formerly lacked.

The increase in the degree of technological ability to do away with large numbers and the concentration of that efficiency in the hands of small numbers of military or police cadres, qualitatively change the issue of genocide from random events to systematic policies. Analytical problems remain: To what extent can one describe the liquidation of peoples through such events as ecological and environmental discrimination as genocidal? Are diseases brought to subject peoples a form of systematic liquidation? How is the issue of ethnocide related to genocide; or is all genocide peculiarly geared to the isolation and elimination of an ethnic, national, or racial group? These problems of definition must be placed in an empirical context which takes cognizance of the statist character of genocide and the technological methods which enable us to transform nightmares into realities.

Why has sociology failed to achieve the status of a fundamental science—not an important or auxiliary discipline, but a fundamental discipline? In the closing plenary address delivered before the 1974 meetings of the International Sociological Association, I tried to distinguish between basic and secondary sciences in a forthright manner. I argued that fundamental disciplines involve some aspect of life and death, or if not death, incarceration and illness. Sociology is denied the status of a fundamental applied science, such as medicine or engineering, because it so rarely comes to grips with issues of life and death. And ordinary people, whatever else may concern them, are moved to seek the advice of others primarily by root considerations. It is axiomatic that issues of importance are related to living and dying; issues of secondary importance are the quality of life and its purpose. Many sociologists exhibit a studied embarrassment about these issues, a feeling that intellectual issues posed in such a manner are melodramatic and unfit for scientific discourse.[2] I am not arguing for a theological view of society, or that auxiliary activities are always less important than fundamental ones, but only that the social status of a science is often measured by such easy-to-make but hard-to-prove distinctions.

This study is an effort to give substance to such a vision; and in so doing to demonstrate that the underlining predicates of sociology as presently practiced give scant consideration to basic issues of life and death in favor of distinctly derivative issues of social structure and function. The underlining rationale of this study is a recognition, tragic in its consequences, that the dominant structural-functional categories of explaining the social system increasingly hamper the empirical description of systems by reducing the social order to formal labels or organizational operations. The rise of sociological formalism leads to a presumed isomorphism among societies in theory that is rarely apparent in fact.

The word *fundamental* is itself value laden and extremely troublesome. While there is an able-bodied literature on the moral demand for social science to consider fundamental questions, such as mastery and misery, or producers and products, the dilemma persists that there are so many such general concerns that one is "left with the feeling that the house of social science is still largely founded on sand."[3] Another view of the sociologically fundamental is contained in the Millsian distinction between "individual troubles" and "public issues," with those items of national or international historical meaning being highest in the rating chart of the fundamental.[4] But while these are important efforts to establish clear-eyed precepts, they remain ethical strategies and moral postures rather than sociological efforts to come to grips with the shank of issues.

Life-and-death issues are uniquely fundamental, since they alone serve as a precondition for the examination of all other issues: public and private, local or historical, products and producers.[5] Life and death alone move us beyond a relativistic framework; those works within social science that have most profoundly gripped our attention over time and through space are linked to problems of life and death. While for the most part our concerns are with life and death as a human, biological fact, we should also consider the life and death of institutions[6] and communities[7] as fundamental social questions. This volume is dedicated to a consideration of genocide within an amplified context of sociology.

Although the entry point in this analysis is sociological, this does not imply either a special meaning or worth to this singular specimen of social science research over others. Each of the social sciences will be compelled, by force of circumstances, to evaluate the structure of genocidal behavior, and more, its involvement in the very process of that terrible phenomenon it seeks to understand. In a sensitive recent effort, Stephan Chorover has explored how psychology—in particular such areas of the discipline as psychosurgery, mental measurement testing, chemical and drug treatment of patients or prisoners—has traversed the field from genesis to genocide. His study of psychotechnology "is intended to illustrate the interplay between meaning and power that necessarily pervades many areas of contemporary social life." What started out as a study of behavioral control, concludes by revealing the "common embeddedness in a larger conceptual, material, and social context."[8] The paradigm of social science is itself transformed under the impact of technological, state-imposed death. The very character of disciplinary boundaries dissolves under the impact of reviewing what has transpired over the course of this century. Advanced societies have indeed shown "the way" to backward societies; and what is revealed is a mixed bag of progress and retrogression. Advanced forms of science such as neurosurgery have shown the darkness behind the light to more macroscopic visions of society. That is why the study of genocide must perforce represent a review and reconsideration of the study of society in general.

It is difficult to avoid comparison between the twentieth century and what Barbara Tuchman refers to as "the calamitous fourteenth century": an era of mad emperors, military plunder, religious persecution and, of course, the omnipresent and ubiquitous black plague. Until the present at least it was a common belief that the fourteenth century, with its "cult of death" and "expected end of the world," was the low point in modern history. As Tuchman puts it:

> Mankind was at one of history's ebbs. At mid-century that Black Death had raised the question of God's hostility to man, and events since then had offered little reassurance. To contemporaries the *miseria* of the time reflected sin, and, indeed, sin in the form of greed and inhumanity abounded. On the downward slope of the Middle Ages man had lost confidence in his capacity to construct a good society.[9]

It is no accident that the fourteenth century was particularly vicious in its treatment of the Jews and all other peoples defined as outsiders in political, economic, or religious terms. But it is also the case that the century provided an optimism of those who survived, a continued belief in chivalry, the emergency of a bourgeois class that was not to be denied, and generally, cultural creativity that led to the emergence of the city as the center of modern civilization. In this sense it is hard to say that the twentieth century is less ambiguous than the fourteenth century in that here too we are faced with unparalleled creativity and achievements in the area of science and technology, if not in art and literature. But the level and technification of the dying system is such as to make the plagues pale in consequence. The plague, if anything, had the capacity to bring people together since it was humans against elemental nature fighting an entity called the "black plague," rather than people fighting each other. This is not to romanticize the black death, since there are all kinds of theories that the black deaths were basically brought about by the effort to undermine Christian civilization. Even the flagellants saw their role as purging the ritual murdering of Christians emanating from a compulsion to reenact Crucifixion. Hence the black plague was not without its social consequences. But these were and remain throughout random rather than systemic assaults. The notion of an engineering of death rather than the individuation of death had not yet emerged.

What made possible the engineering of death was a set of value-laden assumptions that the state, whether to purify its racial base or amplify its economic base, has the right to decide how many sacrifices are required to achieve its goals. As a result, social scientists (along with others) began to raise the issue in terms of how many lives it takes to reach industrialization, political integration, religious hegemony, etc. In this subtle way, a transvaluation of values occurred. Decision making hinged on bookkeeping considerations of how many lives, rather than the more formidable question of the consequence of empowering the state to take lives for any purpose, whatever the ostensible nobility of purpose. Herein lies the essential difference between the fourteenth and twentieth centuries: the distinction between death as unavoidable tragedy willed by providence and death as manufactured purification of society willed by people.

# Notes to Chapter 1

1. Arendt, Hannah. *The Origins of Totalitarianism.* New Edition. New York: Harcourt, Brace, and World, 1966. pp. 460-63

2. Horowitz, Irving Louis. "Science and Revolution in Contemporary Sociology," *The American Sociologist.* Vol. 10, No. 2. May, 1975, pp. 73-78; also see my paper on "National Realities and Universal Ambitions in the Practice of Sociology," *Sociological Praxis: Current Roles and Settings,* edited by Elisabeth Crawford and Stein Rokkan. London and Beverly Hills: Sage Publications Ltd., pp. 11-28.

3. Seeley, John R. "Social Science: Some Probative Problems," *Sociology on Trial,* edited by Maurice Stein and Arthur Vidich. Englewood Cliffs, N.J.: Prentice-Hall, 1963. pp. 64-65.

4. Mills, C. Wright. *The Sociological Imagination.* New York: Oxford University Press, 1959. pp. 3-13.

5. Horowitz, Irving Louis. *War and Peace in Contemporary Social and Philosophical Theory* (originally published in 1957). London: Souvenir Press; New York: Humanities Publishers, 1973. pp. 192-203.

6. Cottrell, W.F., "Death by Dieselization: A Case Study in the Reaction to Technological Change,"*American Sociological Review.* Vol. 16, No. 3. June 1951, pp. 358-65.

7. Caudill, Harry M. *Night Comes to the Cumberlands: A Biography of a Depressed Area.* Boston: Little, Brown/Atlantic Monthly Press, 1963. pp. 305-324.

8. Chorover, Stephan L. *From Genesis to Genocide: The Meaning of Human Nature and the Power of Behavior Control.* Cambridge and London: The M.I.T. Press, 1979, esp. pp. 1-10, 77-110.

9. Tuchman, Barbara W. *A Distant Mirror: The Calamitous 14th Century.* New York: Alfred A. Knopf, 1978. pp. 509-510.

# Chapter 2

# Defining Genocide

*If a crime unknown before, such as genocide, suddenly makes
its appearance, justice itself demands a judgment according
to a new law.*

Hannah Arendt, EICHMANN IN JERUSALEM

The contemporary German social philosopher Ernst Bloch has
aptly written: "We paint images of what lies ahead, and insulate
ourselves into what may come after us. But no upward glance can
fail to brush against death which makes all things pale.[1] Even with a
considerable new literature on the processing of death at an
individual medical level, we still do not possess a political sociology
that properly encompasses the phenomenon of death. Social
psychologists have provided insights into the meaning of death[2]
and into its personal consequences.[3] But we know precious little
about how to account for differences between social systems and
state organs that employ mass murder to maintain themselves and
those that eschew or resist the ultimate strategy of enforcing the
social order by the sacrifice of lives.

What is required is the large-scale movement beyond structures
to processes, from systems to humans, not simply to bring people
back into sociology or because of considerations derived from
humanitarian concerns, but because of basic scientific concerns,
namely, connecting theories employed to explain the world with
what the world itself deems important at any given time. At this
point in social science evolution, the tendency to seek explanations
in terms of organization, structure, and system is common to most
major tendencies of sociology, from functionalism to Marxism.

**9**

Social science at a macro level tends to be satisfied with descriptive statements about trends and stages. As a result, the measurement bias is to infer functional similarities from presumed organizational prerequisites. This trend weakens the validity of scientific measurement and the quality of sociological theory.

Why then employ genocide as a basic framework to overcome the functionalist hubris? The concept of genocide is empirically ubiquitous and politically troublesome. Formal definitions are either too broad to invite action or too narrow to require any; political definitions invariably mean what *other* nations do to subject populations, never what one's own does to its subjects or citizens. Genocide is not simply a sporadic or random event such as the Katyn Forest Massacre in which 15,000 Polish troops were presumed to have been destroyed by the Red Army during World War II.[4] In addition to its systematic character, genocide must be conducted with the approval of, if not direct intervention by, the state apparatus. Genocide is mass destruction of a special sort, one that reflects some sort of political support base within a given ruling class or national group. This contrasts sharply with vigilantism, which represents the maintenance of order without law, or some kind of mass participation without corresponding state support.[5] Genocide is also quite distinct from tyrannicide—the time-honored tradition of seeking redress against a tyrant-ruler—in which murder is perceived not as a crime but as a liberating act.[6]

These are not absolute categories. There is a slim line between systematic and sporadic destruction. Sporadic destruction may take more lives over time than sytematic annihilation. Similarly, vigilante politics often has the tacit support of at least a portion of the state mechanism. For example, the vigilante practices of the Ku Klux Klan had the assistance of legislative assemblies and court houses in Southern states between 1865 and 1920. Nevertheless, the distinction between genocide and vigilantism is significant and of more than academic consequence, for we are dealing with political structures, not just social events.

The concept of genocide is one of the best defined and least adhered to in the lexicon of modern times. Traditionally, genocide simply meant any attempt to destroy, in whole or in part, any one of a number of various groups. With the founding of the United

Nations, the General Assembly, in response to the horrors of World War II, declared in its resolution of 11 December 1946, that genocide "is a crime under international law, contrary to the support and designs of the United Nations, and condemned by the civilized world." It received further analysis by the United Nations Economic and Social Council, which appointed a special committee that approved a convention on the subject.[7] This convention was discussed and finally approved on 9 December 1948 by a unanimous vote of fifty-six to nothing. The crux of the matter is contained in Article 2, which stipulates as follows:

> In the present Convention, genocide means any of the following acts committed with intent to destroy, in whole or in part, a national, ethnical, racial, or religious group, as such: (a) Killing members of the group; (b) Causing serious bodily or mental harm to members of the group; (c) Deliberately inflicting on the group conditions of life calculated to bring about its physical destruction in whole or in part; (d) Imposing measures intended to prevent births within the group; (e) Forcibly transferring children of the group to another group.[8]

This legal definition has had the effect of stimulating intense sociological interest in the subject of genocide. We shall consider only a select number of these social generalizations, albeit some of the more interesting and suggestive approaches.

One approach to genocide is to link it to victimology, that is to a study of those who suffer at the hands of criminals—political as well as sociological. In the work of Drapkin, Viano, Dadrian, and their followers, there is a profound imbalance in studying criminology without a corresponding examination of victimology. Specialty areas as penology or criminal rehabilitation on such a theory deserve a corresponding framework for the rehabilitation of the innocent—those individuals or families dismembered as a result of criminal behavior. Dadrian fully understands that while all genocidal acts are criminal, not all forms of "victimology" are genocidal. Still there is a strong hint that genocide as mass murder deserves an empathic appreciation of those who are the mass victims of such practices; including the study of proper forms of restitution and rehabilitation of those who so suffer.[9]

The difficulties in this paradigm are important. First, it has been argued that many if not most "victims" of criminal behavior are knowing or willing participants. And by extension it has been argued that even racial genocide could not have happened without the willing or knowing participation of those so victimized. Whatever the merits of this argument, it is clear that before any firm "science" of victimology can be erected on foundations other than the conventional one of criminology, it would be necessary to distinguish the precise character and background of victims and criminal perpetrators. One gets the impression that the proposal for a science of victimology is addressed to those special subsets of people caught in the cross fire of criminal, deviant, or Stalinist elements. And that Dadrian's concerns are less with a new science than with a proper sense of respect for the sufferings and outrages inflicted on innocent third parties. In this regard, the victims of genocide, whether Armenian or Jewish, appear as precisely a collective representation of such a victimology.

Second, to make the problem of genocide part of a new science of victimology tends to weaken the claims of genocide on its sociological and historical specificity, that is, genocide becomes one amongst a variety of forms whereby innocents are victimized by a society that does not properly control its criminal elements. This tendency to distinguish the so-called criminal element from the political factor, when in the case of genocide it is precisely the transformation of the criminal into the political—the fusion of deviance to a special form of marginality—gives the question of genocide its special poignance and meaning. While there are some obvious appeals to making the study of genocide part of a larger "scientific" examination of victims and their behavior, it carries the danger of falsifying the terms of discourse by rendering the historical record inept and fragmented into quasi-scientific variables.

One way of formulating the question of genocide is in terms of extrajudicial execution. As outlined by Edy Kaufman, this has come to encompass not only assassination for the purpose of transferring political power, but overwhelmingly, to retain such political power. Essential as a tool of genocide, the extrajudicial execution became a formula by which governments disposed of hundreds, thousands, and even hundreds of thousands of political enemies. Kaufman's main area of interest in the past has been Latin America, where this formula probably has its highest utility; nations like Brazil, Uruguay, and Guatemala employ it extensively.[10]

The advantage of using extrajudicial execution as a category equivalent to genocide is the availability of rendering the genocidal concept in precise numerical terms. Kaufman's work represents a useful catalog of assassinations not legally sanctioned in Asia, Africa, and Latin America. The difficulty with this approach to genocide becomes transparent when one recognizes that most forms of political assassination are not extrajudicial in character, but quite judicial. Sanctions for genocide are strengthened and the prohibition against genocide lifted once the state embarks on such a course of action. As a result, in nations with undisputed high levels of genocidal practice such as Cambodia, the line between the legal and extralegal vanishes. It is precisely in countries such as Uruguay, where strong legalistic traditions pertain, that the law remains a factor in preventing genocide from becoming massified. It is not that the concept of extrajudicial execution is without merit. It is rather that it is so overly formalistic as to make more rather than less difficult the task of creating a useful framework and general model.

One recent and interesting study of ethnic tensions in central Europe was conducted by Feliks Gross. What makes it so relevant to a study of genocide is Gross's belief that genocide, like other systems of state rule, has its own natural history. This approach derives in part from Gross's earlier work (and that of others) on the natural history of the revolutionary process, and represents an extension of this concept to the field of genocide. He claims that the six stages, at least in the Julian Region of Europe, went something as follows:

> (1) The good neighborhood in the Julian Region lasted from 1867 until almost 1920. (2) After 1920 and especially after 1922 there followed the oppression of the Slavic minority. (3) In 1943 the oppression changed into genocide of the Jewish population and cruel persecutions and executions of ideological and ethnic dissidents. (4) A short respite occurred and lasted a few insecure hours, perhaps a day or so at the end of April 1945. (5) Next followed forty days of persecutions and massacres, recorded in the history books as liberation.[11]

Oddly enough, the sixth stage for Gross—the movement from oppression to genocide and massacre—is the reduction of tensions and the liquidation of old hostilities. His claim is that genocide is a function of political tensions between nation-states, and that genocide characterized not only the German Nazi period, but the Yugoslavian interval which followed, since both were authoritarian. Genocide was eliminated only at the point when the authoritarian system was forced to move back, and in what he calls political megasystems as well as subsystems. Ethnic and civil issues fused and tensions were reduced once a relative détente was reached between the Italian and Yugoslav governments. A new ideology advancing a concept of linkages between two neighboring states came into being, and the age of genocide in this area of the Julian Region between Italy and Yugoslavia was ended.

It is to Gross's credit that by placing ethnic issues in the forefront he too was able to see the importance of life and death questions, and hence to characterize states as racist or tribal in character, intolerant or benevolent, universal or pluralistic, or subordinate and hierarchical. Another important aspect to Gross's work, which has been sadly neglected, is the incomplete character of genocidal practices, and the natural history technique allows one to appreciate that even genocidal systems are not eternal and have built-in limits and weaknesses.

The shortcomings in this approach are also manifest. His typology is purely descriptive rather than analytic, and there is no evidence to indicate that the natural history outlined in one area will be equally true in others. For example, Central Europe was an area where parties had great influence on public policymaking. But what about genocide in areas where party processes are virtually nonexistent? Another problem is in seeing the issue of genocide in ethnic terms, and hence closing out the possibility of genocide as a reflection of other variables, such as race in the more exact anthropological sense, and class in the exact economic-developmental sense. Ultimately, the weakness of Gross's approach is that genocide is seen as simply a fifth or sixth stage in a national process without an appreciation of its policymaking ramifications: its utilization by leaders of nation-states.

Still, these criticisms registered, the attempt to create a taxonomy of genocide is itself deserving of more than casual attention, since at least it comes directly to terms with the life and death framework rather than structural and functional prerequisites.

Long before the United Nation's definition of genocide, Raphael Lemkin, in his work on *Axis Rule in Occupied Europe,* gave a succinct account of what genocide was:

> Genocide is effected through a synchronized attack on different aspects of life of the captive peoples: in the political field (by destroying institutions of self-government and imposing a German pattern of administration, and through colonization by Germans); in the social field (by disrupting the social cohesion of the nation involved and killing or removing elements such as the intelligentsia, which provide spiritual leadership); in the cultural field (by prohibiting or destroying cultural institutions and cultural activites; by substituting vocational education for education in the liberal arts, in order to prevent humanistic thinking); in the economic field (by shifting the wealth to Germans); in the biological field (by a policy of depopulation and by promoting procreation by Germans in the occupied countries); in the field of physical existence (by introducing a starvation rationing system for non-Germans and by mass killings, mainly of Jews, Poles, Slovenes, and Russians); in the religious field (by interfering with the activities of the Church, which in many countries provides not only spiritual but also national leadership); in the field of morality (by attempts to create an atmosphere of moral debasement through promoting pornographic publications and motion pictures, and the excessive consumption of alcohol).[12]

This extract is of critical importance, since it represents the first effort at a scientific statement on what was taking place. It also makes possible gradations of meaning in the concept of mass murder.

The distinction between genocide and the Holocaust is the difference between denationalization of selected groups within those out of favor, and the total physical annihilation of members of a community, people, or nation. While there was a justified fear that after the Jews had been liquidated, all other groups such as the Gypsies, Poles, and Rumanians would suffer the same fate, there was no systematic policy to that effect. Genocide is a national policy having adherents throughout the world, whereas the Holocaust was a specific practice of the Nazis which entailed the total murder of an entire population.[13] As bizarre as it may seem, it is the difference between defining people as subhuman and required as economic slaves, and not human at all, not even fit to serve in a slave capacity. It is perhaps the hallmark of the present age that a distinction between genocide as a general practice of state power and the Holocaust as a specific practice of Nazi power has to be made.

George Mosse put the matter in its starkest form: "The Holocaust transformed racial theory into practice." It is extremely important to realize that even genocidal systems have theoretical moorings. In the case of modern genocide such as the Hitler system, the biological mooring was central. Again, paraphrasing Mosse, racism made alliance with virtues such as cleanliness, honesty, oral earnestness, hard work, and family life.[14] Because of the wide penetration of racism, we are directed toward the cultural destruction of the Jewish people, the anthropological dismemberment of the Black people, the destruction of deviants, mongoloids, or what have you. The genocidal society managed to garner adherents, even massive followings—not in the name of genocide, never in the name of genocide; but penetration took place through ideas held to be highly ethical: usually the virtues of both Christians and the middle class. In a telling passage, Mosse notes that racism so infected Christianity that in the end no real battle between racism and Christianity ever took place. As a result, there was no mass resistance to genocidal solutions.

There was no coalescence of opposition either. Since the Blacks for the most part were outside of Hitler's reach, there was no rude awakening that all racism, whether aimed at Blacks or Jews, was cut of the same cloth. Worse, this lack of awareness made possible a much more coalescent system than would otherwise have occurred. On religious and racial grounds alike, there was a greater degree of division among opponents of the genocidal society than its supporters. This ultimately has been the strength of totalitarian systems generally: the singleminded interest in the state concerning the control of large numbers of people.

In addition to legal definitions and historical taxonomies of genocide, there are structural dimensions. Two points must be subsumed under such a structuralist heading: first, genocide represents a systematic effort over time to liquidate a national population, usually a minority; second, it functions as a fundamental political policy to assure conformity and participation by the citizenry. There are exceptions to each point. Sometimes, as it is in the apartheid policy of South Africa, the minority practices forms of genocide on a majority. Also, there are many cases in which overt statements of a government only vaguely reflect its covert actions, for instance, the case of Soviet policy toward its national minorities.

A formal distinction between genocide and assassination is also required. Genocide is herein defined as *a structural and systematic destruction of innocent people by a state bureaucratic apparatus;* whereas assassination designates random and sporadic efforts of people without power to illegally seize power and liquidate paramount central figures in a given regime as a means to that goal.[15] Assassination, like genocide, may take the lives of innocent third parties, but its primary focus is aimed toward the symbolic, and hence selective, liquidation of powerful enemies. The distinction between genocide and assassination is roughly analogous to that between force as the prerogative of state power and violence as the instrument of those excluded from state power. All linguistic devices have built-in limitations, and the fine lines of intellect may be crossed to satisfy the exigencies of immediate practice. Yet this distinction between genocide and assassination does permit a rule-of-thumb separation between death at the hands of the state, the behemoth; and death at the hands of the individual, the anarch.

Still, one must recognize exceptional forms of genocide not directly linked to state power. The assassination-suicide syndrome which took place under the sponsorship of the Reverend Jim Jones in his People's Temple of the Disciples of Christ in Guyana is perhaps the most recent and bizarre such instance. The death by poisoning of 910 members of this cult in 1978 took place in a climate which simulated totalitarian state power: a total institution, an environment closed to a variety of information from diverse sources, absolute reliance on the leader for counsel and support, and a corresponding sense of total dependence on the sealed environment for all forms of existence; to the point where existence outside the total institution (or the simulated state) became unthinkable.

In this instance, once again social life outstrips sociological categories. We have a concept of suicide, but essentially as a private and individuated event; not as social and collectivized. We have a concept of infanticide, but again as something connected with highly refined and unusual ritual, not as a clinical and routinized act of engineered genocide. We have a concept of totalitarianism, but generally as a system of government rather than a subsystem of religious organization. Genocide can thus be an episodic and even sporadic event. It does not have to be, as it was in the case of the Nazis, systematic and sustained. This is small consolation to those seeking precise correlations between totalitarian systems and human destruction. But it would be a large-scale error to conceive of genocide as a peculiar or bizarre entity, rather than as part and parcel of the totalitarian temptation.

A special type of genocidal practice is employed against overseas rather than native populations. One of the fundamental characteristics of nineteenth-century European imperialism was its systematic destruction of communities outside the "mother country."[16] Decimation of Zulu tribesmen by British troops, the Dutch-run slave trade, and the virtual depopulation of the Congo by Belgians, typify this form of colonial genocide. It would be simple to say that such events are merely a consequence of international strife and the division of spoils, and that they do not qualify as genocidal practice. Those engaging in genocide nearly always define the people to be purged and liquidated as alien or enemy populations. This is so even in the liquidation of ancient Indian civilizations by relatively recent White arrivals.[17] Whether they are aliens from within or without is an ideological caveat that disguises the fact of systematic mass extermination by one state power against a relatively powerless group or sector. The conduct of classic colonialism was invariably linked with genocide. It is the hypocritical heritage of European nations that they proclaimed concepts of democracy and liberty for their own populations while systematically destroying others. This was the bequeathal of nineteenth-century "civilized" existence. This bequest of the past became the norm of the twentieth century.

Although concern for problems of genocide fitted into the thinking of the United Nations at its inception, the series of treaties, approved and even ratified, remained largely unenforced. The emergence of the cold war and its attendant polarization of all conflicts along a communist-anticommunist cost-benefit scale, led to a decline of attention to that very feature of the twentieth century that presumably differentiated it from all other centuries: the international protection of the rights of people. As a result, the genocidal norm outlasted any organizational efforts to displace it. As Leon Gordenker recently inquired:

> Who made the destruction of the 300,000 or so Indonesian communists after the attempted coup d'état in 1965 a matter for the United Nations? Who saw the deprivation of the rights of Asians in Uganda as an outrage? Who labelled as genocidal the slaughter of baHutu tribesmen—80,000 or so of them—by the waTutsi elite of Burundi? How much attention was given to the horrors of the civil war in Nigeria? Who has tried to ease the emergence of Angola by protecting the humanity of all involved? Who talks of the operations of the secret political police whose knock at dawn is a common sound in dictatorships of the right and left that occupy most of the world? Well, not the principal organs of the United Nations which for the moment have other priorities in the human rights field.[18]

Quite beyond the process of labelling social systems and then determining whether any assistance should be rendered, is the yet more recent pattern of intense rivalry between odious regimes. Genocidal systems have no more necessary affinity for each other than do other social systems. Thus, for example, the invasion and conquest of Cambodia by Vietnam represented, internally at least, a movement from a genocidal system to an incarceration system. The most authentic claim about Vietnam is that at the end of 1978 approximately 800,000 prisoners were distributed throughout the country, evenly divided between North and South Vietnam.[19] The placement of the internment camps, the conditions of the prisoners, the forms of punishment, are all adequately described in the current literature. But this system has now been extended to a nation where conservative estimates place the number of people liquidated at roughly two million out of a population of approximately eight million. In the grim war of twentieth-century geopolitics, on a scale of living values at least, one might say that Cambodia has improved its situation!

This is not a claim to the legitimacy or legality of such forms of invasion, or breakdown of territorial sovereignty, nor is it to enter a dispute concerning the proxy-like status of the conflict between the Soviet Union and China. For with superpowers too, the question of the internal regimes of the proxy powers must itself be considered part of the grim tragedies of the present era. The fact that societies can be described as genocidal in their essence does not necessarily change foreign policy equations. The question of genocide is once again returned to the nation-state, to competition between sovereigns no less than efforts to prevent opposition to a sovereign from within. If candor is to prevail, statesmen and scholars alike would have to admit that the umbilical cord between genocidal practice and state power has never been stronger.

# Notes to Chapter 2

1. Bloch, Ernst. *Man on His Own*. New York: Herder and Herder, 1971. p. 43.
2. Becker, Ernest. *The Denial of Death*. New York: The Free Press/Macmillan Publishers, 1974; and *Escape from Evil*. New York: The Free Press/Macmillan, 1975.
3. Lifton, Robert J. *Death in Life: Survivors of Hiroshima*. New York: Random House, 1967; also *History and Human Survival: Essays on the Young and Old, Survivors and the Dead, Peace and War, and on Contemporary Psychohistory*. New York: Random House, 1970.
4. Zawodny, J.K. *Death in the Forest: The Story of the Katyn Forest Massacre*. South Bend, Indiana: The University of Notre Dame Press, 1962.
5. Rosenbaum, H. Jon and Sederberg, Peter C. (editors). *Vigilante Politics*. Philadelphia: The University of Pennsylvania Press, 1976.
6. Laqueur, Walter. "Terrorism—A Balance Sheet," in *The Terrorism Reader*, edited by Walter Laqueur. Philadelphia: Temple University Press, 1978. pp. 251-267.
7. Patterson, William L. *We Charge Genocide: The Historic Petition to the United Nations for Relief from a Crime of the United States Government against the Negro People*. New York: International Publishers, 1951 and 1970. See also Patterson's autobiography, *The Man Who Cried Genocide*. New York: International Publishers, 1971. pp. 178-79.
8. United Nations. *Yearbook of the United Nations, 1947-48*. New York: 1949. pp. 595-599; and *Yearbook of the United Nations, 1948-49*. New York, 1950. pp. 958-959.
9. Drapkin, Israel and Viano, Emilio. *Victimology*. Lexington: Lexington Books/D.C. Heath, 1974; and *Victimology: A New Focus—Violence and Its Victims*. Lexington: Lexington Books/D.C. Heath, 1975.
10. Kaufman, Edy. *Extra-Judicial Executions: An Insight into the Global Dimension of a Human Rights Violation* (paper delivered before the International Conference on the Death Penalty, December 1977. In mimeograph form).
11. Gross, Feliks. *Ethnics in a Borderland: An Inquiry into the Nature of Ethnicity and Reduction of Ethnic Tensions in a one-time Genocide Area*. Westport and London: Greenwood Press, 1978. pp. 70-73, 116-17.

12. Lemkin, Raphael. *Axis Rule in Occupied Europe.* New York: Howard Fertig, 1973. pp. X-XII (first printed in 1943).

13. Bauer, Yehuda. "Against Mystification," *The Holocaust in Historical Perspective.* Seattle, Washington: University of Washington Press, 1978. pp. 30-49.

14. Mosse, George L. *Toward the Final Solution: A History of European Racism.* New York: Howard Fertig, 1978. pp. 232, 234-35.

15. Havens, Murray Clark; Leiden, Carl; and Schmitt, Karl M. *The Politics of Assassination.* Englewood Cliffs, New Jersey: Prentice-Hall Publishers.

16. Walter, Eugene Victor. *Terror and Resistance: A Study of Political Violence with Case Studies of Some Primitive African Communities.* New York: Oxford University Press, 1969. pp. 109-263.

17. Davis, Shelton H. *Victims of the Miracle: Development and the Indians of Brazil.* New York: Cambridge University Press, 1977; and Richard Arens (editor), *Genocide in Paraguay.* Philadelphia: Temple University Press, 1976. See in this connection, Irving Louis Horowitz, "Genocide in South American Style," *The Nation,* Vol. 226, No. 6, 1978. pp. 181-183.

18. Gordenker, Leon, "Symbols and Substance in the United Nations." *New Society,* Vol. 35, No. 697, February 12, 1976. pp. 324-326.

19. Toai, Doan Van, "The Penitentiary Regime Under the Communist Government of Vietnam," *Documents on Prisons in Vietnam.* Paris, France (no publisher given). pp. 10-16.

# Chapter 3

# Functional and Existential Visions of Genocide

*In the ashes of the past we can taste the ashes of the future, and from both we try to create the present and to awaken life. We pass by and, precisely because now and again we do awaken life, that which is called real life is so precious to us— precious because we know what society, if it wishes to remain itself for even a week or two, must not allow itself to become aware of: that transience and death are always at the door, that all will turn to ashes.*

*Heinrich Böll*, MISSING PERSONS

Even the most rudimentary examination of the various forms of totalitarian systems reveals serious shortcomings in conventional social science modes of dealing with the interrelations between repressive regimes and mass murder. The attempt to locate "bad" practices in bad states is as flawed an approach as those who would locate "good" practices in good states. Such neat Aristotelian tautologies just fall apart in practice. There are "bad" fascist states like Germany that took lives with impunity; others, like Italy, that rarely took lives at all. There are "good" democratic regimes like England and Belgium that would never dream of violating the civil liberties of their native citizenry. But these same regimes, when operating in imperial contexts, whether in Africa or India, had few compunctions to engage in genocidal practices.

This chapter takes up functional and existential perspectives on genocide. It is an effort not so much to discredit earlier efforts, as to make evident the need to further explore cultural forms ignored by such inherited frameworks. If the theory and practice of social science is to measure up to the needs of understanding some of the most extreme, yet typical, behavioral characteristics of our times, we must engage in a sober look at social systems and their responses to the protection of, or prohibitions against, human life.

Defined in strictly organizational terms, fascism is a system in which the state regulates labor and management functions while the bureaucracy grows exponentially with respect to the rest of society, and in which the state apparatus, from education to the military, is harnessed toward insuring its own survival and expansion. State preeminence creates conditions for authoritarian domination over vast populations, national and even international. There are other characteristics of fascists systems. An organizational chart would show that countries such as Italy during 1920-43 and Germany in 1933-45 had considerable similarities: the one-party system, the permanent charismatic ruler, and the orchestrated mobilization of masses by state-controlled agencies. These are important categories in any discussion of fascism. Yet for those who had to (or rather could) make rational decisions about where to live in the 1930s, Rome in the Fascist period was a far less austere and grim place than Berlin in the Nazi period.

The difficulty with functional description is best appreciated by taking for granted the correctness of Parsons' macroanalysis of fascism as linked to "the generalized aspects of Western society" stretched to the limit. Included in the Parsonian shopping list of fascist characteristics are: the emergence of an emotional, fanatical mass movement closer to religion than to political movements; huge and sudden shifts in population and demographic patterns; the emergence of nationalization and nationalism; the unwillingness of privileged classes to yield their prestige and power to newer, emerging classes.[1] While these are certainly elements in fascism, they do not provide a sufficiently sensitive characterization of fascism as a social system. They offer meager guideposts in distinguishing between fascisms. Functional indicators of fascism are so general that they often serve to describe characteristics of every advanced industrial system. They lack sufficient refinement to permit meaningful distinctions between Fascism in Italy, National Socialism in Germany, Falangism in Spain and elsewhere, or differences between fascist and other social systems.[2]

Few events in the annals of twentieth-century genocide equal the treatment of European Jewry by Nazi Germany. The dropping of the atomic bomb on Hiroshima might well equal it in horror, but not in sustained magnitude. Likewise, the treatment of the Gypsies by the Nazis may have equalled the Holocaust in approach but not in size. On 20 January 1942, Hitler's government held a conference in a Berlin suburb, at which time the central administrative authorities of the Third Reich prepared to carry out Field Marshall Hermann Goering's order to "make preparation for the general solution of the Jewish problem within the German sphere of influence in Europe." The total number of Jews slated for extermination was eleven million.[3] The Nazi war machine fell short of realizing this number by approximately one-half, since the bulk of Soviet Jewry survived the war, and nations like England and Switzerland were never occupied and hence fell outside the Nazi sphere of influence. Even so, available data indicate that nearly six million Jews were arbitrarily executed between 1939 and 1945 at the hands of the Nazis.[4] This figure does not include other groups which also died in concentration camps, such as Poles, Gypsies, and other "undesirables." But treatment of other peoples remained relatively random in contrast to the highly rationalized and total destruction of Jews under Nazi occupation. One-third of world Jewry was exterminated during Hitler's rule. The sixteen million Jews of 1939 were reduced to under eleven million by 1945.[5]

Rationalization of the Nazi program of assassination moved by stages: First came the 1933 declarations that the Jewish problem was uniquely a German curse, the slogan being: "The Jews are our misfortune." Next came the 1935-37 period in which the Nuremberg Laws were enacted, decreeing that only persons of German blood or Aryans could be citizens of the German Reich. The third stage, covering the 1938-39 period, was one in which the first concentration camp was opened at Buchenwald and mass anti-Jewish riots occurred in both Berlin and Vienna. The fourth stage of 1939-40 was one in which World War II began and ghettos were sealed and converted into concentration camps. In the fifth stage, between 1942 and 1944, the bulk of the Jews were exterminated in the many concentration camps that had been developed after the Wansee (Berlin) Conference. It was also during this period that the liquidation of all ghettos throughout Europe was carried out. The sixth and final stage took place in the last year of the war, 1945. Every attempt was made to obliterate all traces of the various and sundry activities committed in the name of cleansing the Third Reich by destroying the Jewish remnants.

The natural history of genocide, its progression by stages, had a powerful psychological deterrent to mounting any resistance. There was the difficulty of large-scale populations to perceive that genocide was actually taking place. The literature on this is legendary as well as legion. Even those taken to the final death marches were willing to believe that they were simply to be taking showers, or in the process of being reunited with families. The very momentousness of genocide as a state practice makes it difficult to recognize the phenomenon by participants—those performing the executions no less than those being executed. Interesting in this regard is the case of the American Jewish community during World War II. Despite its large size, it scarcely placed any pressure on the American adminstration because of its relative disbelief in the magnitude of the Nazi Holocaust. As Henry Feingold reports in *The Politics of Rescue,* a volume on the Roosevelt administration and the Holocaust:

> In the case of the Jews the Roosevelt Administration had no popular mandate for a more active rescue role. Public opinion was, in fact, opposed to the admission of refugees, because most Americans were not aware of what was happening. A Roper poll taken in December of 1944 showed that the great majority of Americans, while willing to believe that Hitler had killed some Jews, could not believe that the Nazis, utilizing modern production techniques, had put millions to death. The very idea beggared the imagination. Perhaps there is such a thing as a saturation point as far as atrocity stories are concerned. In the American mind the Final Solution took its place beside the Bataan Death March and the Malmedy massacre as just another atrocity in a particularly cruel war. Not only were the victims unable to believe the unbelievable, but those who would save

them found it extremely difficult to break through the "curtain of silence." The State Department's suppression of the details compounded the problem of credibility.[6]

Thus the question of genocide is made difficult to comprehend by those living in other social sytems, in part because it continues to be viewed as an aberration rather than a system.

The purpose of reciting these well-known details of Hitler's Germany is to illustrate that the precondition for mass extermination was engineered dehumanization: the conversion of citizens into aliens, first by executive decree, then by legislative enactment, and finally by judicial consent. These legal and sociological events represent the precondition for the technical performance of genocidal policies by totalitarian states. This progressive delegitimization of minorities had its parallels throughout the Stalinist era. There is no question that Soviet citizens were exterminated by the Soviet system and its secret police for failure to conform to the canons of the national question. Still, a strong difference between communism and fascism was the hard-core ideology derived from Leninism, which argued that anti-Semitism and other forms of national discrimination were capitalist aberrations. The Soviet regime has always been torn between attacking Jews and other "nationalities" for their "petty bourgeois" manifestations, and attacking anti-Semites and other chauvinists often on the same ideological grounds.[7] But confusion in theory did not prevent massacre in practice. In the *Gulag Archipelago*, Alexandr Solzhenitsyn outlines the high points of the Soviet system of terror, its origins, duration, and structure. Literary devices notwithstanding, one is reminded that we are dealing with the liquidation of roughly twenty million Soviet citizens by the Soviet state; or a number which roughly parallels those destroyed by the Nazi state.

When people today decry the abuses of the cult, they keep getting hung up on those years which are stuck in our throats, '37 and '38. And memory begins to make it seem as though arrests were never made before or after, but only in those two years. The wave of 1937-38 was neither the only one nor even the main one, but only one, perhaps of the three biggest waves which strained the murky, stinking pipes of our prison sewers to bursting. *Before* it came the wave of 1929-30, the size of a good River Ob, which drove a mere fifteen million peasants, maybe even more, out into the taiga and the tundra. But peasants are silent people, without a literary voice, nor do they write complaints or memoirs. No interrogators sweated out the night with them, nor did they bother to draw up formal indictments—it was enough to have a decree from the village soviet. And after it there was a wave of 1944-46, the size of a good Yenisei, when they dumped whole nations down the sewer pipes, not to mention millions and millions of others who (because of us!) had been prisoners of war, or carried off to Germany and subsequently repatriated. (This was Stalin's method of cauterizing the wounds so that scar tissue would form more quickly, and thus the body politic as a whole would not have to rest up, catch its breath, regain its strength.) But in this wave, too, the people were of the simpler kind, and they wrote no memoirs.

But the wave of 1937 swept up and carried off the Archipelago people of position, people with a party past, educated people, among whom many had been wounded and remained in the cities—and what a lot of them had pen in hand! And today they are all writing, speaking, remembering: "Nineteen thirty-seven!" A whole Volga of the people's grief![8]

The efforts of Wilhelm Reich to place the Soviet and German experience in a similar cultural perspective, despite their differences in social systems, are particularly noteworthy. One may argue with his arcane linguistic formulation, but there can be no question as to the empirical accuracy of his evaluation:

The German and Russian State apparatuses grew out of despotism. For this reason the subservient nature of the human character of masses of people in Germany and in Russia was exceptionally pronounced. Thus in both cases, the revolution led to a new despotism with the certainty of irrational logic. In contrast to the German and Russian State apparatuses, the American State apparatus was formed by groups of people who have evaded European and Asian despotism by fleeing to a virgin territory free of immediate and effective traditions. Only in this way can it be understood that, until the time of this writing, a totalitarian State apparatus was not able to develop in America, whereas in Europe every overthrow of the government carried out under the slogans of freedom inevitably led to despotism.[9]

To see how ubiquitous the use of labels such as fascism can be, one need only contrast the situation in Germany with that in Italy, both in respect to the general nature of Italian Fascism and its particular attitudes toward the Jewish question. In Italy, the Special Tribunal for the Defense of the State was a judicial body created ad hoc by Fascism in the Exceptional Laws of 1926, with a view to prosecuting political opponents of the regime and removing them from the jurisdiction of the ordinary magistracy, which had more respect for legality. The Special Tribunal was therefore by its very nature an extralegal judicial body, which often made no effort to give a coherent juridical basis for its sentences or to conceal the political persecution that was its function. Between 1927 and 1943, the Special Tribunal passed 4,596 sentences for a total of 27,735 years of imprisonment. Death sentences numbered 42, of which 31 were executed. Those sentenced were members of every social class and of various parties.[10] The source of this information on the relatively benign condition of Italian Fascism is no less an authority than Antonio Gramsci. The great distinction between genocidal societies and incarceration societies is precisely what permitted Italian Communism to survive and what made German Communism die—only to be reborn in postwar East Germany as an appendage of Soviet occupation.

In retrospect, the attitude toward Jews seems a touchstone of fascist systems. While both had similar forms of political organization, Italy represented an incarceration society and Germany a genocidal society. The passage of the Racial Laws marked the fundamental rupture between the Fascist state and the Italian bourgeoisie. From 1938 to its collapse in 1943, the bulk of the Italians, and not simply those in one class, began to view the regime as something alien to them. The emergence of official anti-Semitism, restricted though it was to a juridical model, marked the beginning of the rejection of Fascism by large numbers of Italians and began the period that produced the evenual downfall of the regime.[11] It was argued that Fascist anti-Semitism was both unnecessary and extrinsic to the Italian class system and its cultural components. Various observers have seen Italian anti-Semitism as a fundamental component and fatal cause of the demise of the Fascist role in Italy.[12]

With respect to distinguishing Fascism from Nazism, it is exactly the genocidal potentials of each that become crucial. Whatever the formal or structural similarities, for example, between Italian Fascism and German Nazism, it would be dangerous to see the latter as a mere variant of Fascism. There is a need, therefore, to distinguish between the two, precisely because significant differences exist in matters of life and death.

The emphasis on biological determinism within Nazism is in marked contrast to the permissive pluralism of Fascism. This is a crucial distinction, involving the definition of the national idea of Fascism as against the racist idea of Nazism. While the two systems may have in common a high degree of antiliberalism and anticommunism, and may be defined by an excessive amount of government authority in all areas of life, the biological when seen in political terms, that is, in its modus operandi, has to do with nothing less than the purification of race, and hence the survival of certain people and the liquidation of others. Fascism was born of a political tradition; Nazism incorporated a biological tradition. Even if totalitarianism represents a common denominator of Fascism and Nazism alike, this does not necessarily mean that they perform in similar terms with respect to ordinary people.

A sophisticated appreciation of the political character of Fascism is contained in an essay by Zeev Sternhell. He understands that the coming to power of the Fascists in Western Europe was a function of the weakness of the Right, and represented a political standpoint throughout.

> It was where the right was too weak to hold its own ground that fascism achieved its most marked successes. In times of acute crisis, the right turned to the new revolutionary movement—the only one capable of confronting communism—for assistance, but never treated it with anything less than the deepest suspicion. By contrast, where the right was sufficiently confident to face the Marxist left itself, where its positions were not unduly threatened and it had a

solid social base, it did everything in its power to prevent the fascist phenomenon from getting out of hand. It concentrated above all on manipulating fascist troops and spending money to safeguard its own interests. Western Europe, Spain included, is a good case in point. It was not the strength of the right but its relative weakness, its fears, and its fits of panic, which created one of the essential conditions of fascist success.[13]

This stands in considerable contrast to the successes of German Nazism, where the "Fascist phenomenon" did get "out of hand," and where the traditional Right proved inept and incapable of holding the line.

This brief description of the relative absence of mass murder in an incarceration society such as Fascist Italy is offered not only to prove that cultural variables are unique determinants of behavior in a social system, but to demonstrate that defining a social and political system solely in terms of formal characteristics falsifies a comparative analytic framework. To argue the case for a great world-historic struggle between Fascism and Communism on the basis of fine ideological distinctions seems less persuasive when we make central the question of officially inspired deaths. On the basis of raw data concerning their official assassination of citizens, Nazi Germany and Stalinist Russia are more proximate to each other than either is to Italian Fascism or, for that matter, if official murders are a yardstick, to Chinese Communism. When we compare the Italian and German experiences with fascism or the Russian and Chinese experiences with communism, we have the beginnings of a fundamental existential perspective toward social and political life.[14]

Some fascist or socialist countries can employ virtually no death by state decrees, while in others carrying similar political labels, death may be a commonplace event. This existential dimension of the sociological enterprise must therefore be taken seriously. Whether people live or die is a fundamental distinction that may enable us to make a science of society a fundamental discipline; one based on the fusion rather than further disaggregation of social, cultural, and personality dimensions.

It is not my purpose to discuss the entire range of issues related to life and death: deviance, suicide, random assassination, crimes of passion. These are being placed to one side, although they are certainly important; indeed, they are central to any sociological definition of the social system. But here I want to examine a specific problem: the possibility of defining the state not in structural-functional terms of communism, liberalism, or conservatism, but whether and to what degree any state system permits the official and arbitrary termination of the lives of its citizenry.

Conventional war will largely be excluded from the purview of this discussion. Deaths occasioned by conflict between states are subject to so many interpretations, such as the right of survival of the state over and above the obligation of individuals to that state, that it is operationally imperative to distinguish warfare from genocide. This decision is further warranted by the weight of current empirical research that indicates that domestic destruction and international warring are separate dimensions of struggle. "There are no common conditions or causes of domestic and foreign conflict behavior."[15] And while this disjunction between domestic and foreign forms of decimation may seem incongruous, even a brief reflection will reveal how often foreign détente permits internal mayhem.

Life-and-death issues have a bearing beyond particular concerns of class or stratification. The subject of the arbitrary termination of life involves a general understanding of the merits and demerits of the social system as a whole, and the place of social order within the system. Durkheim well understood this relationship.

> The questions it raises are closely connected with the most serious practical problems of the present time. The abnormal development of suicide and the general unrest of contemporary societies spring from the same causes. The exceptionally high number of voluntary deaths manifests the state of deep disturbance from which civilized societies are suffering, and bears witness to its gravity. It may even be said that this measures it. When these sufferings are expressed by a theorist they may be considered exaggerated and unfaithfully interpreted. But in these statistics of suicide they speak for themselves, allowing no room for personal interpretation. The only possible way, then, to check this current of collective sadness is by at least lessening the collective malady of which it is a sign and result.[16]

I would like to extend this line of analysis to the area of deaths due to reasons of state. Genocide differs markedly from suicide. Taking one's life, dying for oneself: anomie, altruism, fatalism; or dying voluntarily for one's state in order to uphold the boundaries of a nation; or to uphold the laws of a nation, such as the Socratic death—these represent a phenomenon apart. We are concerned with the arbitrary termination of life against the will of the individual and on behalf of the collective will of the state. The burden of these remarks is restricted to legal murder in which no one is punished other than the victim; that area of state power that terminates one life or many on behalf of an abstract political principle, whether it be national or international in character.

Hannah Arendt, an astute commentator on the subject of genocide, put the matter in proper perspective when she pointed out that there is a fundamental difference between totalitarian and libertarian concepts of law.

> At this point the fundamental difference between the totalitarian and all other concepts of law comes to light. Totalitarian policy does not replace one set of laws with another, does not establish its own *concensus juris,* does not create, by one revolution, a new form of legality. Its defiance of all, even its own positive laws implies that it believes it can do without any *concensus juris* whatever, and still not resign itself to the tyrannical state of lawlessness, arbitrariness, and fear. It can do without the *concensus juris* because it promises to release the fulfillment of law from all action and will of man; and it promises justice on earth because it claims to make mankind itself the embodiment of the law.[17]

She goes a good deal further in the idea of a legal breakdown as a prelude to the totalitarian temptation. Underlining the notion of absence of legality is the idea that the state demands a higher legality that may be called nature, divinity, or history. The source of authority is no longer human but transcendental. This fanatic commitment to transcendental notions makes death not only possible, but thoroughly justifiable as well. What can one do with those of inferior genetic worth and in opposition to the best of racial man? Not simply a collapse of law, but its displacement by a higher law, permits certain societies to mandate the taking of lives.

In the interpretation of totalitarianism, all laws have become laws of movement. When the nazis talked about the law of nature or when the Bolsheviks talk about the law of history, neither nature nor history is any longer the stabilizing source of authority for the actions of moral men: they are movements in themselves. Underlying the nazis' belief in race laws as the expression of the law of nature in man, is Darwin's idea of man as the product of a natural development which does not necessarily stop with the present species of human beings, just as under the Bolsheviks' belief in class-struggle as the expression of the law of history lies Marx's notion of society as the product of a gigantic historical movement which races according to its own law of motion to the end of historical times when it will abolish itself.[18]

The social system alone does not explain this drive to satisfy the requirements of history or nature by taking the lives of dissidents. Here again, national-cultural differences between Italians and Germans, and Chinese and Russians, loom very large.[19] Cultural traits create their own imperatives: that life is more (or less) important than death; that rehabilitation is always (or never) possible; that rehabilitation is valued and supported by money and effort (or a costly waste of time). The fact that highly genocidal societies cross ideological boundaries like fascism and communism indicates that structural ideological analysis itself does not exhaust the possibilities of understanding social systems.

There is one shadowy area of genocide that permits the state to take lives by indirection, for example by virtue of benign neglect, or death due to demographic causes. The kinds of Malthusian events discussed by Josué de Castro[20] or Lester R. Brown[21] cover areas formerly considered as death by natural causes: Malthusian verities of war, famine, floods, plagues, and so on. The efforts of a government to reduce the naturalness of this phenomenon and to harness technology and natural resources to minimize such disasters is itself a central indication of how a society values life.[22] In certain circumstances, specifically in the Soviet Union, the state may be working at cross purposes: performing an active role in the reclamation of virgin soil, hydroelectric dam projects, reforestation, and so on, while at the same time condemning its own citizens to death in police camps, or sometimes even harnessing manpower in the building of those dams. Thus we must consider the role of even highly genocidal societies in minimizing random death.

Genocidal measurement of the state is to be confined to the area of state power and its attitude toward the sacred or profane nature of the life of its citizenry. As international warfare becomes a decreasing possibility for the settlement of major disputes, and as individuals place greater emphasis on the responsibility of society for their economic or social failures, suicide can also be expected to increase. In this technological vacuum, the fundamental unit for taking or preserving life becomes the state. Measurement of the state's achievements must increasingly be made in terms of demographic mortality factors and the social production of goods in society. The central equation of state achievement is the ratio between the arbitrary consumption of people over and against the necessary production of goods.

Time, too, no less than space, is a crucial element in the characterization of a society as genocidal or pacific. In all social systems, whether in revolutionary or counterrevolutionary causes, moments of great tension lead to a catharsis that often claims many lives. But for a state to earn the appellation of a genocidal society it must conduct the systematic destruction of innocent lives over a finite period of time.[23] Killing must be endemic to the organization of all social life and state activities. On such a scale, one might say that Colombia and Paraguay are close to being the apotheosis of genocidal societies in Latin America, in contrast to such nations as Mexico and Peru which experience officially sanctioned violence sporadically and even spasmodically, but above all, randomly.

A significant task of the state in establishing a genocidal system is its capacity to politically neutralize vast population sectors. This can be achieved in various ways: through careful news leakages of the physical dangers of resistance; rumors about the number of people subject to destruction; delineation of outsider and insider group distinctions to lessen fears of those not targeted for immediate destruction; and finally, rewarding portions of the genocidal society for remaining loyal to the state. (Usually, as occurred in Nazi Germany, such rewards were simplified by the redistribution of Jewish commercial business holdings to a sector of the non-Jewish German population.) Whatever techniques are employed, the tacit support or quiescence of the larger population is necessary for genocidal practices to prove successful even in short-run terms. The differential outcome of Jews in nations like Denmark and Poland—in the former they were saved largely through militant support from all social and political sectors, whereas the absence of such broad support in the latter nation markedly contributed to their extermination—would indicate that either tacit support or complete demobilization are prerequisites to the success or failure of the genocidal society. The general feeling of collective anomie, or isolation, is a powerful stimulant to the success or failure of a genocidal policy.

A crucial existential distinction should be made between genocide and coercion, between the physical and cultural liquidation of peoples in contrast to bending the will of peoples to a presumed common end. The analysis of genocide does not entail a search for distinctions between good and evil, but simply the discontinuity between genocidal societies that may bear a superficial resemblance. Those who widely practice guilt, shame, imprisonment, torture—those malevolent practices with which so many societies are cursed, but which, nonetheless, do not cross a psychological or physical threshhold involving the taking of lives— are qualitatively different from genocidal societies.

The argument is still presented that one does not have to go beyond economic explanations to comprehend the nature of genocide. As we have seen, the presumed need for economic growth and the very real economic consequences of genocide in redistributing property and good do play a considerable part in such practices. However, we come upon other examples that compel us to go beyond an economic explanation for genocidal practices. A particular case in point is the utilization of the German railroads (the *Reichsbahn*) in the destruction of European Jewry. The deployment of railroads for such barbaric ends represented an "unprecedented event that was a product of multiple initiative, as well as lengthy negotiations and repeated adjustments among separate power structures."[24] The political use of railroads was real enough. But significantly, the transport of Jews took precedence over the transport of men and materials going to the battle zones;

such human cargo also took priority over industrial transport. Hence, purely economic uses were superseded by political uses. As a result, the role of the German railroads in the destruction of Jews does indeed open profound questions about the substance and ramifications of the Nazi Reich.

The implications of this "prioritization," this decision to first eliminate the Jews and then pursue the war effort, indicates more than a choice of the irrational over the rational. It also has to do with the primacy of state over economy. For as Anna Pawelczynska has recently noted in her work on Auschwitz: "Concentration camps were state institutions of the Third Reich, operating on the basis of official statutes and a set of strictly secret directive that were binding on the subordinate levels of government, which acknowledges the right of higher authorities to issue orders and make laws of this type."[25] The manner in which genocide was to be conducted was carefully structured: it involved edicts by the state to paid employees of the camps. Given the nature of mass murder as work, a special reward system was set up, and even mechanisms for guilt alleviation in the conduct of such work. But the very nature of such state work involved secrecy, duplicity, and criminal activities which had the effect of undermining state authority and any possibility of it becoming legitimate.

The state character of genocide leads to the conclusion that it is a drastic oversimplification to identify genocide directly with the developmental process. Certainly a considerable amount of invariant correlations between the two might occasion such a general theory. However, the number of instances in which genocidal practices are used to prevent development—for instance, civilizations that have employed genocide, especially racial genocide, to maintain a slave system over and against an industrial one—clearly indicates that something other than the necessity for industrial growth is operative as a stimulant to genocide; that something else, that element which truly distinguishes genocidal societies from industrial societies practicing a wide range of coercive procedures to maintain patterns of economic growth, is essentially political. When the ruling elites decide that their continuation in power transcends all other economic and social values, at that point does the possibility, if not the necessity, for genocide increase qualitatively. For this reason, the chemistry of genocide involves the fusion of strategies and principles common to totalitarian regimes. So much is this the case that even when genocidal practices serve to threaten economic development—as it did in the irrational expulsion and destruction of Jewish scientists from Nazi Germany, or the mass incarceration of trained professionals and their reduction to slave labor until the point of death in the Stalinist experience—they manage to take priority over "rational" economic goals. Genocide is always a conscious choice and policy. It is never just an accident of history or a necessity imposed by unseen economic growth requirements. Genocide is always and everywhere an essentially political decision.

The purpose of an authentic political sociology is to provide a theory of the state based on a scale of its preservation and enhancement of life at one end of the continuum, and death caused by the will of the state on the other end. There are all sorts of intermediary stages that complicate our task—for example, forms of suffering such as mass starvation that might make death a welcome relief. Yet genocide as an essential measure of the state and its purposes seem to provide an eminently significant break-through in linking the *phenomenon* of imposed death with a *system* of organized repression.

Too often those who make the equation between development and genocide are disguising their own metaphysical pathos. They provide a theory of human sacrifice to the god of growth. Too often developmentalists not only claim the necessity of genocide, but also add, as a private agenda, that genocide is worth the price. But what is a satisfactory price for development? Here we get into a type of moral bookkeeping. For example, it is estimated that the human costs of Soviet development have been between twenty and forty million dead souls. Would a smaller number have made the costs of development more bearable? One gets into a *reductio ad absurdum*. The moment it is argued that no human sacrifice is justified for economic development, the other side immediately comes to the fore, arguing that the consequence of such humanistic absolutism is pure stagnation. I do not know the crossover point between the empirical and the ethical. I would welcome research on what constitutes an appropriate number of human losses in the development process. For example: Is the dismemberment of the Indian population, or the emergence of a modern slave system utilizing millions of people and involving an incredible cultural dismemberment and disfiguration worth the developmental achievement? Whether we pose the issue in historical or contemporary terms, the probem of genocide invites moral bookkeeping.

Political leaders join a chorus of social scientists in claiming that a certain number of lives are worth a certain amount of development. But when you are asked what number or which people, then the issues of genocide are joined. As Solzhenitsyn remarks, there was nothing asked about the disruption of Russian society until 1938, because the intelligentsia was not directly involved as a victim. When it was the peasantry there was no outcry. When it was the urban proletariat it was perfectly acceptable that they go to the rack. When it was one ethnic minority after another it was perfectly rationalized in terms of development and nationalism. But when the intelligentsia felt the lash in 1938, questions about Soviet genocide arose. Genocide becomes a problem only when the intellectuals are affected; until then, the latter have an incredible capacity for myopic moral bookkeeping. The intellectuals had no problems with Bolshevism. One problem this raises is the selective values of one person or group over another. Genocide is the great leveling device of state terror; it alone equates classes and elites in the name of higher statist goals—quite apart from judgments based on social or even economic contributions to growth. That is why it is difficult to accept the argument that genocide has any organic connection with development.

## Notes to Chapter 3

1. Parsons, Talcott. "Some Sociological Aspects of the Fascist Movements," *Essays on Sociological Theory*. Glencoe, Illinois: The Free Press/Macmillan, 1949. pp. 124-141. It should be noted, in all fairness to Parsons, that his more recent writings on social systems have tended to emphasize their "evolutionary" characteristics and not just their "structural" components. See for example, "Polity and Society: Some General Considerations," *Politics and Social Structure*. New York: The Free Press/Macmillan, 1969. pp. 473-522.

2. Woolf, S.J. *The Nature of Fascism*. New York: Random House, 1968; see in this connection Renzo De Felice, *Fascism: An Informal Introduction to Its Theory and Practice*. New Brunswick, New Jersey: Transaction Books, 1977.

3. Martyrs and Heroes Remembrance Authority, *The Holocaust*. Jerusalem: Yad Vashem, 1975. pp. 46-63.

4. The most authoritative figure available is 5,820,960 Jews perished during the Holocaust. See Encyclopedia Judaica, "The Holocaust." Jerusalem: Keter Publishing House Ltd., 1971. Volume 8, pp. 827-915.

5. Hilberg, Raul. *The Destruction of the European Jews*. Chicago: Quadrangle Books, 1961. pp. 766-67; and Lucy S. Dawidowicz, *The War Against the Jews: 1933-1945*. New York: Holt, Rinehart, and Winston, 1975. pp. 150-166.

6. Feingold, Henry L. *The Politics of Rescue: The Roosevelt Administration and the Holocaust*. New Brunswick, New Jersey: Rutgers University Press, 1970. p. 304.

7. Korey, William. *The Soviet Cage: Anti-Semitism in Russia*. New York: The Viking Press, 1973. pp. 125-163.

8. Solzhenitsyn, Alexandr, I. *The Gulag Archipelago* 1918-1956. New York and London: Harper and Row, 1973. Volume 1, pp. 24-25. For a fuller treatment of this point, see chapter 6 on "Collectivism and State Power."

9. Reich, Wilhelm. *The Mass Psychology of Fascism* (translated by Vincent Carfagno). New York: Farrar, Straus, and Giroux, 1970. p. 281.

10. Gramsci, Antonio. *Letters from Prison* (selected, translated, and introduced by Lynne Lawner). New York and London: Harper and Row, 1973. pp. 131-132. Perhaps no single research effort equals that of Renzo De Felice in understanding the crucial elements of "conciliazione" and "consenso" in Mussolini's Italy. See especially,

*Mussolini il fascista: L'organizzazione dello state fascista,:* 1925-1929; and *Mussoloni il duce: Gli anni del consenso,* 1929-1936. Torino, Italy: Giulio Einaudi editore, 1968 and 1974.

11. Chabod, Federico. *L'Italia Contemporanea, 1918-1948.* Torino: Giulio Einaudi editore, 1961. pp. 91-100.

12. Ledeen, Michael A. "Italian Jews and Fascism," in *Judaism,* Summer 1968. pp. 278-281; and more recently by the same author, "The Jewish Question in Fascist Italy." Paper delivered at the American Historical Association, December 1973; and "Fascist Social Policy" (section on Fascism and the Jews), in *The Use and Abuse of Social Policy: Behavioral Science and National Policy Making.* New Brunswick, New Jersey: Transaction Books, 1971. pp. 90-108.

13. Sternhell, Zeev. "Fascist Ideology," in *Fascism: A Reader's Guide,* edited by Walter Laqueur. Berkeley and Los Angeles: University of California Press, 1976. pp. 360-362.

14. Steiner, John M. *Power Politics and Social Change in National Socialist Germany.* The Hague: Mouton Publishers, 1976.

15. Rummel, R.J. "Dimensions of Foreign and Domestic Conflict Behavior: A Review of Empirical Findings," in *Theory and Research on the Causes of War.* Edited by D.G. Pruitt and R.C. Snyder. Englewood Cliffs, New Jersey: Prentice Hall, 1969. pp. 226-227.

16. Durkheim, Emile. *Suicide: A Study in Sociology.* New York: The Free Press/Macmillan, 1951. p. 391.

17. Arendt, Hannah. *The Origins of Totalitarianism* (new edition). New York: Harcourt, Brace, and World, 1966. p. 462.

18. Arendt, Hannah. *Ibid.,* p. 463.

19. Contrast for example, Luigi Barzini, *The Italians,* with Ralf Dahrendorf, *Society and Democracy in Germany.* Garden City, New York: Doubleday, 1967.

20. de Castro, Josué. *The Geography of Hunger.* Boston: Little, Brown, and Company, 1952.

21. Brown, Lester R. *World Without Borders.* New York: Random House, 1972.

22. Hadwiger, Don F. and Browne, William P. *The New Politics of Food.* Lexington, Mass.: D.C. Heath & Co., 1978.

23. Arens, Richard. "Death Camps in Paraguay," *American Indian Journal,* Vol. 4, No. 2, July, 1978. pp. 3-12.

24. Hilberg, Raul. "German Railroads/Jewish Souls." *Transaction/Society,* Vol. 14, No. 1, Nov.-Dec. 1976. pp. 60-74.

25. Pawelczynska, Anna. *Values and Violence in Auschwitz.* Berkely and Los Angeles: University of California Press, 1979. pp. 15-23.

# Chapter 4

# Genocide and a New Definition of Social Systems

*A civilization is a struggle to keep self-control, and in this it is like some great tragic person, some Niobe who must display an almost superhuman will or the cry will not touch our sympathy. The loss of control over thought comes toward the end; first a sinking in upon the moral being, then the last surrender, the irrational cry, revelation—the scream of Juno's peacock.*

*William Butler Yeats*, A VISION

There are eight basic types of societies that can be defined on a measurement scale of life and death. I place these broad types within a framework of state power rather than cultural systems. It is not that anthropology was incorrect in its emphasis on the importance of culture, tradition, and language. Without their work the social sciences would be even more bereft of a humane literature than they are at present. The cultural framework has proven unable to move beyond psychological categories of guilt or shame, or to achieve better than a critical radicalism that envisions the life and death systems in terms of paralleling the life and death of individuals. The classical tradition in anthropology, at least until the contemporary period when political anthropology became a recognized area,[1] was unable to show how state authority, bureaucratic networks, and nationalist claims generated their own forms of genocidal patterns. For the internalization of guilt or shame to be effective there must be a set of external, and usually

43

political, restraints on behavior. The potency of guilt societies or shame societies not only entails forms of conservatism and consensus, but also, as has recently been pointed out, is at the heart of the revolutionary processes in many newer societies.[2]

The following definitions of societal types should be viewed as political guidelines with near-infinite shadings, not psychological types such as Spranger's *Types of Men*.[3] Social systems provide a continuum; it is only when one examines the poles of this continuum that the extent of differences in human organization becomes apparent. Beyond that, we are faced with the grim truth that any given nation may exhibit all eight types of patterns over a sufficient length of time. Much depends on the primary and secondary definitions of a society rather than the existence of any one type and the absence of all other types.

The types are: *First,* genocidal societies in which the state arbitrarily takes the lives of citizens for deviant or dissident behavior. Since this work is dedicated to a full exploration of this subject, an extended definition is not required. But it must be emphasized that the break, the gap between genocidal and all other types of societies is qualitative. It is the only form of rule which takes lives systematically. *Second,* deportation or incarceration societies in which the state either removes individuals from the larger body politic or in some form prevents their interaction with the commonwealth in general. *Third,* torture societies in which people are victimized short of death, returned to the societies from which they emanated, and left in these societies as living evidence of the high risk of deviance or dissidence. *Fourth,* harassment societies in which deviants are constantly being picked up, searched, seized, or held in violation of laws that are usually remote from the actual crimes the state feels these individuals have committed. Since laws can be invoked against almost any behavior, the possibility of harassment of individuals through legal channels is infinite.

These four types of societies have in common the physical discomfiture and dislocation of deviant, dissident individuals, employing everything from simple harassment for nonpayment of taxes, for example, to direct liquidation of the person. What is involved is physical. There are four other types of social systems that use what might be called the symbolic method for gaining allegiance and adherence. These are: *Fifth,* traditional shame societies where participation in the collective will is generated through instilling the individual with a sense of disapproval from outside sources, and insured by the isolation suffered as a result of nonparticipation in the normative system. *Sixth,* guilt societies closely akin to shame societies but which internalize a sense of wrongdoing in the individual causing him to respond to normative standards. *Seventh,* tolerant societies where norms are well articulated and understood, but where deviance and dissidence are permitted to go unpunished; they are not celebrated, but not destroyed either. These can be described as a series of pluralisms operating within a larger monism. *Eighth,* permissive societies in which norms are questioned and community definitions rather than state definition of what constitutes normative behavior emerge in the decision-making process.

While at least the last seven of these eight types of societies overlap, they are distinct enough to merit differentiation and understanding on their own terms. Each of these eight types of societies can be found in capitalist, socialist, or any kind of society, whatever its admixture, and it would be gratuitous to claim that the movement from capitalism to socialism requires or involves a movement from less punitive to more permissive, or less permissive to more punitive societies. To attempt such a correlation at this level is a snare and delusion, inviting spurious sorts of measures and variables.

Capitalism and socialism are not strictly economic systems. They yield all sorts of mixed political and ideological persuasions. Thus if we isolate but one item—the number of parties operating in a given social system—we find a similar lack of correlation between types of polity and forms of rule. While it would appear to be the case that single-party states reveal higher levels of coercion than multiparty states, the single-party apparatus of Mexico or Israel (with all due tolerance for the formal existence of smaller, satellitic parties in these two nations) may operate more democratically than the multiparty apparatus in Argentina or Indonesia. In any event, the purpose of this chapter is not to examine the relationship between democratic processes and political parties. Rather it is to develop first a typology and then an explanation for state-perpetrated violence that distinguishes genocidal societies from other types of domination and authority.

To Turkey we owe two developments that were to be of profound impact on the course of the twentieth century: at one end there was the Kemalist Revolution that functioned as a prototype for Third World patterns of development half a century later. Both in practice and in concept, Turkey initiated a revolution from above under military bureaucratic sponsorship that took that agrarian society to the threshhold of the twentieth century.[4] Equally important, and far more ominous, was the final legacy of the Ottoman Empire. From the start of the century until its final demise in 1918, it bequeathed a policy of genocide on a scale unparalleled in any earlier epoch. The destruction of the Armenians was an event whose magnitude was matched only by the silence of the "civilized world" too absorbed in its own horrors of World War I to realize the qualitative uniqueness involved in the mass extermination of the Armenian peoples.

> In 1915, the leaders of the Turkish Empire put into action a plan to remove and exterminate its Armenian population of approximately 1,800,000 persons. The Turks were not particular about the methods they employed to this end: of at least a million and a half Armenians forced to leave their homes, supposedly to be deported, from 600,000 to 800,000 were murdered before ever reaching their destinations. Descriptions of this massacre clearly indicate an attempt to deliberately, systematically exterminate all or most of the group.[5]

The genocide committed against the Armenian people illustrates how different facets of state authority, and even different state authorities as such, can generate an appropriate ideology to perform the necessary dirty work. The Turkish overseers began the destruction of the Armenian minority in the name of the Ottoman Empire. The Young Turks continued the process in the name of Turkish nationalism. The Kemalists completed this process in the name of development and hegemonic integration.[6] Hence, between 1893 and 1923 roughly 1,800,000 Armenians were liquidated, while another 1,000,000 were exiled, without a single political or military elite within the state assuming responsibility for the termination of the slaughter, or for that matter, granting the Armenians national autonomy or territorial rights. This is not to equate the final stages of the Ottoman Empire with the first stages of the Kemalist Republic, only to point out that any effort to establish a precise correlation between a type of state system and the character of response to national minorities or peoples is dangerously mechanical and reductionist.[7]

The fate of the Armenians is the essential prototype of genocide in the twentieth century. The method of identifying the Armenians was simple enough: they were identified by tax collectors, public officials, and neighbors within the Ottoman Empire. After that, a process took place where first they were segregated sexually; second they were required to surrender all weapons; third, Armenian men went into the armed forces in special units called "labor battalions"; fourth, the elites or prominent members of the Armenian community were arrested, secretly murdered, leaving the others numbed by terror; fifth, the remaining males in each village were summoned by the town to report immediately and were then slain out of town; sixth, woment and children were then prepared for deportation, driven into the desert by soldiers, and were then slain out of town; sixth, women and children were then prepared for deportation, driven into the desert by soldiers, and in the Ottoman Empire in 1914 were annihilated or deported to the desert.

Without wishing to engage in an ideological refinement, i.e., whether the genocide perpetrated against the Armenian people was or was not of Holocaust proportions, the fact remains that this people provide a major benchmark for events of the century. The disposition of this people dispels the common illusion that genocide is simply a function of development. The Armenian case is one in which a backward Ottoman Turkish empire, which initiated the first major mass destruction and expulsion of a people, was followed by a Kemalist regime, which made common cause with the Soviet Union to liquidate a nascent Armenian Republic which was recognized as a member of the family of nations by the Paris Peace Conference following the conclusion of World War I. The Armenian question represented a fusion of national, religious, and cultural issues. If the genocidal outcome was "incomplete" in the case of the Armenian people, it was less a consequence of Turkish mercy than it was their lack of systematic techniques of engineered death.

Explanations offered for the genocidal treatment of Armenians provide crucial elements in any explanation of premeditated mass murder carried out by the state. The summary prepared by Dadrian clearly delineates these elements.

> (1) Acute interferences with mainly political, military, and economic goal-directed activities gave rise to anger, or aggressive tendencies. (2) The Armenians were perceived as the available source of much of this frustration, and hostile attitudes against them were amplified. The process of scapegoating added to these hostilities and angers, which could not be directed toward the actual frustrator, i.e., the opposing Allies. (3) Social and cultural inhibitions which might have directed anger into channels other than aggression were minimal or absent. (4) Hostility became so intense and restraint so weak as to allow aggressive behavior of the most violent nature to occur, thanks to the original decision of the Turkish government.[9]

Such social-psychological features as external threat, opposing beliefs, competition for scarce goods, and frustration-aggression-scapegoating syndromes are often present in social systems without genocide taking place. These characteristics are often extant during wartime conditions. In this regard Dadrian has extended his analysis more recently to provide a greater specificity to genocidal systems. In comparing the Armenian and Jewish cases, we are presented with a pioneering typology in the sociological literature.

*Primary Importance Common Features.* Both acts of genocide were designed and executed during the exigencies of so-called world wars. In both instances, the principal instruments for the conception, design, and execution of the holocausts were political parties (Young Turks and Nazis) which invested themselves with monolithic power and literally took over the functions of their respective states.

*Secondary Importance Common Features.* The war ministries and the selected organs and outfits of the affiliated military structures were subverted and utilized for the manifold purposes of genocide. Economic considerations involving official as well as some personal designs of enrichment at the expense of the relatively better off members of the victim group, played a key role. In both members, the victim groups were minorities whose overall vulnerability was matched by the degree of ease with which the dominant groups implemented their schemes of extermination.

*Tertiary Importance Common Features.* Cultural and religious, and in a sense racial differences separated the victim groups from the perpetrator groups—notwithstanding the incidence of certain patterns of assimilation and even amalgamation through which multitudes from both groups were, and felt, identified with one another. Many Ottoman Armenians and German Jews felt politically and socially, if not culturally, identified with the respective dominant groups. The bureaucratic machinery had a crucial role in the administration and supervision of genocidal violence. Sanctions, both negative and positive, were the operationally controlling factor in both cases through which military and civilian personnel, from the highest to the lowest echelons of the administrative setup, were demoted or promoted, punished or rewarded, threatened or cajoled on the basis of their attitudes and performances vis-à-vis the processes of genocide.[10]

Whether a "symbolic interactionist" perspective really flows from available evidence is somewhat doubtful.[11] Rather it seems to move the discussion of genocide away from its promising roots in political economy into a softer theoretical plane of social psychology. The search for metaphor would better take us into the realm of social biology, or more simply, neo-Darwinian survivalist perspectives. Metaphorical reasoning, however attractive, still leaves intact a study of the specifics of genocide; more poignantly, how genocide serves as an ultimate test of the stratification of a society and the prevention of any realization of equities among different races, religions, tribes, and nationalities. For we must try to demonstrate that genocide is endemic to the social structure. And genocide must serve as a basic measuring device for creating a new typology of social and political systems, rather than be viewed as a response to mass contagion or elitist charisma.

The emergence of a new field called victimology, as an answer to criminology, raises fundamental issues. Genocide addresses itself to the problems of those who are victimized by official representatives of the state. On the other hand, if the emphasis on victims is randomized, that is, without concern for sources of violence, a serious dilemma emerges: a breakdown of the notion of criminal rehabilitation at the expense of assistance to the victims. This may also entail abandonment of the notion of meliorative behavior in the political and social systems. The pitfall of victimology as a "science" is its tendency to produce an overly conservative outcome. Victimology tends to emphasize victims as if they existed independently of another entity called the criminal. Victimology in its very outrage, omits from consideration one hundred years of social science research that has placed questions of crime and punishment, victims and criminals, in a larger political and sociological perspective. Victimology is an important new tendency in social research. There is hardly a professional meeting without a victimology panel offsetting the criminology panel. But analysts should be wary of any overreaction to genocidal problems, of seeing every form of deviant behavior as an insult to the dignity of the potential victim. An "institutional" victimization approach to a social problem is risky; it carries with it the further dilemma that identifying the victim is no more self-evident than locating the criminal.[12]

How does one respond to those who engage in genocide? What alternatives are available to its practitioners? Strategies have ranged from the Nuremberg trial of Nazi leaders to the Japanese war criminal trials which seek to enunciate and codify limits to state or official violence. But when all is said and done, such legal codification reduces itself to a much more simplified theory than we like to admit: we punish those who lose rather than those who engage in genocide. While victors have a healthy, spirited reaction to those who participate in mass murder, they are selective about criminal prosecution, based on the degree of loss and gain of those who engaged in these acts. It is hard to distinguish between the persecution of Armenians by Turks and the persecution of American Indians by new settlers of the Western frontier. Yet here is a world of difference in the way popular classes and intellectual elites handle the question of punishment, or even the way in which these problems are framed. There are serious ontological issues in this area of genocide: whether we are punishing criminals or those who made the mistake of losing massive military engagements.

As in all high-level generalizations, one must account for sharp variations in political systems. The most extreme of these is a weak state, which underwrites mass violence and human genocide in order to foster its own survival. The most pronounced and unique illustration of this is Colombia throughout the twentieth century. Here we have a nation characterized by *la violencia* that demonstrates how weak state authority can be yet manage to foster its interests without alleviating mass destruction.[13] The importance of this case is trancendent: the issues of genocidal societies cannot be reduced to a simplistic formula that juxtaposes the anarch with the behemoth, and that presumes that the liquidation of state authority is equivalent to ushering in an age of respect for human rights.

Stokes[14] refers to the Colombian state syndrome as *machetismo*. He notes that Colombia has been in a condition of violence that geographically includes almost the entire country, and worse, the entire century. "When no one caudillo can peacefully subjugate existing opposition, when one or more challengers claim supreme power, *machetismo* becomes a costly and time consuming methodology for establishing authority. Among seventy nationwide examples of *machetismo* in Colombia in the nineteenth century, one conflict alone took approximately 80,000 lives, and the struggle which covered the years 1899 to 1903 took about 100,000 lives." Colombia is an example of a state that exhibits weak central authority and yet manages, by that very factor, to stabilize a genocidal system.

Since we are concerned with establishing the genocidal social system as a basic category of social life, the Colombian case is just as significant as the Turkish case; indeed more extended over time. In most cases of recorded genocide, the ruling class, party, or regime established itself as supreme and exclusive, but in Colombia an entente took place between two aristocratic, patrician institutions that succeeded in maintaining oligarchic domination even in the twilight of their actual economic power. Darcy Ribeiro traces such dictatorial state authority during the twentieth century.[15] Assassination societies have in common a "homogenization period" in which real opposition, usually liberal in character, is decimated in a systematic fashion. "Figures based on statistics of recent years show that in 1960 Colombia had a rate of death by homicide of 33.8 per 100,000 inhabitants, whereas that of the United States, by no means a tranquil nation, was 4.5, and Peru 2.2."[16] Ribeiro plainly states that the entire social structure came to operate "as the generator of lawless forms of conduct on the individual or the family plane, forms that constitute the regular modes of maintaining the overall regime, or in other words, the very function of the institutions."

> The eruption of violence en masse—with its 300,000 officially admitted murders and surely more than 1,000,000 wounded, exiled, robbed, crippled in one decade—occurs when the overall order represented by the regulative institutions of national scope (government, church, justice, army, police, parties, press) becomes confused with local order in the exacerbation of partisan hatred, everything becoming fused and swallowed up in the same generalized dysfunction.[17]

Let us take as a third example of a genocidal society a newly emerged nation: Uganda. The following report on differences between Tanzania and Uganda sums up what a genocidal society looks like, when one considers that the estimated 80 to 90,000 people who have died at the hands of the Amin government represent a considerable slice of the population. General Amin seized power in an overthrow of the Milton Obote government in 1971. Prior to the demise of this regime in 1979, the International Commission of Jurists published a 63-page report of offenses against human rights in Uganda, with some horrifying details of the persecution and murder of individuals and total local communities within this African state. A low estimate is that 50,000 people who were considered "enemies" of the regime have been murdered and another 50,000 have been forced into exile. A relative of Amin, who was Uganda's foreign minister in 1971-72 and then sought exile himself, estimated that 80,000 to 90,000 people have died at the hands of Amin's government.[18] A more recent estimate provided by Amnesty International places the upper limits of the number of Ugandans killed by the Amin regime at 300,000 or more. The report notes that the people killed were drawn from all social classes, religious groups (especially Catholics), and occupational segments such as teachers, lawyers, and doctors. The final tortured twist in the Amin regime was to set up a "Ugandan Human Rights Committee" comprised of the same security organizations and personnel accused of responsibility for the genocidal practices to start with.[19]

The full measure of how a genocidal society operates becomes clear by examining such data. Uganda was, until the fall of Amin in 1979, also a deportation society, having exiled 40,000 Indians within a four-week period of time, against their will. What is especially noteworthy about viewing Uganda primarily as a genocidal society is that one does not become encumbered with lengthy discussions about communism or fascism, and comparative governments of Europe and Africa. Defining Amin's economic system becomes a secondary intellectual task. Ethnocentricities prevent us from viewing nazi Germany or Stalinist Russia in terms similarly unencumbered by ideological definitions.

One should not assume that genocide is unique to movements that claim revolutionary outlooks. It is equally the case that reactionary systems can practice genocide on revolutionary movements. The case of Malaysia between 1948 and 1956 is indicative of the extermination not simply of an internal political movement, but of a political movement deemed to represent a national minority, in this case Chinese. In the Malaysian situation, the linkage between genocide and ethnocide was apparent. The guerilla forces never numbered more than 8,000 men, who were eventually defeated by a force of 40,000 British and 45,000 Malaysian home guards. This huge overkill was based on a profoundly erroneous persuasion that the Chinese minority was interested in setting up a Chinese hegemony. As a result, a genocidal policy was followed that took lives estimated to be anywhere from 5,000 to 20,000 people.[20]

Nor have the Malaysian attitudes toward the Chinese calmed with the years. In 1979, a quarter century after the first massacre, the government of Malaysia, in the teeth of worldwide opposition, initiated the practice of putting to sea and to certain death the 76,000 Vietnamese refugees (most of Chinese ethnic extraction) who landed between 1976 and 1979 from the Vietnam mainland. In further issuing a prohibition against any such further landing, and a "shoot on sight" order, the Malaysian state has taken upon itself the determination, once again, of which peoples shall live and which shall die—blaming the victims in the process. It is noteworthy how, during the course of this century, the unthinkable act of genocide has passed over into the realm of the commonplace.

Nor can any extrinsic justification, such as the acceleration of rates of industrial growth, be employed. When societies are economically backward, the consequence of a high assassination and/or expulsion rate has been to intensify backwardness and stagnation. Uganda, even more than Malaysia, is a prime example of this tendency. The rates of industrial expansion and consumer purchasing power both fell off badly in the final three years of the Amin regime.[21] This is not to deny that when industrially advanced societies turn into genocidal states, they tend to maintain their high levels of economic productivity. Terror can produce at least short-run upswings in economic growth rates. This was the case of Germany under Hitler and the Soviet Union under Stalin in the 1930s. But there certainly is no "iron law" in which human extermination can be coupled with social development.

Recently, attempts have been made to extend the concept of genocide to include cultural repression. Hence, questions have been raised about the position of Black people in America during the contemporary epoch. Questions have been urgently raised as to whether punitive sterilization, breakdowns in advanced obstetrical care, tubal ligations, and hysterectomies do not constitute new elements in genocide.[22] The difficulty with assumptions about genocidal characteristics of family planning and medical care is the ubiquitous nature of the data. The steady increase in numbers of Black people—even beyond the societal norms as a whole—decrease in occupational differentiations, and crude birth and death statistics would indicate that although the punitive treatment of American Blacks continues, such differences are selective; and, above all, do not have federal sanctions supporting such practices.[23]

The ubiquity of the concept of genocide is nowhere better illustrated than in the treatment of American Black citizens by their government. In the antebellum South, the killing of portions of the Black population for the purpose of exploiting the remainder represented a systematic policy. Less certain is the designation of genocide as a national rather than sectional policy in pre-Civil War contexts; and even less warranted is the assumption that every form of vigilante behavior in the post-Civil War context represents genocidal policy. Certainly from 1865 through 1945 one could detect a systematic, state-sponsored pattern of legal persecution, economic inequality, and police harassment against Black people. Beyond that, health, welfare, and educational differentials have constituted a monumental assault by the White on the Black population.[24] As late as 1950 these differential policies toward Black and White accounted for roughly 32,000 more deaths among Blacks than Whites, despite the aggregate difference in numbers of Black and White citizens. There can be no question that racial discrimination endured by American Blacks is unparalleled in American history. What can be questioned is how systematic or structural such practices are at present, in contrast to earlier epochs.

If we are left only with the legal definition of genocide, all manner of empirical problems arise. For example, in speaking of deliberately inflicted measures or forcible transferring of populations, the question inevitably arises: Who carries out such deliberate and forcible actions? In the case of the United States, there seems to be a pattern of vigilantism rather than genocidal practices by the state for the purpose of maintaining social order. The range of additional attitudes by the state toward its Black citizens extends from a long line of federal legislation to diminished racial animus and racial integration, to an assumption that legislation simply will not work and "benign neglect" under such circumstances would be better than forced integration. This relationship between the United States government and its Black citizens is a complex issue made more so by considerable sectional differences and psychological attitudes. Yet it would be both dangerous and hyperbolic to equate the American treatment of its Black citizens with the German Nazi treatment of its Jewish citizens. The demographic information we have concerning crude birthrates and the ever-expanding size of the Black population would move to counter such a mistaken equation. We are not engaged in active apologetics for the brutality of hostile White-power structures toward their Black communities, but this must nonetheless be distinguished from the sort of systematic exter-mination associated with the concept of genocide.

There is a thin line between systematic and sporadic destruction. Sporadic destruction might take more lives than systematic annihilation. Vigilante politics often has the tacit support of at least a portion of the state mechanism. Nevertheless, the distinctions are signficant and of more than academic consequence, for they point to tendencies and trends over time, and also presume the role of resistance to genocide among different peoples.

The end of an era when formal declarations of warfare were made also signifies the beginning of a new era in which the line between war and genocide becomes profoundly blurred. The undeclared war in Vietman, with its mortifiying levels of deaths through air attacks, including napalm and jelly bombings and the wide use of chemical defoliants, all of these have made serious critics of that war argue that this was a case of genocide.[25] Arguments were made on the other side that the Vietnam conflict was not a matter of genocide, since the killings were not systematic, but simply a result of the enemy not accepting the terms of an honorable settlement.[26] The distinction between internal and foreign peoples who are being killed helps little, since it must be confessed that all genocidal practices involve a definition by the perpetrators of mass violence of those destroyed as outsiders. What legitimately can be asserted in such cases is that the widespread use of mass violence by state authorities against one portion of a population clearly has spillover potentials for another part of humanity, sometimes thousands of miles away. This in itself might serve as a deterrent to any further legitimization of a genocidal state.

Peoples subject to genocide have been faced with their strategic requirements for negotiating their own survival. Black resistance to lynchings, hangings, and vigilantism in general served as a major obstacle to genocidal policies, just like in the antebellum South the totality of intimidation weakened such resistance by limiting the social organization of the Black community. The literature on the

Holocaust is filled with similar choices and decisions. The Warsaw Ghetto is perhaps the classical model of Jewish acquiescence being replaced by Jewish resistance once the choices were starkly narrowed to life-and-death concerns. But clearly, whereas in the case of the American Black community its struggle for survival was potentially victorious, the same was not the case in the liquidation of the European Jewish communities under Nazism. There is no *a priori* assurance that either acquiescence or resistance will guarantee survival within the confines of a genocidal regime. This is a constant problem that must be faced not only by those aiming at the death of the minority population but for those negotiating the survival of that population as well. In this regard, the definition of the genocidal enemy as external, as was done in the Vietnam conflict, may assist in the liberation effort.

A major category left unresolved by such an interior or national model is the function of genocide due to imperial aggression or foreign intervention. Here we have the contradiction of fine, upstanding European and American cultures being responsible for the liquidation of masses of native populations. There is the destruction of the Zulu peoples by the British; the decimation and virtual elimination of the Indians by early American settlers; and the impoverishment of the Zaire people in the former Belgian Congo. These are forms of genocide against foreign peoples rather than nationals. A central tendency in all genocidal societies is to initially create juridical-legal separations between citizens and aliens, elites and masses, dominant and backward races, and so forth. This serves as a pretext for genocide and also as a preconditon to the implementation of genocidal policies. We are dealing with an oblique problem that has many ramifications: attempting definitions of social systems, not on economic grounds alone, nor any of the other customary variables of polity, military, and society, but rather on mortality data. American Indians and African Zulus, many of whom sought pacific solutions, were defiled and denied even the remote participation of their numbers in any dominant imperial framework. Again, we have the seeds of a study unto itself. Yet the role of classical imperialism as a critical element in creating the conditions for modern mass genocide cannot be ignored.

A contemporary illustration of the deportation-incarceration society is found in Cuba following the Castro revolution. Without minimizing the enormity of its social reformation, the fact remains that approximately one million Cubans were sent or went voluntarily into exile, out of a total population of less than eight million. One can argue that deportation is an incredibly humane form of treatment compared to assassination, and that, of course, is true. It is also more humane to use incarceration than incineration,[27] although Cuba had its share of the latter as well. There are an estimated 5,000 to 50,000 political prisoners languishing in Cuban jails. The point is not humanity but forms of punishment, and how the state removes deviants and dissidents from its midst. It is exceedingly important to emphasize the difference between assassination and incarceration societies. It is the most fundamental distinction of all since those either deported or incarcerated often live to tell the story; and in the case of Cuba, to confront their tormentors. This is not to deny that deportation and incarceration are fundamental methods of dealing with and eliminating enemies of the state.

Easier to identify as a pure deportation society than Cuba, is France and its policy under Napoleon III in the mid-nineteenth century. After the coup d'état of 1851, Louis Bonaparte inaugurated a system of military dictatorship that entailed expropriation, exile, and acts calculated to restore an empire. With respect to deviants, criminals, and dangerous political elements, no differentiation was made. A "mixed commission" comprised of civil and military authorities passed sentence without concern for evidence, procedure, or appeal. The convicted would be deported to Guiana or Lambassa. In nineteenth-century terms, the numbers were impressive. By the middle of March 1842, over 26,000 persons had been arrested, of whom 6,500 were acquitted and somewhat more than 5,000 sentenced only to police surveillance. Of the 15,000 actually punished, nearly two-thirds were sentenced to deportation to Algeria, while the rest were either handed over to other tribunals *against* common law or expelled from France.[28] Despite the severity of punishment, expulsion was viewed as the ultimate punishment rather than the outright physical elimination of "undesirable elements."

Some societies, like contemporary Brazil, have no capacity to remove or deport enemies of the state. They thus become high-torture societies where police and other agencies of the state minimize opposition and maximize obedience through human disfigurement.[29] The numbers tortured are of course important. In countries like Brazil or present-day Chile the numbers reach into the tens of thousands. One must once again distinguish torture from both assassination or incarceration. For the most part, those tortured quickly return to the larger society. One might argue that the purpose of a torture society is to reinfiltrate these people into the larger society as a mechanism of contagion and mass fear.

When referring to Brazil as a torture society, I specifically have in mind the treatment by state authorities of its urban White citizenry. Like the nineteenth-century United States in relation to its Indian minorities, the twentieth-century Brazilian state has adopted entirely genocidal standards in relation to its Indian minorities.

> The huge losses sustained by the Indian tribes in this decade were catalogued. Of 19,000 Munducurus believed to have existed in the thirties, only 1,200 were left. The strength of the Guaranis had been reduced from 5,000 to 300. There were 400 Carajas left out of 4,000. Of the Cintas Largas, who had been attacked from the air and driven into the mountains, possibly 500 had survived out of 10,000. The proud and noble nation of the Kadiweus—the Indian Cavaliers—had shrunk to a pitiful scrounging band of about 200. A few hundred only remained of the formidable Chavantes, who prowled in the background of Peter Fleming's Brazilian journey, but they had been reduced to mission fodder—the same melancholy fate that had overtaken the Bororos, who helped to change Levi Strauss's views on the nature of human evolution. Many tribes were not represented by a single family, a few by one or two individuals. Some, like the Tapaiunas—in this case from a gift of sugar laced with arsenic—had disappeared altogether. It is estimated that between 50,000 and 100,000 Indians survive today. Brazil's leading social historian believes that not a single one will be alive by 1980.[30]

There are harassment societies where those in opposition to the state are not phyically mistreated so much as legally abused. The range of societies performing such harassment extends from large states like the United States to much smaller societies in Western Europe that likewise engage in mass forms of harassment to guarantee political allegiance. Here the purpose is to harness the legal mechanism to the aims of the state so that all forms of harassment appear to be for real rather than political crimes, and hence punishment becomes a nonpolitical response to political opposition.

The fundamental characteristic of the shame society is the idea of rehabilitation: errors against the state are resonded to by making the individual criminal feel a sense of shame, and hence the need for reformation. China comes to mind as the best example of that kind of system. Both military and civilian authorities are oriented toward the aim that everyone can be rehabilitated; and this rehabilitation is best defined by self-recognition (shame) and the internalization of guilt. In practice, the gulf between shame and guilt societies may be quite narrow.

One reason that torture societies have increased in potency as well as numbers is the growing sophistication of the medical and biological sciences. The same techniques employed by a doctor to reduce pain can also be employed by the torturer to intensify pain short of killing. In some states, such as Iran under the high point of power by the Shah, and Greece under the rule of its military junta, such an abusive extension of science became a method of governing. While antitorture legislation advocated by organizations like the International Commission of Jurists have floundered, the expose of torture societies and their techniques did have the effect of profoundly reducing the use of overt torture among states like the aforementioned Iran and Greece during the last stages of their repressive regimes.

Vigilante groups are a powerful deterrent to crime. Militia patrols tend to deal out rough justice to offenders on the spot instead of bringing them before civil authorities. This usually takes the form of a beating for crimes of theft or pilfering. The militia is also expected to take part in propaganda work and to change the thinking of bad elements. A recent (official) report from Tientsin talked of militia units "organizing, arming, and propagandizing the masses and rebuffing the wrecking activities of a handful of class enemies." The People's Militia appears to do quite an effective job of law-and-order maintenance. Its main drawback is that a paramilitary organization of this sort can sometimes grow too powerful.

The first task of the militia is to back up the People's Liberation Army in time of war. Urban units in large cities are trained in sophisticated techniques of warfare, including antiaircraft defense, rocketry, antitank exercises, and tunnel warfare. The second function of the militia, however, is to assist the public security forces in maintaining law and order, and militiamen and women on patrol with rifles and fixed bayonets are a familiar sight.[31]

Guilt societies are less concerned with psychological manifestations than with the sociological recognition of wrongdoing. The guilt society rests on authorities implanting a clear recognition that there is such a thing as deviance from norms, and that those who perform deviant acts are guilty by virtue of that fact alone, and those who are normative are innocent by virtue of obedience to those norms. Guilt societies rest on the authoritative justification of normative behavior; on the assumption of deviants as well as punishers of the soundness of the social order or public property.

Although we have characterized China as a shame-guilt society, the imposition of such a shame-guilt axis is not without its own form of coercion. In a recent report issued by Amnesty International, it becomes quite plain that between 1949 and 1975 at least, China could be characterized as a nation of legally sanctioned coercion through a relatively high imprisonment system.[32] The trial system was characterized by being closed to the public, or in more serious cases, mass public trials which represent little other than big meetings to announce sentence. The penalty system involved supervised labor, rehabilitation through labor, and control over movement in lesser cases. While the death penalty was not invoked frequently, it did exist. More frequent were detention centers, labor groups, and punishment by long working hours, withdrawing of food, the absence of medical treatment, and harsh discipline within the prison confines.

There is a process of amnesty taking place in which people arrested and incarcerated for years have been rehabilitated—sometimes tragically after death rather than in life. But his does point out a theme I have emphasized throughout the work: that a vast gulf exists between genocidal societies and others which rest upon shame-guilt, or even imprisonment. It is nothing other than a gulf of life and death itself written on the faces of people.

Perhaps the classic model of the tolerant society is Great Britain, where norms, rituals, and rites are fully understood and appreciated, but minority views are also found in great abundance. What characterizes these societies is firm allegiance to normative behavior and nondeviant behavior, while the normal apparatus of the state remains nonpunitive. It is left to the citizenry to apply proper social pressure to obtain obedience to the law. In the tolerant society the practice of intimidation is carried on informally rather than formally, normatively rather than legally. The hegemonic character of island societies, like Great Britain or Japan, help to explain this moral basis of social order.

Finally, there are the permissive societies. They are identified by their open-ended responses to the question of what constitutes moral law or normative behavior. The permissive society not only tolerates deviance and dissidence, but also understands that the role of the state is nothing other than the orchestration of a series of dissident and deviant acts without appreciation or understanding of what constitutes the perfect norm. Every permissive society has its legal limits, but even these tend to be stretched on behalf of the perpetrator no less than the victims of crimes, so that the legal system is involved in a series of plea bargains. They are not only presumed innocent, but also guilt is relatively shared by all concerned in the criminal process.

Where the United States might fit in such a modeling device is a subject for an entire volume. The brief discussion on its treatment of Black people indicates similitudes and continuities with nations elsewhere. Yet there is a special feature: the United States illustrates all eight elements in this typology; from the conduct of genocide toward its Black population in the nineteenth century to permissive liberalism toward a variety of interest groups and deviant forces in the late twentieth century.

One might argue that any typology that cannot adequately settle accounts for the United States (and as we have already noted, countries like Brazil) is not worth much; that we are better off utilizing old-fashioned categories such as capitalism and democracy. Such a typology as herein outlined does provide a new basis for comparison of the United States with other societies. True enough, to be left with an eight-part modeling device as an explanation of the United States raises proper questions as to the generalizability of the model. On the other hand, the mix between these eight items becomes crucial in the case of Western democratic states. Beyond that, the very inability to place such nations as the United States or Brazil in any one (or two) frames of the model itself indicates the complexities of advanced nations, not a need to return to an oversimplified model based on entirely mechanistic variables. The issue of the United States and other Western liberal societies can better be resolved once some clear-cut measures are established for those other countries, and they are in the disastrous majority, which reveal strong tendencies to fit into one or another of these frames.

Why should this be the case? If Mosse is correct that genocide is deeply embedded in the cultural milieu of Central Europe, and there is a tragic amount of evidence to support this contention, then we can better appreciate how such a concept migrated to the New World. In a most unusual thesis on American Frontier mythology, Richard Slotkin suggests that "the Europeans who settled the New World possessed at the time of their arrival a mythology derived from the cultural history of their home countries and reponsive to the psychological and social needs of their old culture."[33] While much of the language of this approach is shrouded in Jungian archetypes, the conclusions drawn by Slotkin stand apart from such theories: "This racial-cultural conflict pointed up and intensified the emotional difficulties attendant on the colonists' attempt to adjust to life in the wilderness. The picture was complicated for them by the political and religious demands made on them by those who remained in Europe, as well as by the colonists' own need to affirm—for themselves and for the home folks—that they had not deserted European civilization for American savagery." While this helps to explain the genocidal attitudes of colonists towards Indians, it does not explain the failure of such attitudes to be translated into genocidal practice against Blacks. For in addition to Jungian archetypes of regeneration through violence, American colonists also exhibited Lockean constitutional persuasions fused with a French utilitarian culture, in which every person was to count as one—no more or less. From the outset, the "three-fifths" doctrine, by means of which Black slaves could be differently punished, came upon hard times. The basis of American values was that individuals rather than collectivities are judged and either punished or rewarded. That is why the myth of genocide in America remained just that, and never had the force of public opinion either on the American frontier or its bastions of advanced European culture.

The problem of applying the model to concrete cases notwithstanding, we at least have a first sketch of eight types of societies (by no means separated into airtight compartments) in terms of a life/death continuum. Almost every society, and not just the United States, has all eight types present in one admixture or another. It becomes the next analytic task to determine the essential characterization of the system and the point where quantity is transformed into quality: at what point the numbers of people involved in sanctions by the state begin to define the character of that state.

Beyond an appreciation of the types of societies that promote or oppose genocidal practices is the final realization that "types" of people are extremely resistant to their own elimination. The Black population of the United States is larger in numbers and percentages than at any time in its two hundred-year history. Despite the utter and near-total decimation of European Jewry at the hands of the Third Reich, the total present-day Jewish population is equal to, if not greater than, at the start of World War II. Even the American Indian population of the United States has doubled between the census reports issued in 1960 and again in 1970. Without becoming self-satisfied or counseling benign neglect about the problem of genocide, it is nonetheless a fact that resistance to destruction of one's group or person should not be minimized; even in this age of maximum state power.

# Notes to Chapter 4

1.  cf. Levi-Strauss, Claude. *A World on the Wane* (translated by John Russell). New York: Criterion, 1961; Stanley Diamond. *In Search of the Primitive: A Critique of Civilization.* New Brunswick, New Jersey: Transaction Books, 1974; and Eric R. Wolf. *Peasant Wars of the Twentieth Century.* New York: Harper & Row, 1969.

2.  Wilson, Richard W. *The Moral State: A Study of the Political Socialization of Chinese and American Children.* New York: The Free Press/Macmillan, 1974. pp. 253-254; also, Amy Auerbacher Wilson. *Deviance and Social Control in Chinese Society.* New York: Praeger Publishers, 1977. pp. 1-13.

3.  Spranger, Eduard. *Types of Men: The Psychology and Ethics of Personality* (translated by Paul J. W. Pigors). Halle: Niemeyer, 1928.

4.  Fidel, Kenneth. *Social Structure and Military Intervention: The 1960 Turkish Revolution.* Unpublished dissertation (University microfilm). Washington University, St. Louis. 1969; and Ellen Kay Trimberger, *Revolution from Above: Military Bureaucrats and Development in Japan, Turkey, Egypt, and Peru.* New Brunswick, New Jersey: Transaction Books, 1978.

5.  Dadrian, Vahakn N. "Factors of Anger and Aggression in Genocide," *Journal of Human Relations,* Vol. 19, No. 3. pp. 394-417.

6.  Boyajian, Dickran H. *Armenia: The Case for a Forgotten Genocide.* Westwood, New Jersey: Educational Book Crafters, 1972. pp. 300-314. For a moving personal statement, see Abraham H. Hartunian, *Neither to Laugh nor to Weep: A Memoir of the Armenian Genocide.* Boston: Beacon Press, 1968. esp. pp. 121-205.

7.  Bryce, James. *The Treatment of the Armenians in the Ottoman Empire.* London, Macmillan Ltd., 1916; and Henry Morgenthau. *Ambassador Morgenthau's Story.* New York: Doubleday-Page Publishers, 1918.

8.  Fein, Helen. "The Armenians: An Example of Genocide," in *Accounting for Genocide.* New York: The Free Press, 1979. Reprinted in *The Holocaust Years: Society on Trial,* edited by Roselle Chartock and Jack Spencer. New York: Bantam Books, 1978. pp. 252-254.

9.  Dadrian, Vahakn N. "Factors of Anger and Aggression in Genocide," *Journal of Human Relations,* Vol. 19, No. 3. pp. 414-415.

10. Dadrian, Vahakn N. "The Common Features of the Armenian and Jewish Cases of Genocide: A Comparative Victimological Perspective," *Victimology: A New Focus on Violence and Its*

*Victims,* edited by Israel Drapkin and Emilio Viano. Lexington, Mass: Lexington Books/D.C. Heath, 1975. pp. 106-107.

11.   Dadrian, Vahakn, N. "The Structural-Functional Components of Genocide," *Victimology,* edited by Israel Drapkin and Emilio Viano. Lexington, Mass.: Lexington Books/D.C. Heath, 1974. pp. 123-135.

12.   cf. Viano, Emilio C. (editor). *Victims and Society.* Washington, D.C.: Visage Press Inc., 1976. pp. 541-592.

13.   Berry, R. Albert; Hellman, Ronald G.; and Solaún, Mauricio. *The Politics of Compromise: Coalition Government in Colombia.* New Brunswick, New Jersey: Transaction Books (in cooperation with The Center for Inter-American Relations), 1979.

14.   Stokes, William S. "Violence as a Power Factor in Latin American Politics," *Conflict and Violence in Latin American Politics,* edited by Francisco José Moreno and Barbara Mitrani. New York: Thomas Y. Crowell, 1971. pp. 446-469.

15.   Ribeiro, Darcy. *The Americas and Civilization.* Translated by Linton L. Barrett and Marie Barrett. New York: E.P. Dutton, 1971. pp. 295-296.

16.   Campos, Germán Guzmán; Borda, Orlando Fals; and Luna, Eduardo Umaña. *La Violencia en Colombia: Estudio de un Proceso Social.* Bogota, 1964. pp. 407-410.

17.   Ribeiro, Darcy. *The Americas and Civilization.* Translated by Linton L. Barrett and Marie Barrett. New York: E.P. Dutton, 1971. p. 296.

18.   Carney, Martin. "Amin's Uganda," *The Nation,* April 12, 1975. pp. 430-435.

19.   Ellsworth, Whitney. "The Structure of Repression in Uganda," *Amnesty International Release,* June 15, 1978.

20.   Fairbairn, Geoffrey. *Revolutionary Guerilla Warfare: The Countryside Version.* Harmondsworth, Middlesex: Penguin Books Ltd., 1974. pp. 125-174.

21.   Schultheis, Michael. "The Ugandan Economy and General Amin, 1971-1974," *Studies in Comparative International Development,* Vol. 10, No. 3 (Fall) 1975. pp. 3-34.

22.   Weisbord, Robert G. *Genocide? Birth Control and the Black American.* Westport, Conn.: Greenwood Press, 1975.

23.   Lerner, William (director of statistical research). *Statistical Abstract of the United States.* 97th Annual Edition. U.S. Department of Commerce. Washington, D.C.: U.S. Government Printing Office, 1976.

24. Patterson, William L. *We Charge Genocide: The Historic Petition to the United Nations for Relief from a Crime of the United States Government against the Negro People.* New York: International Publishers. Originally published 1951. Civil Rights Congress, 1970. pp. 125-132.
25. Bedau, Hugo Adam. "Genocide in Vietnam?" in *Philosophy, Morality, and International Affairs.* Edited by Virginia Held, Sidney Morgenbesser, and Thomas Nagel. New York: Oxford University Press, 1974. pp. 5-46.
26. Lewy, Guenter, *America in Vietnam.* New York: Oxford University Press, 1978. p. 576.
27. Jacqueney, Theodore, "Castro's Political Prisoners," *AFL-CIO Free Trade Union News,* Vol. 32, No. 5, May 1977. pp. 1-2, 7-10; and Edward Tonat. "Castro's Captive Unions," *AFL-CIO Free Trade Union News,* Vol. 33, No. 7, July 1978. pp. 1-5.
28. Bramstedt, E.K. *Dictatorship and Political Police: The Technique of Control by Fear.* London: Kegan Paul, Trench Trubner, and Company Ltd., 1945. p. 39.
29. Della Cava, Ralph. "Brazil: The Struggle for Human Rights," *Commonweal,* Vol. 102, No. 20, 1975. pp. 623-626.
30. Lewis, Norman. "Genocide," *A Documentary Report on the Conditions of Indian Peoples in Brazil.* Berkeley, Calif.: Indigena, and American Friends of Brazil, 1974. pp. 9-10.
31. Jones, Margaret and Ruge, Gero. "Crime and Punishment in China," *Atlas: World Press Review,* Vol. 22, No. 9 (September) 1975. pp. 19-22.
32. Amnesty International. *Political Imprisonment in the People's Republic of China.* London: Amnesty International, 1978. p. 27.
33. Slotkin, Richard. *Regeneration Through Violence: The Mythology of the American Frontier, 1600-1860.* Middletown, Conn.: Wesleyan University Press, 1973. pp. 14-15.

# Chapter 5

# Individualism and
# State Power

*The fact that a man is a man is more important than the fact
that he believes what he believes. Nothing is quite that simple:
I know it. But when circumstances grow unbearably complex,
it is natural that we should grope about for a very simple
credo. And so, after all, we tell ourselves, man's real quidity is
that he is a human being, not that he is a Zionist, a
Communist, a Socialist, a Jew, a Pole, or, for that matter a
Nazi. But any man who cannot recognize this basic maxim is
an agent of Anti-Humanity, and his purpose, whether
conscious or not, is the wiping out of mankind.*

*John Hersey,* THE WALL

Once upon a time, earlier in the twentieth century, individualism
was a doctrine that could readily be dismissed as archaic,
idiosyncratic, and simply out of phase with the modern fashion.
Even those who wanted to make a place for the individual were
compelled to talk apologetically about the new individualism as a
kind of hybrid of social welfare economy in contradistinction to the
old individualism. Henry Steele Commager reminded us that "the
phenomenon of socialization was a logical expression of the
American temperament in the new century. It reflected that decline
of the importance of individualism and that growing awareness of
social responsibility that could be noted similarly in law, education,
business, and legislation."[1] With the triumph of America as a world
empire after World War I, and the rapid emergence of

Communism, Fascism, and Nazism as alternative empire systems soon thereafter, the banishment of the individual seemed complete. Everywhere in Western society good citizens shriveled at the charge of individualism, especially if it was prefaced by the word *bourgeois*. There seemed no place to hide for the person before the onslaught of the collective: the collective conscience, the collective will, and collective plan. In the eyes of a rhetorical liberalism, individualism came to be viewed as an impediment to responsible development, to social change itself. In one recent version of this theme, individualism has gone "too far . . . encouraging narcissism . . . is egocentric, often impulsive-ridden behavior . . has run amok."[2] To listen to most pundits of solidarism, individualism is one "ism" that seemed to violate the spirit of the century. The model of collective action toward predetermined ends was sanctioned by socialism, fascism, and welfarism.

But now that the twentieth century, for all ideological intents and organizational purposes, is behind us, it is rather these other "isms" that have become increasingly suspect. The old individualism failed because of the metaphysical presumptions which underlie Smith's notion of the "hidden hand." Smith seemed to imply some kind of mystical ghost in the machine regulating the behavior of one and all alike to the greater good of society as a whole. But the new collectivism failed because of the "heavy boot"; the widespread recognition that mechanisms to regulate behavior, like machines without ghosts, also worked imperfectly; and that the costs in human terms to achieve economic goals involved such stupendous numbers of lives, that even the most obdurate, dedicated servant of the GNP was compelled to wonder whether the "hidden hand" in its marketplace was not a trifle better than the heavy boot and the barbed wire.

It turned out that inherited doctrines of individualism and socialism were really not at stake. Rather, the ultimate showdown stripped of all "isms," were individuals and their right to self-definition and self-delineation versus states and the authority to destroy invested in them by virtue of their monopoly of power, both presumed and real. The essential Litmus Test became not one of social systems but of personal survival. How people died became a measure of how societies lived. As a result, genocide rather than welfare served to define the limits of state power. Continuities of living and dying, the inalienable rights of individuals in such a cycle, served to show how inalienable rights become subject to deterioration and ultimately dismissal by the state and the powers vested in it.

In a major recent work, Michel Foucault[3] describes the disposition of the body of a condemned man: Damiens the regicide. The officer of the watch left an account which Foucault recites. It provides a medieval horror story only two hundred years old. I ask your indulgence in its lengthy recitation, since it sets the background for the narrative that follows.

> The sulfur was lit, but the flame was so poor that only the top skin of the hand was burnt, and that only slightly. Then the executioner, his sleeves rolled up, took the steel pincers, which had been especially made for the occasion, and which were about a foot and a half long, and pulled first at the calf of the right leg, then at the thigh, and from there at the two fleshy parts of the right arm; then at the breasts. Though a strong, sturdy fellow, this executioner found it so difficult to tear away the pieces of flesh that he set about the same spot two or three times, twisting the pincers as he did so, and what he took away formed at each part a wound about the size of a six-pound crown piece.

> After these tearings with the pincers, Damiens, who cried out profusely, though without swearing, raised his head and looked at himself; the same executioner dipped an iron spoon in the pot containing the boiling potion, which he poured liberally over each wound. Then the ropes that were to be harnessed to the horses were attached with cords to the patient's body; the horses were then harnessed and placed alongside the arms and legs, one at each limb.

> Monsieur Le Breton, the clerk of the court, went up to the patient several times and asked him if he had anything to say. He said he had not; at each torment, he cried out, as the damned in hell are supposed to cry out, "Pardon, my God! Pardon, Lord." Despite all this pain, he raised his head from time to time and looked at himself boldly. The cords had been tied so tightly by the men who pulled the ends that they caused him indescribable pain. Monsieur Le Breton went up to him again and asked him if he had anything to say; he said

no. Several confessors went up to him and spoke to him at length; he willingly kissed the crucifix that was held out to him; he opened his lips and repeated: "Pardon, Lord."

The horses tugged hard, each pulling straight on a limb, each horse held by an executioner. After a quarter of an hour, the same ceremony was repeated and finally, after several attempts, the direction of the horses had to be changed, thus: those at the arms were made to pull toward the head, those at the thighs towards the arms, which broke the arms at the joints. This was repeated several times without success. He raised his head and looked at himself. Two more horses had to be added to those harnessed to the thighs, which made six horses in all. Without success.

Finally, the executioner, Samson, said to Monsieur Le Breton that there was no way or hope of succeeding, and told him to ask their Lordships if they wished him to have the prisoner cut into pieces. Monsieur Le Breton, who had come down from the town, ordered that renewed efforts be made, and this was done; but the horses gave up and one of those harnessed to the thighs fell to the ground. The confessors returned and spoke to him again. He said to them (I heard him): "Kiss me, gentlemen." The parish priest of St. Paul's did not dare to, so Monsieur de Marsilly slipped under the rope holding the left arm and kissed him on the forehead. The executioners gathered around and Damiens told them not to swear, to carry out their task and that he did not think ill of them; he begged them to pray to God for him, and asked the parish priest of St. Paul's to pray for him at the first mass.

After two or three attempts, the executioner Samson and he who had used the pincers each drew out a knife from his pocket and cut the body at the thighs instead of severing the legs at the joints; the four horses have a tug and carried off the two thighs after them; namely, that of the right side first, the other following; then the same was done to the arms, the shoulders, the arm-pits and the four limbs; the flesh had to be cut almost to the bone, the horses pulling hard carried off the right arm first and the other afterwards.

When the four limbs had been pulled away, the confessors came to speak to him; but his executioner told them that he was dead, though the truth was that I saw the man move, his lower jaw moving from side to side as if he were talking. One of the executioners even said shortly afterwards that when they had lifted the trunk to throw it on the stake, he was still alive. The four limbs were untied from the ropes and thrown on the stake set up in the enclosure in line with the scaffold, then the trunk and the rest were covered with logs and faggots, and fire was put to the straw mixed with this wood.

In accordance with the decree, the whole was reduced to ashes. The last piece to be found in the embers was still burning at half-past ten in the evening. The pieces of flesh and the trunk had taken about four hours to burn.

The point that Foucault makes is that in an earlier period, whatever the mode of torture, the body of the condemned was specifically singled out as just retribution for a specific crime. As we moved into the utilitarian nineteenth century, forms of generalized punishment were enveloped by complete and austere institutions called prisons. Punishment was organized around the principle of incarceration; prison life created the framework of rationality and universality which no longer necessitated a direct assault on the body of the condemned. Docile bodies required no direct assault. In an odd way, Foucault missed the point of his own illustrations. For it was not only the system of incarceration in total institutions that was at stake, but the erosion of an entire Judeo-Christian tradition of individual punishment for specific individual crimes. As crimes became massified, punishment too became massified in the form of scientific imprisonment systems. But at the same time, the possibility of heroic death was denied. The prison as a negotiated order, created conditions for a contrite life. Survival through rehabilitation involved a tacit acceptance of the prison system as such. In this way the state did not simply move from a vicious to a benign system, but through the science of human engineering, citizens subject to the penalties of total institutions were denied their distinctiveness, and instead were offered universalist norms of rehabilitation that conveniently included a belief in their own guilt as a precondition to prison life.

However awful in recounting, poor Damiens died a martyr's death. He was recalled and memorialized even by his executioners. If his life was a mixed bag, his death was an unfettered example of heroism. Two hundred years later the problem of death was not one of exact punishment for a well-defined wrongdoing, but an engineering problem: how many people could be eliminated in the shortest possible time with a minimal amount of resistance, retaliation, or public awareness. Even death had become collectivized. At the trial of Eichmann, Peter Bamm, a German army physician, recites the magical technology of genocidal death. Hannah Arendt's summary of the engineering ethic reveals the moral impotence caused by this new technology.[4]

> They were collected by "the others" (as he calls the S.S. mobile killing units, to distinguish them from ordinary soldiers) and were put into a sealed-off part of the former G.P.U. prison that abutted on the officer's lodgings, where Bamm's own unit was quartered. They were then made to board a mobile gas van, in which they died after a few minutes, whereupon the driver transported the corpses outside the city and unloaded them into tank ditches. We knew this. We did nothing. Anyone who had seriously protested or done anything against the killing unit would have been arrested within twenty-four hours and would have disappeared. It belongs among the refinements of totalitarian governments in our century that they don't permit their opponents to die a great, dramatic martyr's death for their convictions. A good many of us might have accepted such a death. The totalitarian state lets its opponents disappear in silent anonymity. It is certain that anyone who had dared to suffer death rather than silently tolerate the crime would have sacrificed his life in vain. This is not to say that such a sacrifice would have been morally meaningless. It would only have been practically useless. None of us had a conviction so deeply rooted that we could have taken upon ourselves a practically useless sacrifice for the sake of a higher moral meaning.

But if this new technology is morally impotent, it certainly does not lack for efficiency in the hands of state authorities. Both the level and types of death imposed on victims is a direct function of the sophistication of technology available to the victimizers. Thus, in states where only an intermediary technology is available, intermediary levels of genocide are practiced. Thus in a regime such as that of Idi Amin, which held power in Uganda between 1971 and 1979, the death system could be described as a half-way house between seventeenth-century France and twentieth-century Nazi Germany. The summary report filed by a former officer of the Gestapo-modeled State Research Bureau, Abraham Kisuule-Minge, gives strong evidence that genocide as a style is directly linked to technological availabilities and not developmental goals.[5]

> Saturday was the cruelest day of all. In the morning he (Farouk Minawa, one of Amin's most trusted Nubian aides) would order prisoners brought to the reception area. With a wave of his hand, he would signal which were to die that night. At 7 p.m. precisely, the cars parked in the courtyard would be started to drown out the screams to come. Each prisoner was brought down and told to kneel before an officer in the yard. He was asked to explain why he had been brought in and was told he was being released. Then guards would leap from the darkness, loop a thick rope round the victim's neck and slowly strangle him. The *coup de grace* was a sledgehammer blow to the chest. It took about ten minutes to kill each prisoner. The bodies were piled in trucks and driven north for five hours to the Karuma Falls to be thrown to the crocodiles.

This strange mix between the primitive and the modern, between state murder as individualistic and mechanical, helps to define the form of genocide, even if it does not precisely explain its causes.

The essence of the modern death system is a deprivation of both individual accountability and individual transcendence in death. In a remarkable new commentary on the reprinting of Horace Bleackley's minor classic on *State Executions,* John Lofland provides a clinical framework for Foucault's type of narrative. He points out the essential distinction between "the open and concealed dramaturgy of state execution." Open executions are characterized by long death waits and death trips; public death places; professional executioners with personal contact with the condemned; death techniques that are noisy, painful, scream-provoking, mutilating, struggle-inducing, odor-causing, and highly visible; corpse disposal is public and prolonged; finally death is announced by the suspension of institutional activities. Concealed executions are characterized by short death waits and death trips; private and enclosed death places; part-time executioners with impersonal and limited contact with the condemned; death techniques which are reliable, fast-acting, quiet, painless, non-mutilating, odorless, and concealed; corpse disposal is quick and anonymous; finally, death involves no suspension of institutional activities. It is to Lofland's credit that he appreciated that however "raucous or crude historic executions may have been, they did provide the condemned with opportunity for dying with a display of courage and dignity utterly denied in modern executions."[6]

The issues of alternative death systems represent considerably more than half a trade-off in humanistic styles. The depersonalization of death is hardly a random event, or even a matter of simple strategic options. At its essence, the modern death system is linked to the emergence of genocide as a centerpiece of state power and the display of its monopoly of power. Orwell quite properly pointed out that one cannot have a worthy picture of the future unless an understanding of the losses occasioned by Christianity are accounted for. Socialism only postpones a consideration of the role of the individual by urging the solution to basic material needs. The modern state may be a useful technique to overcome the anarchy of the marketplace but unlike individualism, it is scarcely a statement of personal moral obligation or commitment.

> Western civilization, unlike some oriental civilizations, was founded partly on the belief in individual immortality. If one looks at the Christian religion from the outside, this belief appears far more important than the belief in God. The western conception of good and evil is very difficult to separate from it. There is little doubt that the modern cult of power worship is bound up with the modern man's feeling that life here and now is the only life there is. If death ends everything, it becomes much harder to believe that you can be in the right even if you are defeated. Statesmen, nations, theories, causes are judged almost inevitably by the test of material success. Supposing that one can separate the two phenomea, the decay of the belief in personal immortality has been as important as the rise of machine civilization. Machine civilization has terrible possibilities, but the other thing has terrible possibilities too, and it cannot be said that the Socialist movement has given much thought to them.[7]

Twentieth-century totalitarianisms created pioneering innovations in the deprivation of meaning to death no less than to life. One's guilt is collectivized and accrues to a class, race or religion as a whole. Once this process is successfully concluded, the problem of innocence is also easily collectivized. Both guilt and innocence are no longer matters of individual conscience, but in a sense accrue to a master race, the historically sanctioned party, or the purified race. Death is its ontological opposite: it accrues to the degenerate religion, the backward race, and the oppressive class. It is indeed the essence of twentieth-century ideology to collectivize the spirit of guilt and innocence; therein lies the banality of evil.

In some measure, this collectivization process was ordained by the breakdown of the distinction between deviance and marginality, between social outcasts and political radicals. Hence a notion that the common danger stemmed from those who would be different, and the character of their transgression vanished. As a result, whatever the nature of the crime, it too became generalized and universalized. The point I made a decade ago in an essay on "Social Deviance and Political Marginality" has only been partially confirmed by time and events. The blend of criminality and politicality, although it defines the essential quality of the collective spirit of the age, does not quite explain the moral superiority of a life of politics over that of crime. The line between the social deviant and the political marginal is fading. It is rapidly becoming an obsolete distinction. As this happens, political dissent by deviant means will become subject to the types of repression that have been a traditional response to social deviance. This development compels social scientists to reconsider their definition of the entire range of social phenomena—from deviance to politics.[8]

The distinction between the social and pathological on one side, and the political and ideological on the other, persists in part because the criminal phenomenon accepts almost unqualifiedly the collective judgment of society. It internalizes its sense of guilt and believes in its wrongdoing, and hence is reduced to working the system. Solzhenitsyn describes this distinction between the common criminal and the political prisoner, the "suckers" who retained their sense of personal worth, with stunning precision in *The Gulag Archipelago*.

> They had their own "original code" and their own original concept of honor. But it was not a question of their being patriots, as our bureaucrats and writers would have liked to have it, but of their being absolutely consistent materialists and consistent pirates. And even though the dictatorship of the proletariat was so assiduous in courting them, they did not respect it even for one minute; they do not recognize the earthly institution of private property, and in this respect they really are hostile to the bourgeoisie and to those Communists who have dachas and automobiles. Everything they come across on life's path they take as their own (if it is not too dangerous). Even when they have a surfeit of everything, they reach out to grab what belongs to others because any unstolen article makes a thief sick at heart.[9]

Political prisoners were not simply morally superior to common thieves, but rather they had not understood the twentieth century nearly as well. They had not understood the role of the collective in mass society, or, put another way, they understood it all too well and refused to go along with that program. What was that program that so collectivized the Archipelago? It was, again to paraphrase Solzhenitsyn, comprised of ten points: constant fear, servitude, secrecy and mistrust, universal ignorance, squealing, betrayal as a form of existence, corruption—the lie as a form of existence—and cruelty, generalized cruelty; and finally, slave psychology—the assumption that the executioner was right because he held the monopoly of power to execute. These propositions so characterize the collective spirit, and do so with such little regard to social system, place, or geography, that we must begin to take seriously the dangers of collectivism as a whole, and the need for some kind of return to an individual framework as a base of all moral and political decision making.

In his essays on the social situation of inmates, appropriately entitled *Asylums,* Goffman makes important points: that the relationship between the totalitarian institution and democratic society may be far closer than one initially anticipates or expects, and that our model forms of democracy have their own way of providing intimidation of the cruelest sorts.[10]

> If the institution has a militant mission, as do some religious, military, and political units, then a partial reversal of the inside of external

status arrangements can act as a constant reminder of the difference and enmity between the institution and its environing society. It should be noted that in thus suppressing externally valid differences, the harshest total institution may be the most democratic; and, in fact, the inmate's assurance of being treated no worse than any other of his fellows can be a source of support as well as deprivation.

What this means, whether we are talking about concentration camps in Germany, slave labor camps of the Soviet Union, or mental asylums in America, is a system which presents itself under various labels, but ultimately reduces itself to a struggle between individuals and the state. Goffman shrewdly points out that getting out of an asylum involves a negotiation of the system and accommodation with its social order. To leave an asylum means to surrender, to presume your own guilt or sickness, your own weaknesses, your own need for rehabilitation. It is only when that need is felt enough that at that point one can be "free" in the collective sense. This is also the basis of Orwell's 1984. Here too, freedom means perfect slavery, not just simply as a literary juxtaposition, but the necessary assumption that to have even a modest amount of freedom in the collective society is to assume a therapeutic position. And that entails manipulating the system rather than changing it. There must be something wrong with the individual in order for a person to be cured. In such a system, resistance, even questioning of authority, whether that authority be psychiatric, legal, medical, or political itself becomes the main danger to state power. What has to be extirpated, uprooted, is not a particular kind of individual resistance, but the very idea of resistance.

An excellent report of a teacher of English who spent several years in Mao's China underscores the elimination of resistance through the annihilation of the individual as a meaningful category. Beneath the heavyhanded sarcasm is the feeling that the anarch individual comes upon the behemoth, and that with the new collectivisms we are once again in a Hobbesian world, but one which is technologically far more proficient than anything known in seventeenth-century England.

All these things helped me finally see the connection: The freedom to have opinions, that is a Bourgeois freedom. And likewise the freedom to have information. The important freedom for a Socialist is the freedom to have correct opinions; that is, the freedom to repeat the Party Line. In other words, people who have opinions are class enemies. Throughout China now the system of "Socialist Courtyards" is in force. This brings Party leadership right to your door. Every three or four families has one person appointed to report to the local Party committee. On everything. The Chang boy is playing truant. The Wangs seem to quarrel a lot. Young Chen is sometimes out late at night. If the appointee doesn't make these reports, that is conspiracy. Counterrevolution. This is perhaps why China is so ardently against the Helsinki agreements. Nowhere in that document is there any mention of the essential human right: the right to Party leadership.[11]

The Chinese, whether as a result of ethnic homogeneity or a refined sense of internal history, are uniquely uninvolved in genocidal solutions to socioeconomic problems. Even their ability to create a society free of individualism has been placed in serious doubt. The need for real material development pushed through the weight of inherited rhetoric. And if China has not yet achieved a level of moral responsibility as a concommittant of personal behavior, it has at least made the first moves in that direction by recognizing the rights of material satisfaction as an individual as well as collective decision.

These remarks are not intended as a contribution to ongoing discussions on the merits or demerits of capital punishment. That issue has received ample if inconclusive coverage in nearly every advanced industrial nation; the same nations which turn strangely myopic when it comes to collective punishment. The genocidal practices of Paraguay, Uganda, or Cambodia can hardly elicit a proper quorum in the United Nations among the very nations which agonize breathlessly over capital punishment. The Caryl Chessmens and Gary Gilmores, however different their crimes from each other, or those committed by Damiens, share in common a strong sense of individuation, or being punished for an exact crime or series of crimes. In this peculiar sense, they illustrate the healthier agonies of a society. In demanding that the State of

Utah carry out its capital punishment clause, Gilmore confronted the society with its legal system and the limits of its own moral foundations. In contrast, the essence of modern genocidal systems is that collective death makes it possible to avoid such issues.

The technological devices which permit collective death are also at work in creating a profound sense of total distance between victims and victimizers. The modern state with its bureaucratic orientation, converts the problem of choice by making death a nonproblem of necessity. People must die because they represent symbolic evil: Jews in Poland, peasants in the Ukraine, Catholics in Northern Ireland, Indians in Uganda, Blacks in South Africa. As a result, in the absence of moral choice, the state exempts or at least suspends judgment for the executioners. Killing becomes a matter of policymaking rather than ethical decision. Thus the individual is reduced to the status of nonperson not simply as victim, but with equal profundity, as victimizer. In this way, the breakdown of individual responsibility opened the pathway toward collective guilt and punishment.

This assertion that the breakdown of individual responsibility opens wide the gates to collective repression, should not be construed as a defense of capitalism or a critique of socialism. True enough, advocates of the former system of economy use a rhetoric of free enterprise and individual initiative, while devotees of socialism celebrate the virtues of social ownership of the means of production. But the character of the economy would appear relatively indifferent to the issue of genocide. There are as many societies presumably following capitalist models of development practicing such mass annihilation as those following socialist models of development. Even if we ignore the obvious fact that the issue of capitalism and socialism has become more a problem in measuring the size and character of the public sector vis-à-vis the private sector, and less a critical cutting point for measuring social systems, Brazil handles the problem of minority groups with at least as much vicious vigor as the Soviet Union handled its unwanted Aryan minorities, or the United States its Indian problem. Those that cannot be entirely eliminated are reduced to enclave status. Such people are permitted a bare cultural survival without structural components for autonomy. The collective will of state power, rather than the presumed needs of economic growth, dictates and determines the character of punishment. In this way the battle is joined at its purest levels, between individuals and the small communities in which they huddle, and the state and its machinery of repression. Economic systems may account for levels of production or rates of growth, but these appear in history as strategic decisions a state takes. Beyond strategy is the omnipotence of the state as such; and the impulse to nullify the individual as sovereign entity.

When, for example, a society comes upon an issue so pervasive and yet personal as abortion, advocacy of socialism or capitalism hardly helps matters at decision-making levels. Whether abortion is a matter of a woman's right to her body or a medically sanctioned form of contraception; whether abortion is even a matter of life or death, given the special status of the fetus; whether poor people should have special access to federal funds for abortion purposes—these are issues disguising basic extensions of state power. For example, the Nazis constantly linked the "final solution" with "racial purification" at birth. What the state does is render moral determinations meaningless by providing a *fait accompli*. The state can argue that all fetuses are the property of the state and that therefore decisions about abortion are in the domain of federal or local directives. Or alternatively, the state can place at the disposal of communities a massive network of sponsored clinics that permit abortions to take place in an atmosphere free of guilt but also free of moral responsibility.

The key issue is not the disposition of laws governing abortions but the absolution from moral responsibility that federal intervention into personal morality so often represents. To pose the issue in terms of sanctioning abortions by untrained midwives brandishing coathangers versus abortions on demand by sophisticated medics brandishing scalpels is to fudge the issue. Such a series of false antinomies disguises the collectivization of decision making within most advanced industrial systems. Both sides in the abortion debate, assuming that it can be resolved by law, take for granted the main danger: state power over personal morality.

Much of the rebellion against authoritarianism is also an assertion that individuals can manage their own affairs best; funds should be left in the hands of wage earners and taxpayers and kept away from the coffers of a federal or state treasury. Viewed in this way, demands for federal abortion clinics seem as wide of the mark as demands that abortions be prohibited as a violation of Providential guidelines. The collectivization of responsibility is the problem, not the "right to life" or "abortion on demand." Only when moral issues are restored to individuals for decision can concrete specific issues be meaningfully resolved in a civilized manner. Otherwise we face an endless series of false alternatives: issue fought without principles enunciated; equities gained while liberties are lost.

There is a continuity of the way people live and die with the way social systems conduct their affairs. It becomes especially instructive to examine the social processing of officially sanctioned death because in this area of universally shared agony we have presumed a higher level of being civilized than all past societies. But in the technical proficiencies in distancing killers and those killed, we stand exposed as the least civilized. We recoil in horror at medieval torture systems, at diabolical inventions that were supposed to symbolize fit punishment for thieves, plunderers, murderers, and assorted others. But their very individuation, their continued existence as figures in history, give them a standing denied to the collective martyrdom of the twentieth century. Engineering as an ideology is no match for religion; or, put another way, it is no moral match. On the other hand, religion as an ideology is no match for engineering as a system insuring mass death with personal sentiment.

As a general equation within a finite social system, more state authority means less individual capacity to survive, and a higher individual capacity to survive means less state authority. This point cannot be waffled by attacks that this represents simply a return to an old-fashioned individualism or conservatism. Such ideological eyewash will not longer suffice. Too much suffering has transpired and too many norms transgressed, to warrant a belief in the state as benefactor.

The state provides not simply its elites, but its masses as well. The state not only provides decision making by experts at the top, but generates mass mobilization at the bottom. Such statements which appear as polarized expressions of social life are in fact a part of the same monolithic entity. The task of individual survival, indeed of individualism as such, is to ferret out not simply one polar expression of this status evil, but to appreciate the dialectic of state power—its mass as well as elite components—the carrots it offers below, disguising the stick it holds above. Only in this way can the opium of the twentieth century be fought in meaningful battle. The outcome may not be clear, but at least the lines of struggle have become clarified.

One should be cautious about stretching this duality between individuals and the state into a Manichaean doctrine of contending principles in which goodness is identified with the person and evil with the state; or the more likely prospect of identifying liberty with individual caprice. In strategic terms, demands for extending human rights, covenants intended to limit national excesses, and legislation stipulating root factors entering into deliberation of rights, these most often proceed through demands for state support. As a result, the state becomes both root problem and the core of any solution. Paradoxically, there seems to be an intellectual consensus that in the long run, the state is culpable; but there is also a short-run belief that the state must aid in fostering human rights and even extending human potentials. Rather than attempt a surgical resolution of this evident dilemma it should suffice for social science purposes to carefully disentangle the web of confusion surrounding such dramatic issues as individual liberties, human rights, and state powers. Demands for improvements must come to rest on a careful delineation of inconsistencies and inequities in present arrangements of structures. If this is a modest proposal for gigantic issues, so too is the foundation of this paper: the social processing of death as a measure of the life-giving potential of any given society.

There is a danger in broadening the concept of genocide so that it becomes symbolically all-embracing and hence meaningless. In raising the slogan of American genocide against Black people, or British genocide against Irish people, we risk confusing colonial dependency with physical destruction. Yet there are more Black people in the United States than there were in 1900, 1920, and 1940. There are more Irish people in Ireland than during the nineteenth-century famine years. We have a complex problem. At what point in this scheme of genocide are we referring to actual, physical destruction of people, and at what point are we talking about the symbolic dismemberment of a people? Is there an entity called "cultural genocide," which somehow is as horrible as physical genocide? Or are we dealing with a different phenomenon? This is not simply a matter for academic disputation; it has to do with the survival capacities of entire peoples.

If we broaden our approach to include an entity called "cultural genocide," the results might be counterproductive. A deflated, pessimistic, and ultimately confused concept of genocide deprives the very people who are presumably genocidal victims of the capacity to resist and retaliate. For that reason, I have come to believe that a restrictive, rather than an omnibus concept of genocide, is the most operationally valid.

Genocide means the physical dismemberment and liquidation of people on large scales; an attempt by those who rule to achieve the total elimination of a subject people. Genocide does not mean simply depriving people of their cultural heritage. It does not simply refer to a special segment of the population being deprived of opportunities for education, welfare, or health, however hideous such deprivations might be. One must avoid liberal fantasizing about people who are victimized in ways short of genocide. Broadening the concept so that everyone somehow ends up a victim of genocide only leads to a tautological reasoning. Physical genocide is tragically large enough, in raw numerical terms, not to require a vision of symbolic genocide. Ideological mannerisms that add fuel to an already grotesque fire are counterproductive to practical efforts to limit or reverse genocidal patterns.

There is a growing realization that the shift in politics from an ideological to a personalistic basis, is not simply another rhetorical form, but a politics based on individuals in contrast to parties, officials, and leaderships. It is a Chilean living in exile in the United States, Orlando Letelier; it is a Brazilian journalist named Vladimir Herzog, and a Russian physicist named Andrei Sakharov who become the focus of attention by Amnesty International. Human rights as a movement is of, by,and for individuals. In such a context the body is a willing hostage to free expression. The theory of this movement is that every individual counts as one—no more and no less. Hence, the death, or torture, or maltreatment of every individual is important, and not just part of a state's calculation of the necessary human costs to achieve abstractly predetermined levels of economic production. Undoubtedly, exaggeration, even mistakes of judgment, will be made by such a new politics of human rights. However, that such a movement even exists, indicates that individualism has found a new source of energy, one predicated on the universal right to live rather than the sovereign requirements of state power.

Individualism has provided the question of genocide with renewed philosophical meaning. As the relationship between nonhumans, robots, and infants becomes hotly debated, abortion comes into question. When does a fetus cease being a human vegetable and become an entity and then a personality? What do the relationships between computers performing human tasks and doing so more rationally than most people, for example, playing chess, do to explode the idea that humans are sacrosanct? The issue requires a volume unto itself, and has received a great deal of treatment.

At the philosophical devel, justifications of homicide are similar to those for genocide. What emerges in the medical literature on euthanasia emerges in the political literature as racial purity. This is no simple matter. But perhaps one beginning at this philosophical level has to place the matter of genocide in the context of a means-ends continuum—what might be referred to as Kant's principle of personality: "that human beings are always to be treated as ends in themselves and never as means or instrumentalities." If this principle has significance it does so by the assertion that the destruction of people can never be simply a matter of social convenience, nor can a personality be regarded as subhuman simply as a convenience or as a racial designation. This meaningful formulation is contained in a new work on *The Ethics of Homicide,* by Philip E. Devine, who points out:

> The principle of personality is both plausible in its own right and capable of making sense of many of our considered judgments about moral issues. The difficulty of arguing with those who do not share our intuitions on this point should not inhibit our acting upon our

conviction, whether as individuals or as citizens. To allow philosophical skepticism concerning the first principles of ethics to paralyze action would be to surrender the practical sphere to immoralists and fanatics, neither of whom is likely to be troubled about such issues. So far as ethics proper is concerned, this kind of reply will have to suffice.[12]

But again, to raise the principle of personality is to argue the case for the restoration of individualism on a new basis, and this I have attempted in another chapter.

# Notes to Chapter 5

1. Commager, Henry Steele. *The American Mind: An Interpretation of American Thought and Character Since the 1880's.* New Haven: Yale University Press, 1950. pp. 176-177.
2. Glick, Peter M. "Individualism, Society, and Social Work," *Social Casework,* Vol. 58, No. 10 (December) 1977. pp. 579-584.
3. Foucault, Michel. *Discipline and Punish: The Birth of the Prison.* New York: Pantheon Books, 1977. pp. 3-5.
4. Arendt, Hannah. *Eichmann in Jerusalem: A Report on the Banality of Evil.* New York: The Viking Press, 1963. p. 232.
5. Kisuule-Minge, Abraham. "Amin's Horror Chamber," *Time: The Weekly News Magazine,* Vol. 113, No. 18 (April 30) 1979. pp. 45-46.
6. Lofland, John. "The Dramaturgy of State Execution," Commentary on *State Executions Viewed Historically and Sociologically: The Hangmen of England* by Horace Bleackley. Montclair, New Jersey: Patterson Smith, 1977. pp. 275-325.
7. Orwell, George. "As I Please" (from *The Tribune,* 3 March 1944), *The Collected Essays, Journalism, and Letters of George Orwell,* Vol. 3: 1943-45. Edited by Sonia Orwell and Ian Angus, New York: Harcourt, Brace & World, 1968. pp. 103-104.
8. Horowitz, Irving Louis. *Foundations of Political Sociology.* New York and London: Harper & Row, 1972. pp. 351-352.
9. Solzhenitsyn, Aleksandr I. *The Gulag Archipelago 1918-1956: An Experiment in Literary Investigation* III-IV (Volume Two). New York and London: Harper and Row, 1975, pp. 440-445.
10. Goffman, Erving. *Asylums: Essays on the Social Situation of Mental Patients and Other Inmates.* Garden City, New York: Doubleday/Anchor Books, 1961. pp. 120-121.
11. Erdal, David. "I Work in Mao's China," *Worldview,* Vol. 20, No. 11 (November) 1977. pp. 4-9. For a general analysis, see, An Amnesty International Report, *Political Imprisonment in the Peoples' Republic of China.* London: Amnesty International Secretariat, March 17, 1978.
12. Devine, Philip E. *The Ethics of Homocide.* Ithaca and London: Cornell University Press, 1978. pp. 208-209.

# Chapter 6

# Collectivism
# and State Power

*Not even the dead are spared when the living become lost and grow evil.*

*Milovan Djilas,* LAND WITHOUT JUSTICE

Much has been written on the subject of collectivism. If the century can be politically summarized in a word, one would be hard-pressed to find a more appropriate term. A few elementary points are in order, foremost of which is that while there are many collectivist societies in the twentieth century covering a range from fascism to communism, there have been few, if any, which have upheld the principles of democratic governance. This has been the unspeakable blemish which has converted ecstasy into agony for devotees of democratic socialism—a fusion easier to erect in theory than to observe in practice. As a result, it is both fitting and natural to focus on the Soviet Union in this discussion of collectivism and state power. The self-proclaimed model of collectivism has been the Soviet Union. This also makes it eminently feasible to focus on the great masterpiece which has emerged out of the ashes of sixty years of Soviet history and legacy: *The Gulag Archipelago.* In the analysis therein provided, personal testimony is added to the shank of modern collective societies. This observation is forcefully summarized by Solzhenitsyn in his Nobel statement.

This twentieth century of ours has proved to be crueler than its predecessors, and its horrors have not been exhausted with the end of its first half. The same old atavistic urges—greed, envy, unrestrained passion, and mutual hostility—readily picking up respectable pseudonyms like class, race, mass, or trade union struggle, claw at and tear apart our world. A primitive rejection of all compromise is given the status of a theoretical principle and is regarded as the high virtue which accompanies doctrinal purity. This attitude creates millions of victims in ceaseless civil wars, it drones into our souls that there exist no lasting concepts of good and justice valid for all mankind, that all such concepts are fluid and ever-changing . . . . Less and less restrained by the confines of long-established legality, violence strides brazenly and triumphantly through the world, unconcerned that its futility has already been demonstrated and proven many times in history. It is not even brute force alone that is victorious, but also its clamorous justification: the world is being flooded by the brazen conviction that force can do all and righteousness—nothing.[1]

The first volume of *The Gulag Archipelago* is a classic statement of social reality. It will rank as a foremost contribution to the literature on power and powerlessness long after the biography of the author ceases to be a point of contention or argumentation. A sure measure of a classic is that any one specialist is unable either to encapsulate or for that matter emasculate its contents. From this flows a second measure of high quality: the desire it arouses in every field and specialist to interpret the book's contents from a particular professional vantage point. In a work such as this, ubiquity and grandeur go together.[2]

Since *The Gulag Archipelago* is a work of autobiography as well as of biography, sociology and history, it is impossible not to comment on Solzhenitsyn, although the efforts to lionize, as well as to dismiss this extraordinary man, are really quite independent of this latest publication. Yet *The Gulag Archipelago* also stands apart from the personal career of a single individual, even its author. The work is more than the sum of the 277 other contributions to the volume, many made by persons Solzhenitsyn has kept anonymous. While it can be considered as all one piece with his other works, *One Day in the Life of Ivan Denisovich* and his more recent novels *The Cancer Ward* and *The First Circle*, this volume is singular. *The Gulag Archipelago* itself is only two-sevenths of a work, only two parts of what the author intends as an experiment in literary investigation. Those who would argue that the book has exaggerations or mistakes must be cautioned, first because of the incomplete nature of what is contained, and second because on the basis of what is herein contained one can hardly doubt that the next five parts, should they ever appear, would prove no less compelling or convincing.

Solzhenitsyn is a writer. It would be a mistake to call him a sociologist, or for that matter, a novelist. He conveys experiences, he recites the truths of an entire society. He captures the essence of civilization in the behavioral degeneration of one individual toward another. On the other hand, in the tradition of literary realism, his individuals typify and represent an archetype within society as a whole. Beyond that, Solzhenitzyn is entirely a product of Soviet society and of the Russian literary tradition. His intellectual vision is fused with a sense of politics characteristic of Soviet Marxism as a whole and with a capacity for irony characteristic of Russian literature, particularly its nineteenth-century classic period. He knows nothing of formal social science techniques, could probably care less about ethnographic safeguards, and is not interested in characterizing a society from the point of view of a general theory of political system of the Soviet union, the history of an organization called the Communist party, or the fate of individuals within the penological system known as the U.S.S.R. Solzhenitsyn takes for granted that the Soviet Union itself is a total institution, a network of integrated agencies of coercion dedicated to the survival and promulgation of maximum state power over minimum state power over minimum human beings. Few have been privy to write from inside the whale, yet even those who have suffered similar outrages have been unable to create such a compendium of horrors.

*The Gulag Archipelago* should be viewed as a series of experiences, a set of lessons in fear and courage, in being oppressed and in doing the bidding of the oppressor, in working the system and in being ground down by the system. Whatever polarities come to the human mind appear in *The Gulag Archipelago*. Solzhenitsyn has written the great Soviet dialectic, the supreme word of literary and social analysis that finally, after fifty-five years, has put the Soviet experience into a perspective that can at least be theoretically tested. Vague, didactic Leninist tracts on the withering away of the state; outrageous Stalinist equations of Soviet life with the principle of happiness; the Brezhnev-Kosygin reduction of détente into a series of statements about mutual stagnation: these mythological politics give way, crack apart in the documentary history of Russian suffering before, during, and after the Russian Revolution. We now have an experiential work that, if tested, may resolve questions about the nature of Soviet society or at least permit a huge step forward in the development of political theory.

This book brings to mind, with its documentary evidence of the slaying and imprisonment of tens of millions of Russians, comparison with the Japanese experience at Hiroshima and Nagasaki as recounted in Robert Jay Lifton's *Death in Life* and the Jewish experience of the Holocaust as recounted by Raul Hilberg in *The Destruction of the European Jews*. But the Soviet experience is unique, precisely because terror was self-inflicted, because Russians killed and maimed Russians. In this sense, the banality of evil spoken of by Hannah Arendt is carried one step further; for the terror is not American airplanes over defenseless Japanese cities, or the destruction of European Jews at the hands of the Nazi Gestapo. However awful these other holocausts may be, the enemy was external.

*The Gulag Archipelago* offers a special sort of Dostoevskian nightmare in which Russian spies upon Russian, Communist betrays Communist, Red Army officers destroy other members of the Red Army. All of this national self-immolation, in Solzhenitsyn's words "cauterized the wound so that scar tissue would form more quickly." But as Solzhenitsyn hints, there is more involved; the Marxist principle of criticism and self-criticism is raised to a pathological new high, in which ideological purification is a consequence of purgation, in which inner-party struggle replaces in principle all party democracy, in which the notion of scientific evidence is overwhelmed by the notion of organization-inspired rumor. For these reasons, *The Gulag Archipelago* has a fascination and a horror beyond even the literature of concentration camps. To die at the hands of a foreign tormentor or of a powerful adversary may be awful, but at least it is understandable. To suffer the same fate at the hands of one's own is a form of barabarism which permits Solzhenitsyn to consider Soviet Bolshevism as almost in a class with German Nazism. This point has thoroughly outraged Soviet commentators on the book who have grown up with the belief that the Fascist hordes were history's worst example of cruelty. Solzhenitsyn's comparison of the Soviet system to Fascism must itself be ranked an act of extraordinary criticism and condemnation. He has stepped over a psychological threshold of commentary few others have dared cross.

*The Gulag Archipelago* is the equation of Soviet political sociology with criminology and penology; that is, Soviet-Marxist praxis turns out to be the theory and practice of penology, of imprisonment. In Solzhenitsyn's paradigm of imprisonment every aspect of the Soviet system is converted into a science. There is a science of arrest, involving a structured system of questioning according to various criteria: nighttime and daytime, at home and at work, for initial arrests and recidivists, independent versus group arrests. Then there is the science of searches: how to conduct body searches, how to check out houses, even urinals; in short, how to flush out people. Then there is the science of purge: how to isolate the victim from his own party apparatus, which Solzhenitsyn calls a grandiose game of solitaire whose rules were entirely incomprehensible to its players. The enormous impact on Communist cadres does not derive from their presumed vanguard position, but the other way around: from their unique ignorance of the real nature of Soviet society. The ordinary Russian peasant, spared the patina of Marxism-Leninism, was better prepared for the terror than the party cadre who bought the package labeled "dictatorship of the proletariat." All of these various and sundry facts of the twentieth-century history of the Soviet science of the destruction of personality had very little to do with the lofty claims of Lenin or Stalin. It is as if Archipelago were a nation apart, as if the Archipelago alone had the right, ironically, to experience social science as social engineering while the rest of society paraded forth under the mythical banner of Marxism.

We have the amazing experience of social science emerging in the Soviet Union as a function of the rise of a prison system involving tens of millions of people. Pavlovian behaviorism, stripped of its humane ambitions, found its fulfillment in the Soviet state. This transition from Marxism to Pavlovianism was made possible because the Gulag Archipelago was more than a geographic sector. The prison system of the Soviet Union was far flung but it was connected psychologically, as Solzhenitsyn said, fused into a context and almost invisibly, imperceptibly, carried forward as a nation of the damned.

In this sense, Solzhenitsyn's *Gulag Archipelago,* while reminiscent of the writings of Raul Hilberg and Robert Lifton, also makes one think of the writings of Erving Goffman in *Asylums.* He combines these two types of macro and micro analysis. It is a study in working within a system, surviving it and operating so as to make the system collapse under the weight of its self-imposed lunacy and limitless bureaucracy. A great deal of the book's social psychology has to do with the counterscience of prisoner life, the grim humor of survival in which a mistake means life, and hence a science that has to be equal or better than the various sciences of arrest, search and seizure, and imprisonment inflicted by the state.

One of Solzhenitsyn's major contributions is to note how terrorism functions as a structural feature of Soviet society rather than as an episodic moment in Russian time. That is to say, Solzhenitsyn does not simply speak about the Stalin era, or special quixotic moments in that era where terror was high, but of the entire period of 1918-56. The Gulag Archipelago existed because the need for terror replaced the practice of liberty within Russian life. Indeed, there was not very much liberty to begin with, since the Czarist era was hardly concerned with the distribution of justice. However, the revolution of mass democracy never took place, at least for Solzhenitsyn, and terrorism immediately became institutionalized. Within this structural framework there were special eras, for example 1929-30, when fifteen million peasants were either slaughtered, uprooted, or imprisoned; 1937-38, when party personnel, intellectuals, and cadres of the military were entirely wiped out; and again in 1944-46 when armed forces personnel, prisoners of war, and all persons having contact with the West were similarly destroyed or disposed of. Only the purges of 1937-38 were remembered because intellectuals and party personnel were able to articulate their mortification. Millions perished in this Yagoda epoch, but still more perished in the other two high-purge periods. Solzhenitsyn indicated that a fourth huge round of purges was being prepared in 1952-53, this time against Jews and other national minorities. However the costs were considered so high that even the other members of the Stalin-appointed Politburo withdrew in horror at the thought of another round. Solzhenitsyn does not clarify matters by confusing waves of terror with Soviet military acquisitions after World War II. The occupation of the Baltic countries was ruthless, but it cannot be placed in the same cautionary note with respect to the civil period of 1918-22. By minimizing the gap between peaks and troughs in the exercise of terror, the need for analysis is thus lessened.

The most fundamental issue of social theory raised by *The Gulag Archipelago* is whether terror is intrinsic to the Soviet system or is confined to the Stalinist epoch covered by the book. Solzhenitsyn's viewpoint is that terrorism is endemic to the Leninist definition of Bolshevism and continues to plague the Soviet landscape. The viewpoint of a rather wide-ranging group of Soviet scholars and observers is that terrorism was a special technique of Stalinism employed to stimulate development and industrialization in a uniquely backward set of social and cultural circumstances. The problem with Solzhenitsyn's position is twofold: terrorism was a technique employed by the Czarist secret police with equally telling (but limited) effects. Hence it was not solely endemic to the OGPU under Bolshevism but is part of the history of modern Russia as such. Beyond that, a second line of criticism must be made: that the terror of wartime conditions is finite and determined by military considerations rather than party idiosyncrasies. This might better serve to distinguish the exercise of violence in the Leninist phase from the resort to terror characteristic of the post-1929 Stalinist consolidation. It might also help us understand the turn away from terrorism (and toward benign authoritarian rule) in the post-1956 Khruschev era.

While Lenin in practice preferred norms of "socialist legality," nothing in the Leninist corpus would or could limit terrorism as a strategy and tactic of development. Stalinism is thus a direct theoretical consequence of Leninism, not its diabolical corruption.

On June 16, 1974, the very day that a *New York Times* reviewer cautioned against reading *The Gulag Archipelago* as more than a Stalinist happening, the same *Times* carried a news item on the resurrection of the Stalin cult. Ivan Stadnyuk, unquestionably the figure in the Soviet Writers Union responsible for the expulsion of Solzhenitsyn, has just published an assessment of Stalin as a man who adapted rapidly to the Nazi attack and pulled Soviet war efforts together in contrast to Khruschev's characterization of him as a man "paralyzed by his fear of Hitler like a rabbit in front of a boa constrictor."

Soviet society has been transformed from totalitarian to authoritarian modalities. The rise of middle sectors, bureaucrats, teachers, party officials, technicians, skilled craftsment, and so on, has created the seeds of a consumer society without a conflict society, a mass society without mass democracy. This authoritarianism permits the continuation of Bolshevik legend and myths but does not permit the reinstitutionalization of the kind of terrorism that existed under Stalin. History, at least Soviet history, moves in a peculiar way: not one step backward to generate two steps forward, as Lenin suggested; but rather nineteen steps backward to permit twenty steps forward, as Max Nomad has suggested. To think in purely communist terms empirically at least, has meant a betrayal of the ideals of mass democracy in favor of a codebook of party elites. The connection between the freedom of individuals and the necessity of development is not an easy issue to resolve, especially in the light of foreign assaults upon the Soviet Union. Rather than speak the unspeakable about the limits of democracy it is simpler for Solzhenitsyn to retreat into religious self-actualization. But the foreknowledge that history rarely moves lock step in place with justice may help us better appreciate the Soviet horror without that collapse of moral nerve always entailed in a categorical denial that the future contains the possibility of improving upon the present.

At the theoretical level, Solzhenitsyn is saying that Russia was not ready for socialism, indeed was unfit for it because of its backward economy and political and social conditions. The Leninists attempted to speed up, even defy history, flying in the face of Marxist assumptions that each social system must run its full course before there can be a normal transformation of capitalism into socialism. But the very backwardness of Russian society overwhelmed the Bolshevik Revolution, and instead of breaking the back of feudalism, the Bolsheviks wound up breaking the backs of their own followers and supporters. The very attempt to speed up the historical process of economic development in the face of lethargy and backwardness became the hallmark of Soviet development.

Coercion is a necessary component of development. In all likelihood the sacrifice needed for high development, would be impossible without a mythic sense of purpose. The Soviet state constantly spilled over, failing to distinguish coercion from terrorism, failing to distinguish the forms of state self-protection from the rights of citizens. Within such a system the Soviet Union achieved a level of development which even today is lower than that of its capitalist adversaries. The outcome was not simply political betrayal, but economic stagnation and a dangerous kind of frustration, not so much within the Gulag Archipelago but among those who might point to the Archipelago as a major source of the central problem of Soviet life—the problem of legitimacy.

A central theme in the second volume of Solzhenitsyn's work is the differential forms of punishment meted out to common criminals vis-à-vis political prisoners.[3] The constant denial of the existence of political prisoners by Soviets (and one would have to add, Americans) becomes a charade to mask the criminal nature of the state itself. Legislation is created to distinguish forms of criminality. "For him [the thief] to have a knife was mere misbehavior, tradition, he didn't know any better. But for you [the political prisoner] to have one was 'terrorism.'" Thus we have the master dialectic between crime and punishment, the individual and the state, the rights of the person and the limits of authority; and perhaps more painfully, the obligations of the citizen and rights of the state. *The Gulag Archipelago* is compelling not simply as an exposé of Soviet Party history or its penal system, but as an introduction to the entire gamut of normative issues that have plagued Western civilization since its inception. Marx and Engels recognized these issues and dealt with them by fiat, declaring in principle that socialism would witness the withering away of the state. But in Stalinist practice such a diminution of authority never occurred: circumstances always blocked the path of true historical necessity; and in the vise of this cruel hoax, tens of millions of Russians were squeezed to death.

Solzhenitsyn's volume suffers the defects of its virtues. Like the American prison literature of Malcolm X or George Jackson, it has a searing intimacy that at times disguises a paucity of theory. No large-scale explanation of the Soviet experience, no cost-benefit analysis is forthcoming. One is left feeling that no meaningful mass involvement in Soviet society was registered in the past fifty-five years, a point of view which is clearly unrealistic, first given the Soviet Civil War experience, and above all, the large-scale popular support for the state generated during the war against Fascism. It may very well be that the Russian people were fighting for the enduring features of Russian civilization rather than the Bolshevik system. Exactly such a Pan-Slavic appeal was made by the Nazis (with mixed results as the archives of Smolensk indicate), an appeal which seems to have left, at least in small measure, a mark on Solzhenitsyn and explains why little is said of repression and terror under Czarism and why he offers so little in the study of continuities in Russian terrorism.

The theory offered to explain Soviet terrorism comes close to a conspiratorial view of history, as if a supreme being were masterminding the takeover of the Soviet world by the Devil and the expulsion of God: "It was essential to clean out, conscientiously, socialists of every other stripe from Moscow, Petrograd, the ports, the industrial centers, and later on, the outlying provinces as well. This was a grandiose silent game of solitaire, whose rules were toally incomprehensible to its contemporaries, and whose outlines we can appreciate only now. Someone's far-seeing mind, someone's neat hands, planned it all, without letting one wasted minute go by."

This is not to deny that real conspiracy existed. Wherever democracy is absent, the potential for conspiracy is present. But to explain such a gigantic event as the death and imprisonment of tens of millions of people as a conspiracy, falls badly short of what is required at the macro level of explanation. The answer is right at hand: the fundamental impulse of both Stalinism and Leninism was rapid development. Industrial development can sacrifice consumer modernization along with the people it involves in the developmental process. One might argue that the amount of terror was not comensurate with the tasks at hand, that less terror and more benign forms of coercion might have achieved the same results: but the denial of the results is what weakens Solzhenitsyn's analysis. His myopia concerning Soviet achievements also denies him the possibility of a real theory explaining Soviet terrorism and returns him to a primitive Christian view of good and evil that even Christianity has later abandoned. Goethe once explained that the trouble with Christianity was its impulse to cast problems in terms of good and evil, when in fact the real ethical problems people face are choices between good and good. This choice of goods, or perhaps of evils, breathes real-life tension into social systems. And it is the absence of this awareness of the struggle between developmentalism and terrorism, between the creative life-giving forces no less than the death-making forces, that makes Solzhenitsyn's work an unrelieved horror, or better, a series of horrors relieved by the author's personal genius as a writer.

*The Gulag Archipelago* has given us what few believed would ever be possible: a case history of the Communist party of the U.S.S.R., not a series of party visions and revisions, not a series of myths and illusions consecrated to the initial holders of power, but a study in state authority untrammelled and unfettered by popular will. The history of the Communist party of the Soviet union is ultimately the history of crime and punishment in the Soviet Union: the ultimate fusion of politics and deviance.

It really matters little that this is not a balanced or fairminded work, that it fails to recount properly and fairly the heroic events of Soviet development and of the Soviet people in the face of all sorts of foreign military adversity. Were this a work balancing the worth of the Soviet system on a cost-benefit scale, we would simply have a volume in economic theory, or even worse, a bookkeeping, double-entry system that fails to measure in qualitative terms the monumental architectonics that made the Gulag Archipelago possible. What is so awful about this book is that one realizes that no one remained untouched by the Gulag Archipelago, that the dirty little secret of the society as a whole was that the Soviet Union is the Gulag Archipelago, and that a description of prison life is a description of Soviet life. It serves little use to recite the joys of industrial achievement in the face of this awful truth. The Soviet Union became, at least between 1918 and 1956, a total institution. What has happened since then to change the parameters of the game, to limit and curb the prison-house atmosphere of the U.S.S.R.? Solzhenitsyn does not tell us whether the Archipelago ended in 1956 or whether he simply stopped his story at a point beyond which he had no first-hand evidence. We are left not so much with a conclusion as with a giant ambiguity. Perhaps the issues will be resolved in the next five parts of *The Gulag Archipelago*. Or perhaps there will be no other parts and we will have to reexamine, in the light of this work, the nature of state power, the workings of an economic system, and the consequences and benefits of making a revolution.

The leit motif of this book is the painful and shameful absence of mass resistance. "Today those who have continued to live in comfort scold those who suffered." Solzhenitsyn adds rhetorically: "Yes, resistance should have begun right there, at the moment of the arrest itself." This sense or moral turpitude, not unknown to a generation of Israelis reflecting on the European Holocaust, is all-pervasive; not the least because Solzhenitsyn survived his own shame of silence. But he learned his lesson well. *The Gulag Archipelago* can be viewed as a lesson in courage, a statement of personal survival through conditions of imprisonment, intimidation, and indignities. In the fusion of biography with history this masterpiece comes to fruition, and the dedication "to all those who did not live to tell it" is redeemed.

"I am finishing it [*The Gulag Archipelago*] in the year of a double anniversary (and the two anniversaries are connected): it is fifty years since the revolution which created Gulag, and a hundred since the invention of barbed wire (1867). This second anniversary will no doubt pass unnoticed." In this way a herculean project began as a testament in 1958 and completed in 1967 came into the world. But now that an additional decade has passed it is quite evident that, although pageantry of the fiftieth anniversary of the Soviet Revolution has long passed and the invention of barbed wire did indeed pass unheralded, we have been given as a gift of suffering a twentieth-century masterwork.

*The Gulag* is classic because it makes plain the essence of the century, not simply because it was written in our times. The dialectic of the century emerges on countless pages and in endless details: in the guise of socialism we receive bureaucracy, in the place of popular control we are provided with elite management, instead of the liquidation of state power there emerges an augmentation of such power; in place of abundance through industrial development we get deprivation as the price of such development. And ultimately, in place of justice we get the law. If before Solzhenitsyn we were able to recite conventional platitudes about this century being the best of times and the worst of times, we are forced to the grim realization that these have become simply the worst of times. Even in comparison to other troublesome ages such as the fourteenth century, one must recognize as a redeeming virtue the unconscious force of nature wreaking havoc with humanity. The conscious force of repression (sometimes called "racial destiny" and other times "historical necessity") destroys so many people that the concept of humanity itself assumes a tenuous dimension.

It shall come to pass that the literate population of the future, if there is to be a future, will be divided between those who have read and understood the lessons of the Gulag, and those who have not read—or even worse, read and not understood—the broad implications of this "experiment in literary investigation." Already, the cloudy voices of cynicism, fused with the fatuous voices of childlike optimism, have begun to assert the exaggerated political manners of Solzhenitsyn. Using as a pretext his Harvard commencement address on "The Exhausted West" (it is far simpler to make statements and render judgments on excerpts from a speech than work through the experience of three volumes of *The Gulag*), intellectual scribblers and political hags are assuring one and all that Solzhenitsyn not only does not understand American society but has already lost touch with Soviet realities. In the meanwhile, like a phoenix *The Gulag* remains; beyond contest, beyond dispute, and as is that rare characteristic of a masterwork: beyond good and evil—doomed to repetition in democratic Kampuchea (Cambodia) and only God knows where else.

The major accusation launched against Solzhenitsyn is his emotivism and presumed mysticism. Underlying this charge is the more serious charge that he lacks adequate analytic categories; hence that his critique is one-sided, that it fails to take into consideration the positive achievements of Soviet industrialization. While it is doubtlessly corect that emotional language is used, it is simply nonsense to claim that mysticism is preached. Irony makes the sufferings described and the outrages committed bearable. The catalogue of evils presented never—*not on a single page in three volumes*—involves any mystical commitment to blind faith or self-destructive acts. To be sure, insofar as any act of heroism, courage, and self-sacrifice involves a transcedent belief in the human condition, Solzhenitsyn stands accused; but to the extent that mysticism is adaptation or surrender to antihuman behavior or acceptance of "man's fate," he is entirely innocent. This is, after all, a special variety of prison literature; and prisoners who write books seek freedom, not immolation. Indeed, the burden of the final volume is a testimony to rebellion, resistance, and retaliation. It is an effort to answer the question: "Can a man's urge to stop being a slave and an animal *ever* be reactionary?"

Solzhenitsyn's *Gulag* has an implicit analytic scheme which deserves to be dealt with seriously, even profoundly. For in this towering statement of prison life in Soviet society there are "lessons" about twentieth-century social systems as a whole. The political sociology of Soviet society illumines the contours of a future that indeed "works." Herein lies its terrors for us all. And if that political sociology spills over into a political theology, it is nothing less than a consequence of universal ideologies confronting each other in mortal, perhaps eternal, combat. And if this creates an aura of Manicheanism, of the substitution of good for right and evil for wrongs, reification in itself must be viewed as a consequence of political systems, of state power reaching out for an ultimate domination of individual life. The "evils" of capitalism which spawned its "goods" was an impersonal dialetical necessity for Marx in the nineteenth century; but the "goods" of communism which spawned its "evils" is a draconian choice made by Bolsheviks old and new and then advertised as a necessity.

Stalin enjoyed posing issues in a pseudo-jesuitical manner. Every phenomenon became a rhetorical question. "Is such the case? Yes (or no) such is (or is not) the case." Hence, he gave us the political question, the national question, the women question, etc., ad infinitum. Solzhenitzyn's *Gulag* can be read as a parody of Stalinism. He takes these macroscopic "questions" and shows how they work in microscopic concentration camp circumstances. The marriage of Marxist theory and Russian realities was stress-laden from the outset. The bitter rivalries and factions within the revolutionary movement attest to this strain. Stalin's great achievement was to have consolidated the Leninist pivot and created a new orthodoxy. But to do so meant an end to rivalries, factions, and debate itself. The doctrine was saved while the intelligentsia was wasted.

The depoliticization of Soviet society is an underlying reality every dissident and deviant must contend with. The ordinary Soviet citizen goes about his business not unlike the ordinary Nazi citizen: learnedly ignorant of events and myopically closed to the human consequences of the Gulag. Rebellion is such an unusual event, that its recording by Solzhenitsyn becomes a major aspect of the third volume. While not quite reaching the epic proportions of the Warsaw Ghetto uprising, the record of resistance from Kengir to Novocherkassk—personal and political—forms the essential core of the third volume. But such uprisings remain sporadic and isolated. They are handled bureaucratically, involving scant potential for resistance. It is therefore not the character of rebellion that becomes startling: but the simple fact that resistance is even possible. Leviathan emerges as a total way of life, cut off from popular limits.

The Stalinist decision to emphasize economic development and industrialization muted any efforts at personal liberty. Only when work norms were not met or when political confusions arose from a series of crises of succession were any displays of resistance tolerated. What Solzhenitsyn depicts is the first society in which economics is completely sundered from politics; or better in which bureaucratic systems management becomes the norm. The U.S.S.R. becomes a country without a polity; and without a people who determine the nature of justice there can be no morality. Only political participants acting in complete freedom can determine the nature of goodness. The U.S.S.R. is not only the antithesis of the Aristotelian paradigm; it doesn't even measure up to Platonic communism—since the dialectic of the best and the brightest is reduced to the dynamics of the mediocre and mindless.

The Christian persuasion notwithstanding, Solzhenitsyn, quite like other exiles who preceded him, continues to be the conscience of a socialism gone awry. Like every Russian of the modern age, he grew up with a belief in the national question as resolved by the socialist system. Lenin and Stalin, in their wisdom, appreciated the fact that no revolution could be successful only in class terms. The ethnic and national variable was the crucial lynchpin to the successful conclusion of the revolutionary phase.

> Only when the twentieth century—on which all civilized mankind had put its hopes—arrived, only when the National Question had reached the summit of its development thanks to the one and Only True Doctine, could the supreme authority on the Question patent the wholesale extirpation of peoples by banishment within forty-eight hours, within twenty-four hours, or even within an hour and a half.

The nations of Russia which did not fit plans for unification were extirpated singly and collectively: Chechens, Ingush, Karachai, Balkars, Kalmyks, Kurds, Tatars, Caucasian Greeks, Germans, Balts, Estonians, Karelo-Finns; and, as Solzhenitsyn reminds us, the Jews were being readied when Stalin came to his end in 1953. The numbers of peoples totally liquidated read like an anthropological Who's Who of European peoples. When one asks who inhabited the Gulag is becomes evident that these millions of minority people were declared the chosen ones.

> Neatness and uniformity! That is the advantage of exiling whole nations at once! No special cases! No exceptions, no individual protests! They all go quietly, because . . . they are all in it together. All ages and both sexes go, and that still leaves something to be said. Those still in the womb go, too, and are exiled unborn, by the same decree.

One might argue that this is the necessary price of national unification. But if that be the situation, it was a price extracted with a gigantic political myth, with the promissory note of the rights of all peoples and nations to self-determination. Ideology and reality were never further apart. What the West did with a melting pot the Soviets did with melting people; a system of hard labor, penal servitude, exile, and death. This has become the style of Soviet substance. Perhaps the end of ethnic groups is an anthropological and historical fact, but the end of people as individuals is a political and military policy. And the Bolshevik authorities saw fit to make no fine, hair-splitting distinctions.

Solzhenitsyn offers a traditional romantic vision of women. If they are not elevated in their nature, they are at least deserving of very special concern. But instead of this being an irritant, one realizes that this is not only a sincere sentiment frankly expressed, but a shrewd antithesis to the Marxist equation of women's liberation with socialism. Indeed, the special pains Solzhenitsyn takes with their camp treatment, the abuse they endure as women, would indicate that the Soviet Revolution has transformed society into a whole cloth: with the treatment of women no better or worse than the treatment of peasants, intellectuals, and ethnic minorities. But what does make matters worse is the special vulnerability of women: the unique torments of an unwanted pregnancy, gang rapes by violent criminals as a reward for their abuse of political prisoners, types of work that are brutal and serve as a special form of demoralization for women.

> The body becomes worn out at that kind of work, and everything that is feminine in a woman, whether it be constant or whether it be monthly, ceases to be. If she manages to last to the next "commissioning," the person who undresses before the physicians will be not at all like the one whom the trustees smacked their lips over in the bath corridor: she has become ageless; her shoulders stick out at sharp angles, her breasts hang down in little dried-out sacs; superfluous folds of skin form wrinkles on her flat buttocks; there is so little flesh above her knees that a big enough gap has opened up for a sheep's head to stick through or even a soccer ball; her voice has become hoarse and rough and her face is tanned by pellagra.

The women came to the Gulag sharing with the men the same illusions, and later, slow emergence of consciousness. Among the early women prisoners were those hauled off into the Gulag driven naked between formations of jailors singing to their tormentors: "I know no other country/Where a person breathes so freely." But by the fifties, these same women became the ferocious defenders of their fellow inmates; fused into solidarity by long sentences and desperate lives.

> Events outsoared the casual contempt which the thieves feel for *females*. When shots rang out in the service yard, those who had broken into the women's camp ceased to be greedy predators and became comrades in misfortune. The women hid them. Unarmed soldiers came in to catch them, then others with guns. The women got in the way of the searchers, and resisted attempts to move them. The soldiers punched the women and struck them with their gun butts, dragged some of them off to jail (thanks to someone's foresight, there was a jailhouse in the women's camp area), and shot at some of the men.

When the prisoners rebelled at one penal colony and won forty days of self-determination, this represented the first real breath of freedom these women had known.

> The runaway escapes to enjoy just one day of freedom! In just the same way, these eight thousand men had not so much raised a rebellion as *escaped to freedom*, though not for long! Eight thousand men, from being slaves, had suddenly become free, and now was their chance to . . . live! Faces usually grim softened into kind smiles. Women looked at men, and men took them by the hand. Some who had corresponded by ingenious secret ways, without even seeing each other, met at last! Lithuanian girls whose weddings had been solemnized by priests on the other side of the wall now saw their lawful wedded husbands for the first time—the Lord had sent down to earth the marriages made in heaven! For the first time in their lives, no one tried to prevent the sectarians and believers from meeting for prayer. Foreigners, scattered about the Camp Divisions, now found each other and talked about this strange Asiatic revolution in thier own language. The camp's food supply was in the hands of the prisoners. No one drove them out to work line-up and an eleven-hour working day.

The Gulag does not offer a confrontation of traditionalism with modernity, but convention against barbarism. and in the Gulag everyone knew barbarism would win out in the end. "Newlyweds . . . observed each day as their last, and retribution delayed was a gift from heaven each morning." Irony of ironies: prisoners know a freedom denied to citizens of the Soviet society as a whole.

The tension of the first two volumes of the *Gulag* largely derived from the loggerheads at which "criminals" were juxtaposed over and against "politicals." Repeatedly, Solzhenitsyn shows how the regime utilizes criminals to intimidate and even assassinate political prisoners. The lumpen proletariat of Marx is deproletarianized under Stalin; but it performs the same tasks on behalf of the state: from strike-breaking to organized mayhem. The cynicism of this is displayed by the offerings of women to the criminals, to moving them into camps where political trouble is brewing. Solzhenitsyn rises above the cheap clap-trap of jailhouse lawyers who try to interpret every act of imprisonment as a political torment. He uses language exactly and precisely; in short scientifically.

> Their commune, more precisely their world, was a separate world within our world, and the strict laws which for centuries had existed in it for strengthening that world did not in any degree depend on our "suckers" legislation or even on the Party Congresses. They had their own laws of seniority, by which their ringleaders were not elected at all, yet when they entered a cell or a camp compound already wore their crown of power and were immediately recognized as chiefs. These ringleaders might have strong intellectual capacities, and always had a clear comprehension of the thieves' philosophy, as well as a sufficient number of murders and robberies behind them. And what did their word "frayersky"—"of the suckers"—mean? It meant what was universally human, what pertained to all normal people. And it was precisely this universally human world, *our* world, with its morals, customs, and mutual relationships, which was most hateful to the thieves, most subject to their ridicule, counterposed most sharply to their own antisocial, anti-public *kubla* or clan.

For two volumes these miserable, incarcerated creatures play out a living class struggle while the Soviet authorities offer metastases about the achievements of the Gulag: "a collective organism, living, working, eating, sleeping, and suffering together in pitiless and forced symbiosis."

In the third volume the tension shifts.[4] Prisoners who are ordinary criminals learn, albeit slowly and painfully, the manipulative nature, essence of the regime, while the abused politicals learn to adopt the cutthroat ethic of the criminals—in a kind of Darwinian trade-off. But it is one that worked for a short time at least.

> By 1954, so we are told, it was noticeably in transit prisons that *the thieves came to respect the politicals.* If this is so—what prevented us from gaining their respect earlier? All through the twenties, thirties, and forties, we blinkered philistines, preoccupied as we were with our own importance to the world, with the contents of our duffel bags, with the shoes or trousers we had been allowed to retain, had conducted ourselves in the eyes of the thieves like characters on the comic stage: when they plundered our neighbors, intellectuals of world importance like ourselves, we shyly looked the other way and huddled together in our corners; and when the submen crossed the room to give us the treatment, we expected, of course, no help from neighbors, but obligingly surrendered all we had to these ugly customers in case they bit our heads off.

It turns out that a third category of prisoner exists in Soviet labor camps, distinct and distinctive: the religious prisoner. This well-represented group was extremely important. They bore witness to tragedy; but they did so in a way which confronted the vacuum of Soviet ideology with the force of some higher belief. In their nonviolent commitments, they were the touchstone of conditions for all prisoners. When religious prisoners were tormented, maimed, or shot, that became a cue that all hope was lost. Resistance was the only recourse—futile and folly-laden though it might appear.

The Jews are represented in all three categories. Solzhenitsyn does not make much of it; he doesn't have to . The surnames of Gulag residents reveal this fact. Hence, Jews suffer a sort of triple risk: if they engage in entrepreneurial acts they are reviled as bourgeois remnants; if they engage in human rights activities they were condemned as Zionist plotters; and if they assert their religious commitment to Judaism they are obscurantists and fossils substituting ancient dogma to the "science" of Marxism-Leninism. This threefold persecution makes the Jewish condition especially poignant and dangerous. The liquidation of the Jewish population of the Soviet Union is just as much an agenda item as their liquidation by Nazi Germany. The Nazis were cruel: they wanted dead bodies as dead souls. The Soviet authorities are willingly ready to settle for dead souls only; hoping, like the Inquisition, that the living bodies will convert to communism, becoming in the process productive workers of the state.

One perplexing, haunting, question that remains is why Solzhenitsyn's *Gulag* has the capacity to shock and disturb its readers. Surely, it is not for lack of a literature on the subject of Soviet state terror. The archives are filled with scholarly treatises and personal testaments alike. And such early efforts as Vladimir Tchernavis' *I Speak for the Silent;* Pitirim Sorokin's *Leaves from a Russian Diary;* and Ivan Solonevich's *Russia in Chains* have the capacity to evoke similar powerful moods and sentiments. To be sure, Solzhenitsyn exhibits an exactitude as well as a collective judgment rarely before assembled in such force. And there can be no question that his fame as a great writer, not to mention the circumstances of his exile from the Soviet Union, also played a part in making the *Gulag* special.

Another element is present, one with ominous consequences. Our anlysis of Soviet society is, like our analysis of nuclear conflict, too easily based on a spurious exchange theory; on a trade-off between industrial growth to postwar survival and the number of deaths involved. We are inclined to accept certain levels of death or even mass annihilation if the ends in view can be achieved. Thus if it takes thirty million lives to create a Soviet beatitude, then so be it. But which thirty million? And why one number and not another? could the same results be achieved with fewer deaths or less suffering? What in past centuries was a sense of historical cost, even necessary cost, for social change and economic expansion, in our century has become a willing, and even an enthusiastic endorsement of the idea of costs to achieve not infrequently spurious benefits. I submit that the special nature of Solzhenitsyn's impact derives from his keen awareness of the substitution of engineering for ethical criteria in evaluating the human soul. He does not speak against development, but rather for those countless millions who paid the price for development. And in compelling a fresh review of the actual costs paid and the dubious benefits received, he has restored the balance between political realities and moral possibilities.

Even a masterpiece may have flaws. Solzhenitsyn's single-mindedness would make that inevitable. The major problem in the final volume of *The Gulag Archipelago* is the rather weak empirics of concentration camp life between 1957 and the present. The transition from totalitarianism to authoritarianism in Soviet life is left unexamined in favor of a vaguely stated premise that only a total overhaul in the Soviet system, indeed a counterrevolution, would change the internal dynamics of Russian life. And yet, even Solzhenitsyn despairs about a present generation of Russian youth who walk about with their portable radios and shaggy girls under their arms, and who couldn't care less about the Gulag system. But is that system the same? Is it merely a shell of its former self? Is this a work of history or social life?

In terms of values and norms Solzhenitsyn answers in the affirmative; that Gulag lives. And we have every reason to believe this to be the case. Predetermined prison sentences of dissidents continues unabated. Persecution of the politicals has few rivals in the world. The identical dried-out Leninist rhetoric continues unrivaled. Still, there does seem to be growth in the middle sector, and concommitant demands for observing legal norms that did not formerly obtain. The sheer reduction in numbers within Gulag requires some sort of explanation that Solzhenitsyn is seemingly unable to provide. In this sense, the depoliticization of Soviet society has been so thoroughgoing that the need for an immense Gulag has been reduced to manageable proportions. Perhaps this is more frightening than the Gulag itself, implying as it does a society which has itself become a willing penal colony, where good people are given time off for good behavior as long as they strictly observe one rule: thou shalt not question the political regime and its bureaucratic processes.

By the time this extraordinary work was completed, a work the author never saw in its entirety prior to publication, Solzhenitsyn realized its literary imperfections: repetition and jerkiness. What he calls the mark of a persecuted literature. But such repetitions far from being superfluous are essential. The apostles each repeated the story of Christ's crucifixion and redemption. The magnitude of human suffering is no easy lesson absorbed at one sitting. The Afterword offered by Solzhenitsyn is one of those rare moments when the "hyphen" in the Judeo-Christian heritage is breached: and the Father of historical redemption fuses with the Son who bears special witness to human suffering. "I want to cry aloud: When the time and opportunity come, gather together, all you friends who have survived and know the story well, write your own commentaries to go with my book, correct and add to it where necessary. Only then will the book be definitive. God bless the work!" When the *Gulag* is published in full, and in one of those huge editions Soviet publishing has become famous for trumpeting, then we shall have an operational test of Soviet freedom. Until that blessed event this towering set of volumes will stand between us and going gently into the totalitarian temptation.

With remarkable agility, Solzhenitsyn has become an international political figure. Traveling through the West, and finally assuming residence in the United States, he has become a symbol of the new exile: an unwilling cosmopolitan, who retains more sentiments for a world left behind that any sense of adventure in a "new world." He is a political figure pushed into exile, rather than an economic figure pulled into exile by things to come. Solzhenitsyn is sufficiently aware of Western mores to appreciate the degree to which sponsorship is legitimacy. He has thus chosen his forums as carefully and as prudently as he has spoken to issues boldly and fearlessly. For example, his premier addresses in the United States, after being forced into exile, were sponsored by the American trade union movement, specifically by the national office of the American Federation of Labor / Congress of Industrial Organizations.[5] As the main root and branch of American labor, it is unlikely to be called reactionary or aloof from ordinary people. The choice of sponsors, no less than the selection of topics, in no small part explains why established political leaders have been upset with him. Whether at Washington or Cambridge, Solzhenitsyn has spoken on the essence of Western democratic values, and denied a monopoly on this subject to American nationals or elite politicians.

Solzhenitsyn fused and organized a welter of critical sentiments and feelings that most ordinary Americans still retain toward the Soviet government. The cold war may be over and spaceship diplomacy may be the next step toward political paradise, but there is still that undigested residue of mistrust, with thirty years standing. There are differences between us and them, between Americans and Russians, and even more, between democrats and communists. This is not simply a matter of sentiment, but of continued and intensified competition in the military and economic arenas. Solzhenitsyn tapped that sentiment, and understood how to fuse it and how to use it to develop a broad coalition. His speeches have revealed a high level of sophistication. He employs the organizing symbols and myths of American political life, extending from the antibourgeois spirit to the civil-religious sentiments still strong after two hundred years.

The Helsinki accords were viewed by the president of the United States as a new opportunity for humanitarianism, and by the premier of the Soviet Union as a final termination of all Western interference in East European affairs. The agreement settled very little, but that is not the point. The point is that a writer, Solzhenitsyn, became, albeit briefly, a counterforce to the conventional rhetoric of American political life. In rocking the policy consensus, the foreigner and exiled dreamer had the weight of American tradition on his side.

Much has been made of Solzhenitsyn's religious mysticism and pan-Slavism. If these elements have been reflected in his literary works, they are not the paramount concerns of Solzhenitsyn as a political figure. There is nothing mystical or theological about his political judgments. He reveals himself to be an old-fashioned Western liberal, a believer in democratic pluralism and laissez-faire individualism. In part, his position derives from his role as a writer in Western exile. In part, too, it derives from a clear decision to assume a posture to the political Right of dissidents who remain in the Soviet Union, such as Sakharov,[6] Medvedev[7] and the other Samizdatists.[8] There is a tactical consideration involved. By reintroducing fundamental concerns, Solzhenitsyn has created an opening, not only for authentic dialogue, but for more moderately toned criticisms to be treated with greater respect and realism within the Soviet Union.

Solzhenitsyn is the premier exilic figure, possessing a political potency not found since Trotsky. Not only was he permitted to emigrate from the Soviet Union with a family and library intact, but the West treated him as a celebrity (quite unlike Trotsky). Solzhenitsyn's responsibilities to Russian politics remain central, even in exile. Even more unusual, he is not a Communist party member in opposition like Sakharov. We are presented with a living Russian anti-Communist who sees value, not in the interior Marxist "dialogue," but only in the dialogue between autocracy and democracy. The drama itself is indicative of new times: the Soviet Union, whatever its social structure, now has the capacity and the confidence to permit exile as a solution rather than death, and equally, the United States is in the odd position of having this lonely exile serve as the organizing principle of opposition to détente and a focus of animosity for upsetting a delicately evolved delicate diplomatic equilibrium.

The inaugural speech given by Solzhenitsyn in Washington several years ago was in part a brief history of the Communist party in the Soviet Union. It surveys the ways in which that nation has been bolstered by the United States and Western Europe during its nearly sixty-year history. It is a call to moral arms demanding a quid pro quo in the way of human rights for economics and political concessions. Solzhenitsyn clearly feels the United States has never gotten any bargaining advantages from its recognition of the Soviet regime to the present. There is a strange Manichaeanism about Solzhenitsyn's presentation: the United States is represented as naive while the Soviet Union is represented as cunning. It provides a counterrevisionist reading of history with respect to the origins of the cold war. For while the revisionist historians have been busy working out the ways in which the postwar Truman administration undermined the World War II alliance, Solzhenitsyn shows how the prewar Roosevelt administration may be characterized by its genteel capitulation to Soviet terrorism as well as Soviet expansionism.

Anyone acquainted with the whitewash of the Soviet Purge Trials surely cannot scoff at such an approach.[9] If Truman was suspicious of Soviet postwar intentions, Roosevelt was ingenuous with regard to Soviet prewar performance. From Finland, to the Baltic States, to Bessarabia, the United States acquiesced in geographic and demographic changes of a sweeping order. The "booty of war" overwhelmed the "rights of man."

Solzhenitsyn has been careful not to oppose détente, which he considers to be "as necessary as air." What he perceives in the present moment is no East-West détente but Western capitulation. World War III is being won by Soviet diplomats without firing a shot. What is one to make of the constant Marxist claims that imperialism is shrinking, that the United States is collapsing, that the forces of socialism are expanding, that the forces of communism are inevitable and victorious? Is this not simply the other side of Solzhenitsyn's claims—spoken in an optative rather than pessimistic mood? We are partially involved in empirical questions. What is occurring on a worldwide scale with respect to global politics? Is the United States losing and the Soviet Union winning? Are the forces of imperialism shrinking while the forces of communism are enlarging? Here is where Solzhenitsyn seems to have his greatest difficulties. Because in some measure, whether he would care to admit it or otherwise, he is employing the intellectual coin of the realm of Spengler.[10] The theme of creeping barbarism is the linchpin which, if pulled, collapses the argument and would compel the dialogue to become more realistic and sober on both sides.

In economic terms, capitalism had a period of "long-wave" growth between 1945 and 1973 (the so-called Kondratieff effect) that not even its most severe critics seriously challenge. The emergence of new forms of production, distribution, and organization, labeled multinationalism, has not only "rationalized" capitalist relations by internationalizing them, but further, created a mechanism for dealing with multinational socialism. We are at a point where no pure theory of capitalism or socialism can be sustained because no pure example of either system exists. Bureaucratic centralization, mass social welfare services, and state allocation and manipulation of the economic system typify both American and Russian realities. The United States and the Soviet Union may not be converging, but certainly there are parallels between their economic systems that make détente functionally as well as strategically plausible—if not downright inevitable.

Overall characterizations are inevitably impressionistic and subject to modification. What seems to be taking place is not so much the demise of capitalism or the creeping triumph of Bolshevism, but a trade-off reaching toward an equilibrium point. Solzhenitsyn is correct to note the considerable triumph of the Soviet Union in Eastern Europe and Southeast Asia. but it is likewise the case that Western capitalism has also expanded, rather than contracted, its sphere of influence since the end of World War II. In both political and military terms, the capitalist sphere of influence has been extended to include vast stretches of Latin America, Africa, and Asia. Even the Arab Middle East is shaping up a a new player in the capitalist orbit. While the political forms of Third World nations are often highly centralized, totalitarian, and overtly military, their economic forms remain clearly entrenched in the capitalist world system. The trade-off is thus not simply on a nation-for-nation basis, but also give sway to communism or totalitarianism in the political network and increasing capitalist control in the economic sector. The current mood of China gives further evidence of this trade-off.

This may not be a pleasant outcome of the postwar drama for reconstruction, nor does either option offer much hope in the way of individual freedom. Yet Solzhenitsyn believes, and quite properly, that an enormous gap exists between those nations fully under Soviet dominion and those that retain a measure of democratic self-determination. The point is that Solzhenitsyn's Manichaeanism breaks down under the weight of empirical guidelines. The West is neither entirely naive nor blameless, while the East is neither victorious nor immoral. What makes Solzhenitsyn's response especially poignant is the relative absence of moral considerations in the conduct of foreign policy. If the Soviets can readily wear the mask of evil, the United States does not nearly do as well wearing a crown of thorns. For this reason, the morally centered political universe of Solzhenitsyn fails to convince under careful examination.

Solzhenitsyn's charges and claims tend to fall on deaf ears and to be viewed as the ravings of a literary romantic because empirical and historical events tend to be viewed as ethically neutral or ambiguous. The time machine has passed him by—one might say for worse rather than for better. But in all ages writers have claimed the prerogative of looking backwards as well as forward. After all, even the most hard-boiled of us can say that in the Soviet Union we have seen the future and it works, if by "work" we mean stumbling along. Under such circumstances, it is easier to say we have seen the past and it worked even better.

Solzhenitsyn says that under the rubble of Czarism one found less terrorism, less imprisonment, and less genocide than under Stalinism.[11] But he never quite answers the question of whether Czarism was superior to Stalinism. He cannot quite bring himself to confront the central issue of revolution: Is the price in suffering worth the pain in output? The absolute moralist in him disallows an acceptance of the present Soviet regime; whereas the shrewd historian similarly disallows advocacy of any return to the Czarist regime. Hence Solzhenitsyn must end in a cul-de-sac from which he is incapable of extricating himself.

There is a growing isomorphism and similitude between the internal workings of the United States and Soviet Union. Political and economic differences while real, seem less pronounced on both sides of the Iron Curtain. At the very historical juncture when there seems to be a growing intensity in ideological debates within each major power, there is a noticeable decline in functional distinctions between major world powers. It is simply too risky to undertake armed struggle or its economic equivalencies in a thermonuclear age. Ideological debate is taken down one notch to international levels. Today, all major problems are managed bureaucratically. Political controversies become ambiguous, if not in their nature, then in their solution. From the point of view of the major powers, struggles between Greece and Turkey, Israel and Egypt, Uganda and Tanzania, Flemish and Walloons, are all trivial, dangerous only to the extent that they might conceivably ignite the world in nuclear holocaust.

What has happened in recent years to create an elitist reaction to critics of the Soviet regime like Solzhenitsyn? Certainly it has not been any dramatic democratization of the regime. To be sure, a profound curb to internal genocide has taken place. The very release of Solzhenitsyn indicates as much. But the accusations now leveled by him have often been made in the past. I suspect that the officialist resentment for Solzhenitsyn is a part of the American experience with defeat in military adventures in Southeast Asia and social and economic stalemate domestically. As a consequence, big-power chauvinism has become a new style, wrapped in the phraseology of détente. It is a last effort to turn defeat into victory, even if it means sharing the fruits of such success with a much feared Soviet adversary. Along comes Solzhenitsyn to remind us of the chasm between democracy and autocracy and the schism in twentieth-century history between the United States and the Soviet Union. Official policy continues to believe that by ignoring the past, defeat can still be turned into victory, cold war into détente.

As a result, détente resolves itself in big-power management of small nations and their affairs. The price of such management is less autonomy for small nations and less freedom for individuals. Human rights are guaranteed by power. In this connection, Solzhenitsyn cannot easily by confounded. There may be few options to current policy, perhaps the risks are too great to steer a different geopolitical course. In fact, American policy is part of an anomaly. The end of the cold war is bringing relief from the possibility of military destruction , but it has not yet brought in its wake relief from political terror or personal insecurity.

Détente, to the extent that it is successful, makes mass politics even more remote; decisions are made on high. Solzhenitsyn is responding to this alientated sense of the genocidal condition. He is the perfect Orwellian: one who understands that history is memory and that injustice, like justice, is indivisible. There can be no justice for a prisoner in the United States without justice for prisoners in the Soviet Union. There can be no terrorism in the Soviet Union without opening up that possibility in the United States. The monistic sense of political events, the feeling that the world is one and that Russians have as much right to speak with candor about the United States as Americans about the Soviet Union, makes Solzhenitsyn a special figure: an Amnesty International of One.

# Notes to Chapter 6

1. Solzhenitsyn, Aleksandr. *Nobel Lecture*. Translated by R.D. Reeve. New York: Farrar, Straus, and Giroux, 1972.

2. Solzhenitsyn, Aleksandr. *The Gulag Archipelago, 1918-1956: An Experiment in Literary Investigation* (I: The Prisons Industry; and II: Perpetual Motion). Translated from the Russian by Thomas P. Whitney. New York and London: Harper & Row, Publishers, 1973.

3. Solzhenitsyn, Aleksandr. *The Gulag Archipelago, 1918-1956: An Experiment in Literary Investigation* (III: The Destructive-Labor Camps; and IV: The Soul and Barbed Wire). Translated from the Russian by Thomas P. Whitney. New York and London: Harper and Row, 1975.

4. Solzhenitsyn, Aleksandr. *The Gulag Archipelago, 1918-1956: An Experiment in Literary Investigation* (V: Katorga; VI: Exile; and VII: Stalin Is No More). Translated from the Russian by Harry Willets. New York and London: Harper & Row, 1978.

5. Solzhenitsyn, Aleksandr. *Détente: Prospects for Democracy and Dictatorship*. New Brunswick, New Jersey: Transaction Books, 1976 (second edition, 1979).

6. Sakharov, Andrei D. *Sakharov Speaks*, edited with a foreword by Harrison E. Salisbury. New York: Alfred A. Knopf, 1974.

7. Medvedev, Roy. *Détente and Socialist Democracy*. Nottingham: Spokesman Books, 1975.

8. Voronel, Aleksander and Viktor Yakhot. *Jewishness Rediscovered: Jewish Identity in the Soviet Union*. New York: Academic Committee on Soviet Jewry and the Anti-Defamation League of B'nai B'rith, 1975.

9. Davies, Joseph E. *Mission to Moscow*. New York: Simon and Schuster, 1941.

10. Spengler, Oswald. *The Decline of the West*. Translated by Charles Francis Atkinson. New York: Alfred A. Knopf, 1932.

11. Solzhenitsyn, Aleksandr. *From Under the Rubble*. Translated by A.M. Brock. Boston: Little Brown & Company, 1975.

# Chapter 7

# Bureaucracy
# and State Power

*Once it is fully established, bureaucracy is among those social structures which are the harder to destroy. Bureaucracy is the means of carrying "community action" over into rationally ordered "societal action." Therefore, as an instrument for "socializing" relations of power, bureaucracy has been and is a power instrument of the first order—for the one who controls the bureaucratic apparatus. . . . The consequences of bureaucracy depend therefore upon the direction which the powers using the apparatus give to it. And very frequently a crypto-plutocratic distribution of power has been the result.*

Max Weber, ECONOMY AND SOCIETY

In examining postindustrial society and the future of public administration, we would be well advised to follow the dictum of the theoretical physicist John Archibald Wheeler, who warns us that "no elementary phenomenon is a phenomenon until it is an observed phenomenon."[1] Rather than a postindustrial society, we observe a series of societies at relative plateaus of socioeconomic development and a variety of administrative networks responding to and influencing different levels of development. As long as we distinguish the empirical from the speculative, we may talk about postindustrialization as a generic type, and the future of public administration as an extrapolation from its past and present.

Postindustrial society has no recognizable denotive content. If it means a world in which knowledge replaces artifact as central, then the connection of knowledge to production like the relationship of head work to hand work, is a matter for study, and simply to be assumed. The character of mechanization has shifted, and the role of policymaker has enlarged, but in itself this is not postindustrial, but simply an evolution of the industrial order. We still inhabit a universe largely defined by preindustrial characteristics. The industrial sector remains far from a universal characteristic of social systems.

The major axioms of postindustrial society are evident: Western societies are characterized by private property and the private control of investment decisions, but also by an industrial base whose primary logic is technological efficiency. Using such a division we can identify different sequences of development. Along the axis of technology we have preindustrial, industrial, and post-industrial. There is a built-in contradiction between the principle of bureaucratization, based on hierarchy, and the principle of equality, based on participation. Bureaucracy segments people into roles. The social tensions in Western democracy have been framed by the contrary logics of bureaucratization and participation, under-girded by a change of scale in institutions leading to a profound shift in functions. The major principle of postindustrial society is the cod-ification of theoretical knowledge, specifically new technological-scientific activities oriented around computers, telecommunication, optics, polymers, and electronics. Control of the means of information augments struggle over the means of production in such a society, and hence the character of work alters significantly. Work becomes struggle between persons rather than against nature. In a postindustrial universe, society becomes a free choice by free people, rather than a banding together against nature or an involuntary joining together in routinized relations imposed from outside.[2]

The phrase *postindustrial society* is infelicitous. The metaphor is inherently transitional, arguing about a movement from before to after something called "industrial." The phrase is ambiguous, since it refers to cultural norms in the most advanced nations and is subject to a variety of interpretations; few are operational and even fewer are consonant with each other. Societies do not emerge de novo; we are still trying to ascertain meanings to ascribe to industrialization. Much has happened since the end of World War II: above all the ability of mankind to "totalize" destruction, engineer genocide, and to engage in atomic warfare. Authoritarianism is no longer confined to a single state apparatus, but expands to the global decimation of peoples. Whether we use the phrase *postindustrial society,* or some equivalent labeling device is less important than arriving at a meaningful framework to handle life and death issues.

The term *postindustrial* is often employed as a hygienic way of saying "authoritarianism" in an age of public-sector dominance, or at least the ascendance of policy over politics. The postindustrial vision admits only of a "deeply pessimistic" view of society. Postindustrialism conjures up the image of engineered totalitarianism. "A technocratic society is not ennobling"; it lacks a "rooted moral belief system" and despite the "cockpit of decisions" it permits, the "cultural contradictions of society" are buried rather than expressed by this new postindustrial environment—or more simply, this totalitarian temptation.[3] Implicit is a deep mistrust of bureaucratic administration, one shared by a host of ideological standpoints common to our age.

Whether such a series of postulates adds up to postindustrial society or a neotechnocratic state with authoritarian tendencies is a choice of language and an amplification of different pessimisms. However, that the contours of social structure and social stratification have shifted dramatically is beyond contest.[4] Determining how public administration intersects and interfaces this new reality becomes central. Before doing so, the same yardstick of linguistic rigor must be applied to the notion of public administration as to postindustrial society; a not inconsequential task in a field of strong sentiments and polarized frameworks.

The most essential fact about public administration is that it came into existence prior to any theory. Whether things, people, or ideas are administered, administrators clearly preceded any general theory. Public administration emerged in a context of justification and celebration, rather than general theory, i.e., making "something happen in the public interest." It has an inevitable bias toward the practical, toward getting things done; an uneasiness, even discontent, with frustrating questions that in their breadth and scope may prove to be incapacitating.[5] The private woe of public administrators has been theory writ large. Their preference has been for middle-range theories, and if those are unavailable, no theory at all. This is the first time that practical people have lived a full and useful life without always knowing what they are doing.

The relationship of public administration to economics, sociology, political science, and psychology bespeaks of an insecure search for broader meaning. As administration is distinguished from its parts (forms of administration at different levels covering different subject areas) it simply is no longer possible to make do with makeshift definitions. How does one train a public administrator involved in the Department of Commerce over and against one involved in Health, Education, and Welfare? How does one train public administrators who operate at city levels in contradistinction to those who operate at national levels? These are but the most obvious questions.

General theory emerges in pedagogic contexts when the need to know becomes overriding. Determining entry level skills becomes more exacting in an era of affirmative action. There are questions of the relationship between those who administrate through political appointment and those who administrate through civil service appointment. These issues emerge in the literature on administration; but in a context of search for a simplified paradigm of general theory, as if this alone could transform administration from craft to science.

If not a science, what is the art of public administration? Here the giant assumption which is central to understanding government per se, is that administration is a function of state authority, or authorities as the case may be. One administrates things, peoples, and ideologies on behalf of an employer called the state. Therefore the lineage between administrator and state offers a direct link between administration and policies. The conventional nineteenth-century image of social classes manipulating bureaucracies to gain advantage is not accurate. Rather, a big administrative machinery manipulating other sectors that become decisive: labor forces decrease in size and increase in power.

Public administration takes place in a context of policy inversion: a transformation of power from the economy to the polity; mediated by the monopoly of allocation and distribution of public funds. Public administration does not service one class or sector, but the state. The class interest of the middle administrator is the class of top administrators insofar as they are directly linked to forms of state power. Public administration is therefore inextricably linked to state power. To say that administrators are politically neutral is a naive statement of politics as an elite activity. To be neutral with respect to a party or an interest group is perfectly reasonable, even a prerequisite of sound administrative procedures. But for the administrator to be neutral to the existence of state power as such is a contradiction in terms. For the essential politics of the administrator is the survival, prolongation, and strengthening of the apparatus. This is administrative politics writ large, whatever disclaimers are made about political participation writ small, i.e., as party loyalty or partisan activity.

The essential contest in class terms shapes up as one between elites and masses, or expressed ideologically, statism versus populism. Those who have a vested interest in the state and its organized activities must view with suspicion populist activities that would move against state power. On the other hand, those with populist concerns can no longer rest easy with old-fashioned formulations concerning class. The lesson of the current era is the confrontation of classes, sexes, races, and ethnic groups directly with state authority. The legal mechanisms and financial systems make possible broad layers of social change in attitudes and behavior precisely through reinforcing the ascribed features of the status system.

Administrators do not oppose change. Rather they demand that changes occur legally, through yet a further enlargement and acceptance of the administrative apparatus. Insofar as the system as a whole can manage a reward and punishment framework that appeals to the state, to that extent does state power become enhanced and public administration enlarged. However, to the degree that the state cannot manage rational rewards and punishments, or cannot orchestrate and mobilize the economy to do its bidding, it invites populist rebellion and popular opposition.

The postindustrial world resembles the postfeudal, monarchical era of Machiavelli and Hobbes more than it does entrepreneurial capitalism. The reason a postindustrial world is so comfortable with Machiavelli and Hobbes is that the relationship of ruled to ruler, as in the preindustrial age, has become simplified. Mediating institutions such as parties and pressure groups have less clout and ability to deliver basic services than do state managers. In such a postindustrial climate, interest groups are reduced to fundamental conflict and competition. In the dialectic of postindustrial conflict the manipulation of funds and forces rather than the administration of people becomes a rallying cry within administrative work, much as it did for the nineteenth-century utopians who argued for the withering away of state power.

A central aspect of this rationalization process is the need for the state to confront new Leviathans, ranging from multinational corporations to NASA-type space programs, which involve budgets equal to conventional government expenditures. In substantive areas, public administration turns to the state as an essential monitoring and evaluating tool of potential threats to the commonwealth. The emergence of regional trade and national associations also requires a tighter framework for state decision making; everything from arranging sales to supervising contracts involves administrative servicing. While mediating agencies within a nation lose some of their potency, the need for state power grows as a response to external agencies.[6] The state must negotiate with a wide variety of foreign and domestic agencies and interest groups; public administration does not lack for new areas to conquer.

Much is taken for granted in public administration; even its size and scope remains obscure. As late as the mid-1930's, people were recruited for public administration posts among a wide variety of professions and disciplines. But by the postwar period, public service had become a field unto itself. One writer recently described this evolutionary process as the development of a new mandarinate.

Syracuse University started the first American school of public administration back in 1924, and the University of Southern California followed a few years later. But the idea has really come into its own during the 1970s. In 1972 the National Association of Schools of Public Administration boasted 101 affiliates; today it is up to 220. The number of students graduating from such schools each year doubled in the same period—up to 6,000 in 1977. That may be a trickle next to the floodtide of government bureaucracies (the federal Department of Energy alone employs 20,000 people). But it is an increasingly influential and well-regarded trickle. And with growth in the number of university-trained administrators has come insistence that there should be more.[7]

Administrative personnel include first, those who service the executive and legislative branches of government; second, those involved with interest groups ranging from veterans and homebuilders to the handicapped and police chiefs; third, those who service regulatory and monitoring agencies; fourth, those who manage the roughly five hundred separate grants-in-aid programs sanctioned by congressional action; fifth, lobbyists who support every program enacted or proposed in the first four layers. The magnitude of the federal administration is enormous.

As has been recently observed, the rising tide of administrative expertise stands in inverse proportion to the electorate's sense of diminishing returns. "What is happening in Washington is a fragmentation that feeds defensiveness. Almost every elected official in Washington from the President on down is an independent, the end result of the steady decline in the party system. The White House has put together a different coalition for every issue, and frequently it is as dependent on Republicans as Democrats to win a vote."[8] These considerations pertain only to the federal bureaucracy located in Washington, D.C., a city of three million inhabitants in which administration is the central occupational role. Recent demographic estimates of state and local government administrators—excluding salaried managers and those working in private, nonpublic, administration—count nearly five million people working as public administrators, broadly defined. Between 1950 and 1979 public administration trebled in size. For example, in the census tables covering industrial distribution of employment in the tertiary sector, public administration nationwide jumped from 2,491,000 in 1950 to 4,202,000 in 1970.[9] The 1980 census will undoubtedly show further growth in this sector. Public administration represents a large segment of the labor force: well educated, increasingly subject to specialization of roles and functions, and quite willing to execute and interpret the will of state authority.

The postindustrial concept is organically related to public administration. Public administration's enlarged role is part of a changing pattern of class relationships. Weber's trepidations over the growth of bureaucracy were well grounded.[10] Public sector activities have grown at a pace and in power far beyond older classes: the proletariat has declined as capital-intensive industry replaces manual labor; the peasant-farmer sector has shriveled in size as technology has improved food and agricultural production; the bourgeoisie as an owning group has been allowed to remain constant in numbers, but its decision making has been reduced by the need for federal public sector supports.

Middle management in industry has become the corollary to growth in the public sector. The decision-making function permits one to think of industry, no less than government, as a set of bureaucratic institutions or leaders with divergent ideas.[11] But if neither government nor industry offers a single rational actor, they do offer a picture of two central facets of advanced industrial society operating with profoundly different models of economic well-being. The contrast in economic philosophies between the public and private sector is well known. The critical contradictions between these two sectors prevent any new class of administrative workers from emerging despite similitudes at the functional level.[12]

Public administrators function as a subclass of the public sector, and industry managers function as a subclass of the private sector. The character of class competition also changes dramatically in the postindustrial world. The familiar competition *within* the private sector between bourgeoisie and proletariat yields to the less familiar but more potent struggle *between* the administrative vanguards of the public sector and the private sector. The coterminous existence of older forms of class competition remain intact, but even these are mediated by new administrators and their authorities, interests, and regulations.

The Sherman Antitrust Act of the late nineteenth century introduced a tension between public and private sector economies which has not yet abated. It is precisely the tilt toward the public that permits one to characterize our epoch as postindustrial. Implied is a change not only from goods to services, or commodities to ideas, but more exactly, a shift in locus of power and the force of numbers.[13] Public administration is properly perceived as a subclass functioning as an independent social force, representing public sector requirements in its great struggle to involve the private sector in the goals of equity and opportunity. The public administrator functions in the classic bureaucratic mold, as representative of the national interest over and against managers of industrial interests. Whether the public administration can do so without collapsing the innovation, initiative, and inventiveness of an advanced society becomes the challenge during the next decade.[14]

As in other areas of applied research, the power of the American style emerged with raw pragmatism that rests on a problem-solving context in which "means and ends are sometimes impossible to separate, where aspirations and objectives are in constant development, and where drastic simplification of the complexity of the real world is urgent."[15] Public administration in particular grew in a context of only a barely disguised animus for theorists, those for whom a "rational comprehensive" model has meaning. Public administration was celebrated as "the science of muddling through," and the only widely acknowledged problem was the swiftness of technological innovation so that there was an "absence of enough persons who are knowledgeable in computer use." The solution was better functional division of technology and more extensive training.[16]

To look back even a short decade is to observe a brave new world of public administration, in which technological breakthroughs are constant and solutions to thorny problems are registered through improved data control. Governance through data control reached its crescendo in the United States with the Vietnam war, the Watergate scandals, and a series of uncovered deceptions at the legislative level. As the mechanics of administration became unmanageable, the science of muddling through led to a series of overseas defeats and domestic miscalculations. As a result, there was a dramatic contextual shift from America to Europe in the theory of public administration.

The major theses of the 1960s were delineated and articulated in advanced texts and by major figures but left unresolved. Little more could be expected when even the most advanced researchers proposed that public administration overcome its "crisis of identity by trying to act as a profession without actually being one."[17] The implications were clear: the main issues were turned from the social conditions of administration to the professional status of administration. As a review essay of the ten leading public administration texts points out: "Only one author devotes much space to posing the question of which groups and social classs are best served by the administrative structure of the state."[18] As the emphasis inexorably shifted from issues of broad social meaning to narrow professional issues, micromethodology replaced theory construction: problems of measurement, evaluation, and even monitoring of programs and plans rapidly displaced more fundamental concerns. Under such circumstances, the source of new inspiration in public administration inevitably shifted to technique and away from service.

The cutting edge of public administration theory shifted from the 1960s to France in the 1970s. The reasons for this geographic change are socially complex, but the facts are clear.[19] In the preceding decade, the major divisions were between those who thought about government in functional categories and those who saw government as a total system, i.e., in structural terms. The debate raged between ideologists who preferred the language of bureaucracy because it reflected the actual hierarchy of government, and technocrats who preferred public administration precisely because of its nonhierarchical or functional characteristics. Those who urged a general systems perspective were denounced by those wishing to construct theory at the partial theory level. Some viewed bureaucracy as a generic term; others saw administration as generic, with public administration as one of its aspects. Finally, the argument revolved about whether public administration is a separate discipline or part of the social and political sciences.

The 1970s in France began with the collapse of the May 1968 student rebellion. The higher functionaries, disturbed by the anarchism on the Left and the fascist potential on the Right, began to examine the premises of postindustrialism as a question of elitism versus populism, rather than in 1930s terms of social class, or even 1960s terms of social function. In the hands of public administrators, the state became the guardian of public interest over and against private interest. Two schools of though emerged: one led by Michel Crozier, who argued that the administrative apparatus had as its unique charge superseding social stagnation by making an institutional investment to render habits, negotiations, and systems of rules more complex, more open, more comprehensive, and more efficient.[20] The investment was not impeded by financial constraint or lack of political will, but by the need for an intellectual change of course toward serious analysis, real understanding of change, and deeper personal involvement in institutions.

In contrast, Nicos Poulantzas, in a series of seminal works, announced that the decline of legislative power, the strengthening of the executive, and the political role currently assumed by the state administration now constitute the tripariate leitmotiv of political studies.[21] Mandel elaborates on this theme by noting the heavy increase in the service sector and hence the expansion of administrative state power. Unlike Poulantzas, he feels that such a shift does not "lower the average organic composition of capital."[22] For the French intellectual Left, bureaucracy should mainly be viewed not as impediments to inefficiency, but as responses to structural deformities within the private and entrepreneurial sectors. The economic role of the state undergirds the expansion of public administration, and not the need for efficiency or innovation. In Poulantzas's view administration becomes the terrain in which an "unstable equilibrium of compromises" between the power elites and the popular masses takes place and is elaborated.[23] His view is a far cry from the characterization of bureaucracy as serving a class from an earlier period in Marxist history.

Crozier is arguing the central role of administration in adjudicating the claims of interest groups and in bringing about innovations that otherwise would not be made by the private sector.[24] Poulantzas for his part has become profoundly antitotalitarian, centering his attack on the giganticism of state power. He concludes his most recent work with a vigorous and full-blown critique of Stalinism as an extension of Leninism.[25] But it remains the case that the 1970s are ending with the same sad indecisiveness as the 1960s. Resolution of the issues on the basis of dependence versus the autonomy of public administration is but a more advanced form of the same theoretical bind characteristic of American thinking in the 1960s. The reason for this is not too difficult to locate: researchers like Crozier are essentially policy-oriented meliorists, interested in getting society going again; whereas theorists like Poulantzas and Mandel hold no hope for moving forward through administrative efficiency as long as a market economy remains the essential motor for economic development.

The problem is partially the reification of administration itself. It makes little sense to argue an anticapitalist premise when state power grows with equal force in planned as well as market economies. As Jean-Jacques Servan-Schreiber shrewdly noted, the ability of the Soviet Union and its East European satellites to insure a minimal living wage to their entire population depends on maintaining a high degree of coercion.[26] It makes little sense to argue that American administration is innovative in contrast to European administration which is stagnant, since the problems of racial strife, sexual conflict, and interest group tensions are just as powerful in the United States as in Europe. What is needed to establish an appropriate theory of public administration is a sense of the administrator as both part of the larger state apparatus and as a relatively autonomous sector with its own interests. At a concrete level the politics of administration is only its own expansion and extension. But at a more generic level, its specific political aims are circumscribed by the larger forces of state and economy.

The concentration of administrative power is common to socioeconomic systems designated as postindustrial. One reason for employing the term *postindustrial* is that it avoids the reductionism of identifying the concentration or curtailment of power with any one kind of economic environment or party apparatus. Differences between social systems and nations have not evaporated. They remain potent cultural forces. In any democratic culture, control is in the hands of the popular sectors. The struggle between such popular sectors and bureaucratic regimentalism is real. The personalism of leadership is common to all types of economic systems. The contradiction between public administration, with its impersonal norms, comes up against the political apparatus it presumably serves, with its continuing norms of personalism and charismatic authority.

The administrative apparatus, however close it might appear to the state apparatus, must remain responsive to the led no less than the leaders, to the broad stratum of people who are outside the decision-making process but support it through their taxes. Public administration cannot be characterized as part of the state any more than it can be viewed as a buffer against that mechanism. They must both operate in a context that negotiates the machinery of power and the interests of the public while trying to control the budget. This sort of conflict becomes an essential proprietary consideration in postindustrial environments, where older forms of conflict have collapsed. Polarization remains deeply embedded in advanced social structures, only it takes the form of efforts to dominate funds rather than classes. In consequence, postindustrial society is in some respects close to postfeudal society: it simplifies social relations just when technological forms of negotiating those relations become ever more complex.

The relationship between planners (the policymaking element in advanced states) and the financiers (middle management bureaucrats or public administrators) becomes a most intriguing issue to monitor.[27] It can either evolve into an area of severe friction between those who make policy and set the nation on its long-range course, and those who carry out policy and hence do not easily take to interference or sudden shifts of direction; or it can become a symbiotic relationship in which forces are joined to preserve and extend state power. Given the natural antipathies of those at the top of decision making versus those in middle management, one might well expect antagonism. Increasingly, these antipathies are held in check by decision making, which has itself become postindustrial in the special sense that data determine decisions. In this evolution, decision making has increasingly been removed from the political arena.

Certain characteristics of bureaucracy prevail over policy-making concerns. The growing professionalization of government work, whatever the type or level, moves to counterpoliticization. As a result, one should not anticipate the end of public ideologies so much as the decline of party politics. The essential danger is closure on political participation. The main issue is not how administrators function in postindustrial societies, but how government administration—local, state, regional, and federal—begins with a theory of negotiating between policymakers and political officials, but ends with assuming the reins of state power.

Politics becomes the national interest. The defense of those presumed interests against overseas transgressions becomes central. Hegel overwhelms Marx: but the state, not the class, becomes the main organizing premise. Public administration is uniquely situated to take full advantage of the new conditions. Reared in a tradition of professionalization before politicization, organized to serve the needs of the state directly and not any one subset of special interests, and being directly tied to the process of governance without the encumbrances of electoral affairs, such a group becomes the basic sponsor of the national interest, the guardian of the state, and the definer of its specific survival capacities.

This implies growing conservatism within the public administration sector, not in traditional ideological terms, as a philosophical desire for community and order, but to preserve the state and its interests against military incursion from abroad and fiscal disintegration from within. Public administration creates a solid phalanx because mass politics has long since dissolved in the narcotizing impact of the communications media. The steady expansion of public administration, particularly at local, state, and regional levels (the federal level seems saturated at this point), also provides linkages between the administrative apparatus and further inhibits the emergence of any "grass roots" or local, state, or regional opposition. A certain equilibrium longed for by federal administrators, becomes the norm. Conservatism emerges as a consequence of this political stasis.

The attempt to distinguish adminstration from politics is understandable, but ultimately remains an exercise in futility. The bifurcated vision derives from a Western democratic belief that professionalism is somehow uniquely antipolitical, or better, purely instrumental.[28] Gordon Tullock puts the issue properly:

There is no way this sort of ultimate policy formation by low ranking personnel can be avoided; it will arise on occasion in all organizations, no matter how efficiently these are organized.... Not only the initial decisions, but all subsequent decision, may be made by men operating at the lower reaches of the hierarchy. The sovereign neither ratifies nor disapproves of these decisions either because the chain of command is so clogged that he does not hear of the issues at all, or because he is lazy, or because he fears that any decision on his part will, in turn, annoy his own superior in the hierarchy. In such an organization as this, the lower ranks, after perhaps vainly trying to get the higher officials to take action, may be forced to make decisions. Out of a series of such events, a sort of organizational policy may develop by precedent, and the higher officials may never have to make any choices of significance at all.[29]

In a period of computer technology, administrative decisions by fiat become more frequent. The danger in this equation between expertise and administration is that vox populi gets left out of the reckoning. However, the demos as the ultimate repository of power compels elected officials to take responsibility for decision making. Opposition to this enlarged federal administration apparatus will come from a revived populism—from opposition to government and its services that will undoubtedly cut across traditional Left and Right lines. The Jarvis-Gann Amendment in California is one indication of this development. It is impossible to convert this populism into a Left or Right impulse, any more than one can identify government administrative actions as Left or Right. The shape of things to come is already plain: a struggle between the state and its organized participants and the people, its interest groups, tax clout, and ultimately, sheer numerical force.

Violence, such as sabotage and terror, is more likely in a depoliticized context than in a political one. Politics is an essential cement of moral authority, since it alone guarantees a sense of participation and control over matters of state power. But in the antiseptic climate of top-down rules and regulations, where party identification is low and political allegiance shaky, the legitimacy of the state can be severely threatened. In such a context the administrative machinery of government may be seen as the government itself. Popular actions will become less symbolic and increasingly oriented toward direct action. Getting things done is achieved by threatening bureaucrats with the dire consequences of a given interest group. Hence the web of government, that delicately laced network of authority and legitimacy, can easily become unhinged in a brave new world of bureaucratic determinism.

Postindustrial technology has been unevenly absorbed. Line managers have been afraid of the new technology, while those staff who procure it have emphasized the efficiency of machines rather than the effectiveness of programs. As one recent report indicates: "The impact of computers on the federal government's operations and procedures is pervasive; and federal expenditures for computer-based information systems exceeded $10 billion in fiscal year 1977."[30] In the immediate future much more effort will be devoted to developing symbiosis between electronic information systems and administrative tasks, involving the modeling of complex systems no less than simply processing routine data. Forecasting and assessment of technology are linked to greater use of advanced computer systems. Until now, public administrators have focused on short-term uses of advanced technology. In the next round, long-term planning is likely to prevail. The danger is that complex decision making will become the responsibilty of machines rather than human political actors. Here is an area of maximum potential danger for future public sector policymaking.

The "good" or "evil" potential of technology is moot, but we must not forget that public administrators not only react to a postindustrial technology but have long been involved in guiding it. The military and nuclear areas are particularly vulnerable. "The direction of technology involves two kinds of activity which, in a sense, act against each other yet are also opposite sides of the same coin. We refer to the activities of promoting and controlling technology, the former referring to the encouragement of technology and the latter to its regulation."[31] Because of the enormous costs in research and development and the consequent impact on profitability, the role of technology is not simply external to public administration but organic to it in an advanced postindustrial setting. Technology becomes integral to decision making.

Administration is a service as well as a system. Advanced societies evolve toward increases in this service sector. But over and against this inexorable tidal wave of paperwork over hardware production, allocation over innovation, and decision making in lieu of mass politics, stands the specter of a new public managerialism, a new class that loses intimate contact with ordinary events and plain people and so jeopardizes the political system as a whole. Even if bureaucratic administration is impervious to internal assault, its removal from the taproots of incentive and innovation make any society susceptible to destruction from without.[32] The need to consider public administration as a servant or at least an agency for developing incentive, and not a master of government, is the alpha and omega of democratic life, and also insures the future of public administration as an entity apart from special or private interests.

It is dangerous to conceive of postindustrial technology as necessarily feeding the fires of administrative domination. Mindless slogans and irrational specializations tend to thwart any sense of citizen participation. But certain developments, like cybernetic systems design, can facilitate radical, technological, and social decentralization. The distinction drawn by Manfred Stanley between technology and technicism is useful, since the aims of education—whether of an administrative or political sort—are serviced by redesign of social research methods, the institutionalization of linguistic accountability, and the critique of irrational specialization.[33] The pace of technological innovation and the size of bureaucratic administration have both quickened. On the presumption that historical clocks cannot be turned back, the need to harness the former and counterbalance the latter becomes a major task of democratic culture. The democratic culture must itself be sensitized to new patterns of administration.

There will still be opposition between branches of government in a technological context. The executive branch will still mobilize its bureaucrats to disprove the claims of legislatively appointed bureaucrats. But such conflict among administrators should become less significant as the tasks of governance become more complex. The entire arsenal of populist politics will be required to offset the advantages of bureaucracy. Electoral politics are episodic, sporadic, and ideological in character. Administration is continuous, fluid, and rationalistic. If the two sides need each other, in a more proximate sense, such a need is tempered by realization that different constituencies, functional prerequisites, and ultimately different visions of law and order are involved. Holding this dialectical chain intact, maintaining unity through opposition, becomes an essential task for constitutional law and a pivotal function of the modern judiciary. Democracy has been and will continue to be affected by the rise of public administration in a postindustrial society in which state power grows and in which the relationship between politics and economics is inverted, with politics becoming the base and economics the superstructure.[34] Democracy will also be attacked for its inefficiencies. That is the essential meaning of totalitarian postindustrialism: the adjudication of the innate tensions of mass demands and organizational rules becomes the essential role of public administration in a democratic community.

Democracy is decreasingly definable as a system and increasingly as a process of mutual setting forth of interests that can be adjudicated and negotiated in an orderly and maximally noninjurious way.[35] To the extent that such an admittedly rarified definition of democracy has meaning, conflicts between public administration and mass politics should be viewed only as a late twentieth-, possibly a twenty-first-century possibility. As old conflicts between judicial, legislative, and executive branches of government decrease in importance through increase in the technology of scientific decision making, a clustering effect may occur in which the process of government which takes lives is pitted against the process of being left alone. The private sector will come to mean those areas of individual performance left intact, without genocidal incursions, rather than a portion of the economy left under entrepreneurial control.

A new system of checks and balances might evolve in accord with emerging characteristics of the political process as a whole. The basis for such programmed differentiation of tasks and distinction in goals may not be spelled out constitutionally except as a series of mandates permitting administrative functions to operate in a pluralistic context. The specific functions of various branches of government will appear more rational in a context of opposition, or at least functional differentiation of administrative-bureaucratic tasks. At one level, this is the politics of the last word: the executive head who spends twenty hours on the budget has the final say interpreting the annual message, not administrators who spend thousands of hours preparing the budget. The congressman or originator, purveyor, and mediator of preferences must vote on legislation even though bureaucrats and managers may inundate a legislator with evidence that a bill is too costly or not operational.

Major movements of our time revolve around the size and strength of the administrative bureaucracy. The task becomes making it responsible, increasing its efficiency while decreasing its omnipotence. Insofar as blockage to further political development is administration itself—either through tax pressure or through withholding of political legitimacy; insofar as the blockage to further development is the narcissistic propensity of the popular will, one can expect political elites to assert their own claims over popular forces.

Whatever the nature of the economic system, our epoch bears witness to a constant expansion in state power, growth in bureaucratic norms, and an increase in administrative domination and disposition of people. The economic system a nation lives under has become less important than the fact of state growth and its allocative mechanisms. We have seen new forms of popular rebellion having little to do with class membership and crossing traditional social boundaries. Advanced technology helps insure a simplified society. Not necessarily a more pleasant one, but certainly a society more direct in its conflicts of choice and interests. The new technology offers potentials for both dictatorship and democracy. The outcomes are in doubt not because of the feebleness of social research, but due to the willfullness of human actors. Before the torrent of populism the wall of every known elitism threatens to crumble. But populism itself comes to provide a new form of irrational solidarity. The owl of Minerva gazes upon different social forces and relations than in the past, yet bears witness to the endless search for the utopia underwriting the dystopia.

# Notes to Chapter 7

1. Wheeler, John Archibald and Gardner, Martin. "Quantum Theory and Quack Theory," *The New York Review of Books,* Vol. XXVI, No. 8 (May 17) 1979. pp. 39-41.

2. The two most prescient sources on defining the nature of postindustrialism are: Daniel Bell. *The Coming of Post-Industrial Society: A Venture in Social Forecasting.* New York: Basic Books, 1973; and *The Cultural Contradictions of Capitalism.* New York: Basic Books, 1976. For an earlier evaluation of mine on Bell's latter work, see Irving Louis Horowitz, "A Funeral Pyre for America." *Worldview,* Vol. 19, No. 11 (November) 1976.

3. Daniel Bell. "Is There a Post-Industrial Society?" Transaction/SOCIETY, Vol. 11, No. 4 (May-June) 1974. pp. 11, 23-25.

4. For a general introduction to Post-Industrialism, see Krishan Kumar. *Prophecy and Progress: The Sociology of Industrial and Post-Industrial Society.* New York: Penguin Books, 1978.

5. Cleveland, Harlan. "The American Public Executive: New Functions, New Style, New Purpose," *Theory and Practice of Public Administration: Scope, Objectives, and Methods,* edited by James C. Charlesworth. Philadelphia: The American Academy of Political and Social Science, October 1968. pp. 168-78.

6. Singer, H.W. "Multinational Corporations and Technology Transfer," *The Stategy of International Development: Essays in the Economics of Backwardness.* White Plains, New York: International Arts and Science Press, 1975. pp. 208-233.

7. Kupferberg, Seth. "Teaching the Unteachable," *The New Republic,* Vol. 180, No. 15 (April 14), 1979. pp. 18-21.

8. Herbers, John. "Washington: An Insider's Game," *The New York Times Magazine* (April 22), 1979. pp. 33, 84-92.

9. Bruce-Briggs, B. "Enumerating the New Class," *The New Class?* New Brunswick, New Jersey: Transaction Books, 1979. pp. 217-225.

10. Weber, Max. "Bureaucracy," *From Max Weber: Essays in Sociology,* edited by Hans Gerth and C. Wright Mills. New York: Oxford University Press, 1946. pp. 196-244.

11. See, March, James G. and Simon, Herbert. "The Theory of Organizational Equilibrium," in *Organizations.* New York: Wiley, 1958. pp. 84-108; and also Dorwin Cartwright, "Influence, Leadership, Control" in *Handbook of Organizations,* edited by James G. March. Chicago: Rand McNally & Co., 1963. pp. 1-47.

12. Horowitz, Irving Louis. "On the Expansion of New Theories and the Withering Away of Old Classes," Transaction/SOCIETY, Vol. 16, No. 2 (January/February) 1979. pp. 55-62.

13. Horowitz, Irving Louis. "Methods and Strategies in Evaluating Equity Research," *Social Indicators Research,* Vol. 16, No. 1 (January) 1979. pp. 1-22.

14. Horowitz, Irving Louis. "Social Welfare, State Power, and the Limits to Equity," *Growth in a Finite World,* edited by Joseph Grunfeld. Philadelphia: The Franklin Institute Press, 1979. pp. 21-35.

15. Lindblom, Charles E. "The Science of Muddling Through," *Public Administration Review,* Vol. 19 (Spring) 1959. pp. 79-88; and by the same author, "Policy Analysis," *American Economic Review,* Vol. 48 (June) 1958. pp. 298-299. *See also* Lindblom's more recent work *Politics and Markets: The World's Political-Economic Systems.* New York: Basic Books, 1977. esp. pp. 119-143.

16. Schumacher, Bill G. *Computer Dynamics in Public Administration.* New York: Spartan Books, 1967, pp. 163-171.

17. Waldo, Dwight. "Scope of the Theory of Public Administration," *Theory and Practice of Public Administration.* Philadelphia: The American Academy of Political and Social Science, 1968. pp. 1-26.

18. Bacharach, Samuel B. "What's Public Administration? An Examination of Basic Textbooks," *Administrative Science Quarterly,* Vol. 21, No. 2 (June) 1976. pp. 346-351.

19. Rose, Michael. *Servants of Post-Industrial Power? Sociologie du Travail in Modern France.* White Plains, New York: M.E. Sharpe, Inc., 1979. pp. 144-173.

20. Crozier, Michel. *The Bureaucratic Phenomenon.* London: Tavistock, 1964; and more recently, *The Stalled Society.* New York: Viking Publishers, 1973.

21. Poulantzas, Nicos. *State, Power, Socialism.* London: New Left Books, 1978; and his earlier, albeit less decisive enunciation of the same theme, *Political and Social Classes,* London: New Left Books, 1973.

22. Mandel, Ernest. *Late Capitalism.* London: New Left Books, 1975. pp. 405-407.

23. Poulantzas, Nicos. *State, Power, Socialism.* London: New Left Books, 1978. pp. 127-139.

24. Crozier, Michel. *La Société Bloquée.* Paris: Editions du Seuil, 1970. p. 20; see the discussion of this in Michael Rose, *Servants of Post-Industrial Power?* pp. 113-127.

25. Poulantzas, *State, Power, Socialism.* pp. 251-265.

26.  Servan-Schreiber, Jean-Jacques. *The Radical Alternative.* New York: W.W. Norton & Co. Inc., 1971. pp. 59-61.

27.  Wildavsky, Aaron. *Budgeting: A Comparative Theory of Budgetary Processes.* Boston: Little, Brown, & Co., 1975. pp. 155-157.

28.  LaPalombara, Joseph. *Bureaucracy and Political Development.* Princeton: Princeton University Press, 1963. pp. 48-55.

29.  Tullock, Gordon. *The Politics of Bureaucracy.* Washington, D.C.: Public Affairs Press, 1965. p. 181.

30.  Gammon, William Howard and Hattery, Lowell H. "Managing the Impact of Computers on the Federal Government," *The Bureaucrat,* Vol. 7, No. 2 (Summer) 1978. pp. 18-26.

31.  Johnson, Ron and Gummett, Philip. *Directing Technology: Policies for Promotion and Control.* New York: St. Martin's Press, 1979. pp. 13-14.

32.  cf. Peacock, Alan. "Public Expenditure Growth in Post-Industrial Society," in *Post-Industrial Society,* edited by Bo Gustafsson. New York: St. Martin's Press, 1979. pp. 91-95.

33.  Stanley, Manfred. *The Technological Conscience: Survival and Dignity in an Age of Expertise.* New York: The Free Press/Macmillan, 1978. pp. 251-253.

34.  cf. Apter, David. *Choice and the Politics of Allocation.* New Haven and London: Yale University Press, 1971. pp. 128-154; and Edward R. Tufte, *Political Control of the Economy.* Princeton: Princeton University Press, 1978, pp. 110-145.

35.  For strongly contrasting statements about democracy, which yet manage to appreciate the processual and symbolic nature of the entity, see Dorothy Pickles, *Democracy.* New York: Basic Books, 1970. pp. 9-28 and 169-182; and C.B. Macpherson, *Democratic Theory.* London and New York: Oxford University Press, 1973, esp. pp. 3-23, 29-76.

# Chapter 8

# Democracy and Terrorism

*People are too readily resigned to fatality. They are too ready
to believe that, after all, nothing but bloodshed makes history
progress and that the stronger always progresses at the
expense of the weaker. Such fatality exists perhaps. But
man's task is not to accept it or to bow to its laws. If he had
accepted it in the earliest ages, we should still be living in
prehistoric times. The task of men cf culture and faith, in any
case, is not to desert historical struggles nor to serve the cruel
and inhuman elements in those struggles. It is rather to remain
what they are, to help man against what is oppressing him, to
favor freedom against the fatalities that close in upon it. That
is the condition under which history really progresses,
innovates—in a word, creates. In everything else it repeats
itself, like a bleeding mouth that merely vomits forth a wild
stammering.*

Albert Camus, RESISTANCE, REBELLION, AND DEATH

The question of terror, the organized or sporadic effort to
overthrow existing systems, has in common with genocide its
transcendent characteristics—the direct confrontation with
matters of who shall live or die. The role of terror must be assessed
and responded to by all social systems. Neither capitalism nor
socialism, democracy nor totalitarianism, market economies nor
collective economies can remain aloof from it. The state can
monopolize the power to coerce, but it cannot prevent responses
to such coercion. Merleau-Ponty said it well in noting that "the
human world is an open or unfinished system, and the same radical
contingency . . . threatens it with disorder and prevents us from

**141**

despairing of it, providing only that one remembers its various machineries are actually men and tries to maintain and expand man's relations to man."[1]

Current attitudes toward the uses of terror range from a belief that it is the only possible means to bring about social change to a view of terror as the last refuge of scoundrels. Terrorists themselves are seen either as the only authentic heroes in a notably unheroic age or as petty criminals who coat their venal acts with an ideological gloss.

In such a polarized climate of opinion, attempts to introduce shadings into the analysis of terror invite instant rebuke from both an impatient Left and an outraged Right. Only "reformists" and "bleeding hearts" are apparently willing to challenge the common rhetoric. Yet communist dictatorships, socialist democracies, and capitalist systems must all face the problems of terrorism. Skyjackings, assassinations, bombings, extortions, and sabotage do not stop at any national or regional borders. While different social systems react differently to terror, in accordance with their particular ideological premises, no society can be indifferent to the problems raised by terrorism.

For social scientists who have a civil libertarian viewpoint, any analysis of terrorism must consider not only the attacks on civil liberties by those acting in the name of terror but also the potential damage from those responding in defense of organized society. They must also consider the need for legitimate dissent if the world community of nations is not to become frozen into its present political positions, along with its economic and social inequities. By exploring how and why terrorism arises, who the terrorists are, and what the costs and benefits of antiterrorism are for civil liberties, we should bring more precision to the analysis of the various terrorist activities now facing world society.

The minute one attempts to profile the terrorist, considerable problems of definition arise that inhibit possible remedial action. Can the IRA (Irish Republican Army) operating in Northern Ireland really be compared to the PFLP (Popular Front for the Liberation of Palestine)? And if so, on what basis? Membership in the former is large-scale, with the support of wide numbers, operating on a well-defined home terrain. Membership in the latter is extremely small, with more covert than overt support in the Middle East. Yet there are similarities: the militant Palestinians believe that the destruction of Israel is a prerequisite for a general peace settlement, while the leaders of the IRA for the most part believe that the defeat of Protestant Northern Ireland and its reunification with the rest of Ireland are necessary for peace.

A large factor in ascertaining the differences between guerrilla warfare and terrorist activities is linked to the size of the movements, their organizational efficacy, and geographic locale. And even when ideological predispositions are similar, one may still claim a difference between guerilla organizations and terrorist operations.

The essential difference seems to be that the Irish Catholic militants are involved in an internal struggle for political control, whereas the Arab Palestinians are involved in an external struggle for geographic control. It is this gulf between national liberation efforts and international symbolic acts that seems most emphatically to distinguish guerrilla warfare from terrorist activity. Rather than emphasize the points of similarity between terrorists and guerrillas, it would appear more worthwhile to draw a profile that makes plain the differences. This is not always easy; for example, the psychological characteristics that lead some to guerrilla movements may be similar, if not entirely identical, to the psychological characteristics of members of a terrorist group. Nonetheless, despite the difficulties a tentative evaluation of the essential nature of the terrorist threat is required.

A terrorist is a person engaged in politics who makes little if any distinction between strategy and tactics on one hand and principles on the other. For him (and for the most part terrorism is a male activity), all politics is a matter of principle, and hence, nothing beyond the decision to commit a revolutionary deed of death and personal commitment requires examination, planning, and forethought.

A terrorist is a person prepared to surrender his own life for a cause considered transcendent in value. A terrorist assumes not only that taking the lives of others will lead to desired political goals, but that the loss of one's own life is a warranty that such a cause or political position is correct and obtainable.

A terrorist is a person who possesses both a self-fulfilling prophetic element and a self-destructive element. The act of destruction of another person or group of persons itself becomes the basis upon which future politics can be determined and decided, and the absence of terror is hence held to signify the absence of meaningful events. The self-destructive element is coincidental with the previous point, namely, that one's own death is the highest form of the politics of the deed: the only perfect expression of political correctness.

A terrorist is a person for whom all events are volitional and none are determined. The terrorist, in contrast to the revolutionary, perceives of the world pragmatically as a place to be shaped and reshaped in accord with the human will or the will of the immediate collective group. Beyond that, there is no historical or sociological force of a hidden or covert nature than can really alter human relationships, geographic boundaries, and so on.

A terrorist is a person who is young, most often of middle-class family background, usually male, and economically marginal. Collectively, persons caught as terrorists, whether hijackers, assassins, or guerrillas, are remarkably similar: aged twenty to thirty-five, relatively well educated, with some college or university training, but rarely of the uppermost achievement levels, and clearly not of peasant or working-class stock.

A terrorist performs his duties as an avocation. That is to say, he may hold a position in the larger society quite unrelated to his terrorist actions. This anonymity provides an essential cover for his activities. It also makes the contest between police power and political terror far more problematic, since sophisticated weaponry is relatively useless without adequate methods of detection and prevention.

The terrorist defines himself differently from the casual homicide in several crucial respects: he murders systematically rather than at random; he is symbolic rather than passionate, that is, concerned with scoring political points rather than responding to personal provocation; and his actions are usually well planned rather than spontaneous. Terrorism is thus primarily a sociological phenomenon, whereas homicide can more easily be interpreted in psychological terms. Terrorism essentially has a group nature rather than a personal nature.

The terrorist by definition is a person who does not distinguish between coercion and terrorism because he lacks access to the coercive mechanisms of the state. The essential polarity is not between pacifism and terrorism, which is mechanistic. The essential choice that those responding to terror can make is either coercive mechanisms—which may range from the mild presence of police or the military in the body politic to imprisonment and limitation of the rights of opposition groups—or outright counterterrorism—which goes far beyond coercion, since it violates the sanctity of life itself as an overriding perspective. The believer in coercion must also assume that the victims of coercion can be rehabilitated; the terrorist denies the possibility of rehabilitation for the victim.

A terrorist is a person who, through the act of violence, advertises and dramatizes a wider discontent. The advertising function does more than make evident public displeasure with a regime. It provides instantaneous recognition of the person performing terrorist acts through mass communications. Terrorism becomes a fundamental way of defining heroism and leadership.

A terrorist believes that the act of violence will encourage the uncommitted public to withdraw support from a regime or an institution, and hence make wider revolutionary acts possible by weakening the resolve of the opposition. Practically, however, such acts often work to lend greater support to the regime, by drying up fissures and contradictions in the name of opposing a common enemy, the terrorist.

A terrorist may direct his activities against the leadership of the opposition by assassinating presidents and political leaders; such terrorists usually tend to function alone and in the service of an often poorly defined ideology rather than a political movement. Other terrorists may direct their activities against the symbols of establishments and agencies; such forms of terror are less concerned with the individuals against whom terror is performed than with the organizations and agencies of which they are a part. For example, the Munich massacre of Israeli athletes was directed at the State of Israel; the specific people eliminated were not an issue. This kind of terrorist is usually himself under a strict political regimen and is responsible to counterorganizations or guerrilla groupings that define and determine the extent and types of terrorism.

A terrorist does not have a particulary well-defined ideological persuasion. He may work for the state or against the state, for an established order or in an effort to overthrow one. The level of his ideological formation is generally poor and half-digested, reflecting a greater concern for the act than for alternative systems that may flow from the act. It is important in a morphology of the terrorist not to confuse such rhetorical features with the generic nature of terror, which transcends personality and even social structural characteristics.[2]

These items stated, we must now turn to a consideration about the generic nature of terror and not just the biographic nature of the terrorist. The definition of someone as a terrorist is a labeling device. The act of homicide, or at rare times even terrorist suicide, cannot disguise the moral aspect of such definitions. What is usually referred to as terrorism is unsponsored and unsanctioned violence against the body or bodies of others. However, whether violence performed with official sanction against the leadership or the membership of other groups and institutions is nonterrorist in character, it is part of a continuous process of definition and redefinition in political life. And in the current ambiguous and even ubiquitous conditions, performing a terrorist act does not uniquely make one a terrorist, any more than random nonviolence alone defines the pacifist.

This raises the entire matter of legitimation and labeling, since terrorism is not uniquely an act but a response to an act; and further, since terrorism is a set of punitive measures taken against those so defined, the problem of definition is compounded by the existence of subjective factors in the body politic—factors which in some measure help define and even determine the treatment, punishment, and reception of acts of political violence.

When terrorism is an "internal matter" and not a minigroup invasion of a nation by foreign citizens and alien subjects, the approach must be more sensitive to the ills in the society being addressed. The armed forces and police have a much easier time dealing with foreign nationals, such as the Japanese in the Lod

Airport raid in Tel Aviv, or Arabs in the Munich Olympic encampment. The difficult chore comes in handling native populations. Here we must make a fundamental distinction between guerillas and terrorists. The distinction must be made on the basis of whether the participants in assassination attempts, bombing of buildings, and so on, are nationals or foreigners. In the case of the latter, true terrorists, it is possible to employ the police and the armed forces to defeat and destroy them. In the case of nationals or guerrillas, the aim of the state must always be to contain, restrain, and finally reconcile. This distinction between guerrillas and terrorists is significant not simply as a typology but in terms of operational responses to terror as distinct from national guerrilla movements, which frequently are a response to long-smoldering inequities.

In a special sense the question of terrorism, quite apart from the characteristics of the terrorists, is an "internal concern" of Marxism and the socialist tradition. Within Western liberal democratic thought, from Locke to Montesquieu to Mill and Dewey, there has never been any doubt that terrorism is largely counterproductive for real social change and that excessive use of terror to put down terrorism is even more counterproductive, since it calls into question the legitimacy of the entire body politic. Of course, there have been bourgeois and populist traditions of romantic violence. Theories of the will emanated from the bowels of European irrational and mystical traditions. Yet overall, and especially in the Anglo-American framework, terror has been declared outside the purview of the legitimate exercise of protest and opposition.

The socialist and Marxist traditions are quite different. From the outset, Marx contested Proudhon, and Lenin and Stalin argued with the Russian Narodniki and anarchists. In general, the organizational tradition has been dominant. The argument against "spontaneity" rests at its core on a disbelief in the efficacy of violence. Even the Chinese representative before the United Nations debated on whether the discussion of terror should be on the agenda of the General Assembly, admitted to a parting of the ways with the Arabs on the question of the political payoffs of terrorist tactics.

The Chinese, insofar as they respond as Marxists and also insofar as the whole Maoist notion of the revolution involves armed military struggle, react negatively to the current wave of Arab "petit bourgeois violence" associated with leaders like Yasir Arafat, not on the basis of long-range goals but on the basis of belief in slow-paced military operations, performed in conjunction with the support of a mass peasant people, in contrast to the *foco* belief that one can have successful hit-and-run military operations. The Chinese position if anything, demands even greater adherence to organizational constraint than the Soviet position does, since Russian Bolshevism was based on party organization, whereas the Chinese party position is based on military organization. Both in the past and present, the orthodox Marxist vision has been one of high organization, disciplined assaults on class enemies, and a strong sense of leadership to reduce random acts in politics. A belief in history rather than in human volition dominates this tradition: faith in violence is tempered by a belief that the laws of history are inexorable, only the timing of such historical inevitabilities remains to be ironed out by human action.

A minor motif has run through the socialist-Marxist tradition. it extends from Sorel's vision of the general strike that spontaneously brings down the system to Régis Debray and the theory of the *foco*. It is based upon the idea of the unattached group effecting revolutionary change. Given the current political behavior and posture of China and Cuba, no less than that of the Soviet union and Eastern Europe, it seems unlikely this approach has much appeal to the Marxist world of this day.

The reasons the debates within the Western world seem so much beside the point is the assumption that the existing order of things can somehow either survive or only be changed through parliamentary mechanisms. As a result, one finds a lumping together of quite distinctive phenomena, class conflict such as mass guerrilla warfare with minoritarian phenomena such as urban terror. They all seem to be linked as one of various pieces in the same red garment of rebellion; and hence so much discussion on terrorism in the West is a surrogate for discussions on social change of any sort.

The new wave of terror is both menacing to those singled out for assault and novel in the random internationalization of victims as well as terrorists. The use of Japanese terrorists to perform essentially Arab actions is but the most refined aspect of this randomization of violence. The question of terror, however, is not going to be significantly altered by finely worded judicial statements calculated to appease the intended victims of random terror. It can be altered by a recognition within the Socialist camp that gains of a substantial sort have been made without terror, for example, in Allende's Chile; and that the resort to terror may have become counterproductive to the maintenance and growth of socialism in the Third World. Of course, if there were a collapse of this phase (of what was once referred to as "legal socialism" in pre-Bolshevik Russia) the question of terror might well create an East-West confrontation all over again. But this seems unlikely given the present era of good feelings between the big powers—East and West, Communist and capitalist, authoritarian and democratic. And with so much at stake in terms of a broad-ranging Metternichean settlement now under way between the Great Powers, it is extremely doubtful that random terrorism will be countenanced in the Communist bloc nations, any more than it is within the Western bloc. This international rapprochement of power, rather than the cries of anguish by the powerless, will probably lead to an early end to the current terrorist wave.

The definition of terrorism I employ is this: the selective use of fear, subjugation, and intimidation to disrupt the normal operations of a society. The power to inflict such injury is a bargaining power which in its very nature bypasses due process of law. It seeks an outcome by means other than a democratic or consensual formula. The act of terror—whoever performs it—in some sense violates civil liberties. All the cries about redressing injustices cannot disguise this fact.

Terrorism is based on a calculation of what its victims can and cannot tolerate. A threshhold of pain replaces the articulation of shared values or the rationality produced by consensus politics. The act of terrorism—again without regard to who performs it— involves a substitution of pain for reason as the way to determine political and social issues.

A policy of terror also assumes the social system to be inherently and necessarily law-abiding. It presumes that the desire to return to rationality in the maintenance of a system will help those engaged in terror. In this sense, observance of civil liberties is also a normal state that the attacked society wants to get back to as soon as possible.

Terrorism as a policy is both antidemocratic and anti-civil libertarian because the terrorists' ultimatums are addressed to leadership elites rather than to the people. Because terrorism demands instantaneous decision making, it places great strain on conventional legal mechanisms, which require due process and a strong evidentiary base to take action. Thus the appeal for swift action shifts power in the attacked society to its elites.

Finally, terror violates the civil liberties of those who are nonparticipants or noncombatants. Terrorists usually have as their victims people who are innocent of any crime. Whatever else civil liberties involves, it rejects holding people who have committed no specific criminal acts responsible for the alleged acts of others. In this sense, terrorist acts violate the civil liberties of individuals and collectivities alike.

Increased incidents of terrorism, whether spontaneous or organized, inevitably invite countermeasures. These extended from increased security checks, greater police surveillance, and improved search and seizure measures to changes in the basic legal code, such as the restoration of capital punishment. There are also ideological and organizational changes in the society affected. In place of criminology there emerges a new emphasis on victimology; alongside national organizations dedicated to civil liberties there arise organizations dedicated to maintaining civil order. The costliest aspect of terrorism is not the destruction of physical property and loss of life but—as terrorists intend—the weakening of the social and political fabric, that complex series or norms and laws upon which democratic conflict-resolution ultimately rests.

The seeming inability of national and international legislative bodies to curb terrorism derives, at least to some extent, from an appreciation of the political costs involved. To be sure, when a particular society is attacked, the victim's demand for "action" usually follows. Yugoslavs who resist formal condemnation of Palestinian terrorists are outraged by American passivity in the face of Croatian nationalist hijackings. Soviet officials, intransigent toward the idea of a United Nations ban on skyjackings, are equally harsh to Jews who expropriate planes to escape to Israel. Syrians who are quite willing to see citizens of Tel Aviv randomly blown up, publicly hang the same PLO representatives when their acts are committed in Damascus.

It is easier to stretch the notion of what civil society can tolerate than to establish inflexible legislation that would probably escalate levels of terrorism without leading to international tranquility. The idea of prohibitory legislation as a cure-all, or even a limiting element against terrorist actions, is itself dubious.

In 1968, in the aftermath of American urban disorders, President Lyndon Johnson established a major Commission on the Causes and Prevention of Violence. The analyses of the historical and social causes for the disorders proceeded smoothly enough. The real problems arose at the policy level: what to do about preventing violence in the future. The issues were rather similar to those raised now by terrorism. At one meeting of the National Commission in 1968, I put forward the following position:

> The destruction of the antiwar movement, whether in its abstract universalist or pacifist form, or in its nasty, brutish, or opportunistic form, would represent a far greater loss to the integrity of American democracy than any silence in the streets of our major cities or quiescence in the hubs of our major universities. Obedience is not tranquility. Seething heavily is not the same as breathing easily. The antiwar movement has caused destruction in government operations, increased the cost of domestic military preparedness, stimulated disaffiliation from major parties, and has been a general nuisance for an already burdened police force. But these are costs that can be borne by a society still capable of distinguishing between national concern and national celebration. Those who want law and order, of whom there are many, as well as those who want lawlessness and disorder, of whom there are a few, must weigh carefully the premium price to be paid in a punitive state in which a rage for order displaces a rationality of innovation. That price would be nothing short of a total militarization of the nation.

To be clear about the issue, we must recognize that a society largely free from terrorism is quite possible to achieve. Fascist systems manage to reduce terrorism by a series of devices: mass organizations in which membership is compulsory; block-by-block spying networks; mandatory police identification certificates; and clear delineations of "friends" and "enemies" of the regime. With the increased sophistication of computerization techniques, such mechanisms for social and personal control loom ever larger. The question remains not one of technique but of social policy: Does a citizenry wish to pay such a price for tranquility?

The acceptance of some terrorism, like some protest violence, is a sign of a society's acceptance of the costs of liberty. The potential for terror is also a reminder that the state's force has its counterforce. Of course, the hardware of the state is almost always greater, more pervasive, and more devastating than the disruptive possibilities available to terrorists.

One need only consider the activities of the CIA and the FBI. American intelligence operations involve hundreds of thousands of individuals and the expenditure of billions of dollars. They are carried out by a complex community of organizations whose functions interact and overlap. As the Senate committee assigned the task of investigating the CIA and FBI noted in its final report, "the very effort to deal with problems of terror, violence, and domestic intranquility, has led to this kind of incredible malaise within the legal system, whereby the entire country has been rendered under the control of a paralegal system, a paramilitary system, in terms of dealing effectively with threats of violence." One need only remember Watergate to see how counterterrorist activities can erode our civil liberties.

To make greater sense of the terrorism dilemma, we must discuss large-scale political events and their impact on us in terms of political processes. This means seeing how terrorism affects particular actors in the political dramaturgy. If we evaluate terrorism in terms of the number of people that have been killed by design or by accident, there is clearly no comparison to the genocidal behavior of Stalin in Russia and Hitler in Germany. The autocratic state has nearly unlimited power to terrorize entire communities, ethnic or racial groups, and, or course, religious networks. If terrorism is judged simply in terms of lives dispatched, the Nazi Holocaust—the genocidal benchmark of our century—outstrips the desultory performances engaged in by contemporary terrorists.

If we consider terrorism in terms of its disruption of local political systems or social organizations, again there is scarcely any comparison between what terrorists achieve and the disruption caused by a major automobile accident on an urban superhighway or the massive temporary breakdown occasioned by a power failure in a big city. But it is the symbolic effect of terrorism that represents its real impact. When persons are assassinated or kidnapped because of their national origins or religious affiliations, this threatens the entire structure of intergroup toleration and support. Because terrorism involves death and destruction by design, it is clearly different from the random character of highway accidents or technological breakdowns.

Terrorism is sometimes defended as a special method for speeding up social change. In the sense that terrorists believe their actions can shape the outcome of historical events, they reflect those outlooks in radical thought that stress the will of human actors to affect the outcome of social drama, as opposed to those—Marxists and others—who conceive of political events as moving in fixed, inexorable patterns.

We have no satisfactory method of determining what history's timetable really is, or when the full potential for growth of an old social system has been realized and the next revolutionary step becomes possible, as Marx felt necessary. But we should avoid treating terrorism as a form of "madness"—psychological or political—on the unprovable assumption that terrorists cannot really change history.

Take, as one example, the question of whether terrorism in the United States during the past decade should be regarded as successful. Measured in terms of overthrowing state authority, it failed. Yet consider how far a small number of terrorist acts have disrupted the normal character of the American political system. For even when a terrorist act is committed by a presumably unaffiliated individual, that same individual often comes with an ideological baggage inherited from organized terrorist groups. Can one really deny that the assassination of John F. Kennedy, Robert Kennedy, and Martin Luther King, Jr., and the attempted assassination of Governor George Wallace, have changed the structure and not just the style of American presidential politics in the past decade? The very nature of the political process was interfered with profoundly. The traumas involved in terrorist assassinations of a president, a candidate for that presidency, and the leading figure within the Black liberation movement espousing nonviolence, and the attempt on the life of a major figure in Southern conservatism, helped create the crises that led to Watergate.

The measurement of terrorism's success therefore is not only its ability to loosen that order in symbolic terms, by weakening the legitimizing capacities of elected officials and casting doubt on our concept of the rights of a society and the obligations of a state. Take the situation well known by all who travel. The act of boarding an airplane involves an acceptance of commonplace procedures which a few short years ago would have been deemed a direct violation of civil liberties. A passenger has to have all luggage examined and one's person scanned or frisked. Then there is a separate waiting area to which only those with boarding passes can go. The ordinary pattern of being greeted by or departing from loved ones is no longer permitted. In addition, passengers can no longer place luggage in a locker room in most major airports, bus stations, and rail terminals—the consequence of one solitary airport bombing at La Guardia Airport in 1975. Most people accept the frisking and new baggage procedures as the necessary cost of a safe flight. Nonetheless, one has a perfect right, even a duty, to raise questions about these new social costs of travel, certainly to enquire whether the new frisking procedures are permanent or transitory.

Still another problem with current approaches to terrorism is the presumption that terrorism demoralizes populations and disintegrates societies. This is an oversimplified view. A successful response to terrorism may serve to bind people together in a common cause. The Israeli response to the hijackings of 103 people from an Air France flight in June 1976—the raid on Entebbe Airport in Uganda—served to galvanize and unify Israeli society as no other event since the Six-Day War of 1967. Sporadic acts of terror can thus mobilize sentiments to strengthen the very system the terrorists aim to destroy.

Resolutions or recommendations for controlling terrorist activities, no matter from which quarters they emanate, are scarcely going to be enacted if the leadership of a nation feels that its interests are served by a particular form of terrorist engagement. But certain frameworks can be devised in the international community that might delegitimize, if not entirely curb, acts of terrorism.

Terrorism as a primary tactic will tend to be viewed negatively by "socialist" states as well as by "democratic" states. It should be possible to draw up a bill of human rights under United Nations sponsorship, indicating a universal belief in the right of the citizen to life, including the rights of people to free international travel and communication. Such a bill, to have teeth, must be built into legislation concerning postal regulations and international sea and flight rules. Random populations cannot become the objects of political actions without all norms of international association becoming dismantled and unhinged.

Insofar as possible, a statement of what measures a nation will employ in responding to terrorism should be outlined in advance, so that those engaging in terrorist activities of a specific or random variety will at least be aware of the consequences of their acts. At present, every situation involving terrorists, from kidnapping embassy officials to bombing department stores in crowded neighborhoods, becomes a dramatic confrontation treated sui generis, without a uniform standard of response.

Since the state is the repository of authority and of mechanisms of coercion, it can not only refuse employment to terrorists but can also punish the random use of violence. This it must do, for national polity and national survival depend in part on maintaining a monopoly of the means of violence. Indeed, when the state can no longer do so, its very survival becomes conjectural. The inability of the United States Congress to enact tough gun-control legislation may thus be viewed as a limitation of the American state to control its citizenry.

Through such mechanisms as Interpol, a file and fact sheet should be maintained on terrorists who cross national boundaries. Just as those who cross state boundaries to perform illegal actions within a nation such as the United States are subject to heavy penalties, so, too, should this principle be applied to terrorist movement across national boundaries. In that way, legitimate national liberation movements will be able to survive and grow insofar as they reflect a national consensus or dissensus, while the use of terrorism abroad, precisely because of an absence of true national support, would be profoundly curbed, if not entirely thwarted. The problem here is that legislation that would reinstate the death penalty, for example, might be considered retrogressive rather than ameliorative.

The lines of distinction between guerrillas and terrorists are hard to establish, just as the definition of legitimate geopolitical boundaries may vary. For example, if the Cubans define their activities as the liberation of Latin America as a whole, can the incursion of Che Guevara into Bolivia be considered a terrorist invasion of foreign terrain? The point here is that the Cuban government, and not a small band of uncoordinated terrorists, made this decision. Similarly, the Egyptian government has recently urged upon the Palestinians that they form a government in exile. This suggestion was rejected, and in a sense, the idea of national legitimacy and responsibility was repudiated. So what one witnesses in the Arab context, in contrast to the Cuban context, is precisely a continuing reliance upon terrorism as a method of political pressure and a rejection of government legitimacy as a means for realizing such demands. Such problems are real and must be presented fairly. However, the problem of terror is also real and must be faced.

Terror is a disruption in the modern technological order. The number of people involved can be exceedingly low and the amount of damage created exceedingly high—that is in the nature of a high velocity military and weapons technology. But in another larger societal sense terrorism has always been with us and always will be, as long as a monopoly of terror is reserved for a small fraction of society called the state and as long as people are divided into units called the nation. Perhaps in that sense, the very existence of terrorist groups is a warrant to the health of a particular nation-state: if it can survive terrorism, if in the face of personal tragedy it can forge public solidarity, terrorist acts will be proven counterproductive. But if such terrorism forges links with the broad masses, if it articulates the feelings and beliefs of large numbers, and if the states involved are indecisive and insecure in the face of such unsanctioned violence, then the state is doomed to perish; and here the purposes of terrorism will be proven quite productive.[3]

What must be said in conclusion, is that terrorism can indeed be stamped out—or at least drastically limited—but that in doing so, society does not necessarily offer a demonstration of its health but perhaps a reflection of its weakness. If the capacity for totalitarianism is completely exhausted in an effort to combat random terrorism, the social costs and political consequences alike become so grave that the very foundations of the system become more menaced than they could possibly be by any set of random terrorist activities. Indeed, if it is correct to point out that such random terrorism has a highly mobilizing effect on the masses of the population, rallying that population to the political commonweal, then one might also reasonably infer that the total repression of terrorism could have a demobilizing, and even worse, a demoralizing effect on these same masses, and would ultimately serve as a catalyst for a new round of social revolutionary actions that ironically serve the purpose of terrorists more nearly than they do established authority. Such then is the dialectic of terrorism: its existence may prove the health of a society, and its absence may be a demonstration of the stagnation of a society.

The conduct of genocide is most often determined by the state, but terrorist operations are performed by individuals. As a result, the translation of "state power" into "state punishment" becomes a matter of intense legal concern. Individual responsibility for specific acts is exceedingly difficult to negotiate. Hence the punishment for acts of genocide is usually far less exacting than the performance of terrorist acts. In a recent work on the Malmedy massacre of 1944 in which Leftist troops of the Waffen SS battlegroup murdered hundreds of American prisoners of war and Belgian civilians, punishment was muted, sentences commuted, and the legal situation left unclear because of the gulf between systems and people, leaders and gunmen.[4]

Arguments have raged for three decades on individual culpability for genocidal acts: Can an individual really be blamed for carrying out orders, and on the other side, is collective guilt transmissible to individuals serving the very state which denies such individual responsibility? In some measure, the focus on punishment is a separate and discrete work, one that perhaps defies legal definitions and yet transcends universal propositions about good and evil.

It is more important to focus on the termination of genocide by states than upon forms of punishment. Little if any evidence exists that punishment is a deterrent to terrorism, and much evidence that it has no such deterrent value, especially in the context of a state which condones rather than condemns acts of genocide. Random terrorist activities of marginal groups in society are more readily identifiable and hence more easily punishable than are the systematic genocidal activities integral to continuance of state power. As a result, the issue of punishment too often has a minor meliorative worth, that just as often as not, permits genocidal state practices to go undetected, much less punished.

Social scientists today, are being called upon increasingly to focus their skills on the terrorism problem.[5] Research is being conducted on possible future events: i.e., the ability of small bands of terrorists to steal atomic weapons or fissionable materials, and then hold the country for "ransom." Yet there are serious doubts that terrorists, even if successful in obtaining fissionable material, would have either the scientific or technological capability to produce atomic weapons. Furthermore, the anticipatory research being conducted on this subject may invite a tightening of counterterrorist techniques which would seriously threaten the vitality of individual rights and political protest for decades to come.

There is high risk in researching ways to prevent future occurrences. Not only does such research plumb events that have not happened, but researchers are led to develop structures of analysis that can be self-fulfilling. This can produce an antiterrorist industry under whose banner enormous erosion of civil liberties could be made to seem all too rational and enlightened to the general public.

Risk is part of the nature of the democratic system—to permit modes of behavior that are uncontrolled and experimental. To insist that new mechanisms have to be created to prevent terror may be more risky than accepting the possibility of certain terrorist acts, or questioning the need for pursuing some developments, such as plutonium recycling, for which heavy antiterrorist measures would be inevitable. What needs distinguishing, especially in terms of civil liberties, is society's readiness to respond to an immediate and dangerous threat from its readiness to install built-in "protective" structures to anticipate every form of terrorist behavior.

The solution to the problem of terror is invariably beyond the framework of counterterror. Responses to terror must be accompanied by a strengthening of the social fabric as a whole and the economic order specifically. But strength cannot be reduced to a code word for increased surveillance; it clearly entails real changes in the social sytem, including new weightings in the distribution of wealth, power, and status.

Social scientists asked to indulge their penchants for applied research and futurology ought to be extremely wary about joining the organized search to prescribe and enact antiterrorist programs. If they join in discussions *about* such matters, they should insist on taking a hard-nosed view of the evidence as to how much terrorism actually has been committed, what its nature really is, and how much more of it a democratic society can—indeed *must*—be willing to suffer rather than slide into the conversion of democratic systems to totalitarian ones.

The same conclusion applies to the general public and civil libertarians. Whether put forward by political leaders or social science experts, programs to forestall terrorism should be examined closely to see what their costs are for individual privacy, group protest, political competition, and social change. There are more than a few wolves among those offering to help guard the lamb from the tigers. Defending a somewhat strengthened status quo against the advocates of garrison-state security should be today's battle position by all those who cherish a constitutional order.

# Notes to Chapter 8

1.  Merleau-Ponty, Maurice. *Humanism and Terror: An Essay on the Communist Problem.* Boston: Beacon Press, 1969 (originally published in French, 1947). p. 188.
2.  This profile of a terrorist is derived from an earlier essay of mine. See, "Political Terrorism and State Power," *Journal of Political and Military Sociology,* Vol. 1, No. 1 (Spring) 1973. pp. 147-157. A more recent effort along these lines provides independent confirmation based on a large sample of 350 presumed terrorists. See, Charles A. Russell and Bowman H. Miller, "Profile of a Terrorist," *Terrorism: An International Journal,* Vol. 1, No. 1, 1977. pp. 17-34.
3.  Horowitz, Irving Louis. *The Struggle Is the Message: The Organization and Ideology of the Anti-War Movement.* Berkeley: The Glendessary Press, 1970. pp. 114-120. Frank Kitson, *Low Intensity Operations: Subversion, Insurgency, Peace-Keeping.* London: Faber Publishers, 1972. Robert Jay Lifton, *History and Human Survival.* New York: Random House, 1970. Martin Oppenheimer, *The Urban Guerrilla.* Chicago: Quadrangle Books, 1969. Milton J. Rosenberg, ed., *Beyond Conflict and Containment: Critical Studies of Military and Foreign Policy.* New Brunswick, New Jersey: Transaction/ E.P. Dutton, 1972. Jerome Skolnick, ed., *The Politics of Protest.* New York: Ballantine Books, 1969. Eugene V. Walter, *Terror and Resistance: A Study of Political Violence.* New York: Oxford University Press, 1969.
4.  Weingartner, James J. *Crossroads of Death: The Story of the Malmedy Massacre and Trial.* Berkeley and Los Angeles: University of California Press, 1979. esp. pp. 239-264.
5.  See Arendt, Hannah. *On Revolution.* New York: Viking Press, 1963. James Chowning Davies, ed., *When Men Revolt and Why.* New York: The Free Press, 1971. Harry Eckstein, ed., *Internal War: Problems and Approaches.* New York: The Free Press, 1966. Ivo Feierabend, Rosalind L. Feierabend, and Ted. R. Gurr, eds., *Anger, Violence and Politics: Theories and Research.* Englewood Cliffs: Prentice Hall, 1972. Ted Robert Gurr, *Why Men Rebel.* Princeton: Princeton University Press, 1970.

# Chapter 9

# Human Rights and Foreign Policy

*The kind of faith or obedience that is bought with bread is evil, and so is any constraint on man's conscience, in whatever form, even if the constraint is exercised for ostensibly good ends. Freedom is not to be confounded with goodness or happiness. Goodness festers if bred by constraint, and happiness turns into brutish contentment. Only when freely chosen do they acquire a human content.*

Philip Rahv, ESSAYS ON LITERATURE AND POLITICS

At first glance it might well appear than human rights and social science are perfectly isomorphic terms; the conduct of organized reason called science should issue into an expansion of human rights; and conversely, the unfettered exercise of human rights should allow for the expansion of social scientific research. While there is an obvious moral sentiment that leads us to wish for such a combination of human rights and social sciences, any sort of careful reflection makes clear that the two are quite distinct; occupying discrete realms of reality no less than ideology. Tragically perhaps, the connection between human rights and social science is less one of aesthetic balance than of creative tension.[1]

Specifically, social science must examine the issue of human rights with the same critical dispassion and reserved cutting edge that it would any other political slogan or social myth. To do less

**161**

than this is to substitute aspirations for experience: a fatal confusion that may itself issue more into human misery than human rights, by using up, exhausting meaning to words. Social scientists too have a bill of particulars: the first human right is that of criticism, the second human right is that of analysis, and the third human right is that of construction. Let me take up the subject of human rights in terms of these three notions: criticism, analysis, and construction.

I shall first criticize the human rights movement, insofar as it has political coherence, for its conceptual failure to take into account human obligations. I shall then analyze how rights are frequently in competition with each other, hence still require the exercise of social science for rendering analytic judgment. Finally, I shall indicate those mechanisms by which the human rights question can be monitored and evaluated to determine its centrality in social and political practice. This as admittedly a tall order for a short chapter, but one which at least should be broached if we are to get beyond the present state of political opportunism followed too frequently by moral bluster.

The widespread disregard, even disdain, for a concept of human obligation paralleling that of human rights, has generated the sort of one-sided, interest group politics that has tended to sacrifice the whole for the parts, all but destroyed a notion of international or national community in favor of regional, local, even entirely personalistic "issues." Single interest politics, and its attendant special issue lobbying efforts, has made the political process a jungle of impenetrable hazards. Any sort of political statement on matters ranging from taxation to education to defense policy becomes part of a concerted effort either to depose or impose the public official. A government of laws runs the risk of being reduced to one of lawyers, the force of institutional affiliations is eroded and transformed into a baser force of personalities and influentials. To have an obligation to more than the bottom line, or to perceive of obligations as anything beyond a payoff matrix, becomes absurd in this perfect world of an exchange system in which one hand continually washes the other.

When human rights becomes a demand for sameness, a hedonist calculus of statistical claims, in which the least reward differential within a society becomes a cause célèbre and a reason for public outcry, then social science and human rights must part company. At such a point, the question of human rights becomes one of private avarice. Demands for statistical parity also raise serious questions as to whether a national structure can exist, or creative powers can be acknowledged, or whether incentive and reward can be recognized. This transvaluation of human rights into perfect egalitarianism holds open the spectre of Robespierrism: in an ideology and a system in which democracy is secured through a totalitarian mechanism such an approach to rights becomes all-absorbing and hence quickly dispenses with democracy, in favor of massification.

With human rights, as with other public concerns, political events often dictate public discourse. Since the begininning of the United Nations, in the mid-1940s, the question of human rights has remained in the province of UNESCO conferences; in the late 1970s it emerged, suddenly, as a central issue. Certainly, this new sense of concern cannot be explained on the basis of an intellectual breakthrough in the past thirty years. Rather, human rights have become a major instrument of American foreign policy. It should be evident that the passion for human rights, however genuine, is a measured response to the interests of this (or any other) nation.

Yet one should not be cynical about the subject of human rights simply because the sense of concern appears so clearly related to national interests and mandarin policies. Intellectuals, and social scientists in particular, have long inhabited a world where desultory issues locked away in library archives, become dramatic events of considerable public consequences. The War on Poverty was a political invention long after the emergence of a literature on poverty; and even though that particular rhetorical war has passed into oblivion, the realities of poverty remain. No matter how the major collective issues of the century are placed on the agenda of public discourse, the best efforts of social scientists must be put forward, however cynical one might be with respect to the national origins or even the frivolous nature of such commitments.

Politics is a game of vulnerabilities, and the human rights issue is clearly one in which the "socialist" world has proven most vulnerable, just as the economic rights issue is where the "capitalist" world is most open to criticism. The very interplay of forces, the competition of world historic systems and empires provides an opportunity for individuals and smaller collectivities to register marginal advantages over the systems they inhabit. Because of the practical potential of concerns for human rights, rather than because of an effort to capitalize on a policy quirk of this specific moment in time, social science can provide a useful, albeit limited, role. The various social science disciplines have pioneered in transforming the question of human rights from a series of indecisive philosophic propositions to a precise sense of measurable statistics and theorems.

The debate on human rights can be conceptualized at its most general level as a struggle between eighteenth-century libertarian persuasions and nineteenth-century egalitarian beliefs—that is, from a vision of human rights having to do with the right of individual justice before the law to a recognition of the rights of individuals to social security and equitable conditions of work and standards of living. Whether human rights are essentially a political or economic concern is not a secondary issue. However, the social sciences need not choose between politics and economics. They have enough on their hands in demanding an accountability system for monitoring and evaluating both.

The social sciences have introduced an element of accountability not only into their disciplines, but also into the policy systems and networks that social scientists find themselves in. As a result, the measurement of human rights has become the monumental contribution of social science. Big words are rightfully suspect, but concepts doubly so. It therefore becomes a central act of faith to translate the abstract into the concrete. This is largely what has been accomplished by economists, sociologists, psychologists, political scientists, and anthropologists through the use of social indicators.

The right to justice, or formal education, are concepts easy enough to absorb within the framework of almost any social system. But when rights become carefully stipulated in terms of costs, when freedom of beliefs becomes translated into freedom to impart information and ideas without harassment, when social security is translated into old-age insurance, when rights to privacy are viewed as the right of every individual to communicate in secrecy, when rights to work involve protection of actual workers, when social rights are translated into the rights of mothers and children to special care and protection, when rights to work involve the right to form and joint trade unions and the right to strike, when rights to personal security involve measures to protect the safety of conscientious objectors, when rights to fair trials include protection against arbitrary arrest or detention—then the entire panoply of rights assumes an exact meaning that lifts them from the realm of sermon to one of seriousness.

The habitual interest in human rights in part reflects the absence of these rights. There is a great deal of concern on matters of cruel, inhuman, or degrading treatment because there is so such cruelty, inhumanity, and degradation present in world affairs. There is concern about the rights of self-determination because there are so many violations of those rights in the name of national integration. International law calls for the punishment of genocide because the twentieth century has seen the alarming development of mass homicide practiced for statist ends.

There is a colossal dichotomy between practices and principles. This split between reality and rhetoric gives the human rights issue its volatility. Yet the one enormous breakthrough that has evolved over the century is the sense of right and wrong. A common legacy of democratic and socialist politics, of marketing and planning systems, of libertarian and egalitarian ideologies, is the assumption that there is such a goal as human rights. When one recollects that it was only one hundred years ago that slavery and serfdom were vital forces in human affairs and that wars were fought to protect chattel slavery as states' rights, then the extent and velocity—at least conceptually—of how far we have come becomes evident.

The central characteristic of the twentieth century, what so profoundly demarcates it conceptually from previous centuries, is that a world in which obligations were taken for granted has been transformed into one where rights are presumed to be inalienable. Our institutions were largely concerned with theories of human obligation: what individuals and collectivities owe to their societies and to their states—an automatic presumption that one has an obligation to fight in wars whatever the purpose of the war, or the notion that economic failure is a mark of individual shortcoming rather than societal breakdown. The hallmark of the twentieth century and the achievements of the social sciences is to have made the question of human rights the central focus, while placing the question of obligations on the shoulders of institutions rather than individuals.

There are risks in this transvaluation. One might well argue that the tilt has turned into a rout; that issues of the duties of individuals to the community, or the limitations of human rights to ensure national survival, have not received proper attention; that social research has so emphasized the minutae of imbalances of every sort that even homicides are now blamed on violence on television. But such transvaluations carry within themselves potential for hyperbole; and there is little point in discarding the baby with the bathwater. The literature of the past was written in terms of dynasties, nations, and empires. As long as that was the case, the matter of human rights hardly counted. Only now, when these larger-than-life institutions—these dynasties, nations, and empires—are dissolving, can it be seen that the individual is the centerpiece of all human rights and that the expression of these rights must always remain the province of the free conscience of a free individual. In this very special sense ours is the century in which individualism has emerged beyond the wildest imaginings of previous centuries. Paradoxically, it is also the century of the most barbaric collectivisms, which put into sharp and painful relief the subject of human rights by assuming the right of states to terminate individual life for political reasons. If the momentary strategy of the political system is such that the subject of human rights now is central, the principles of social research must convert those strategies into durable gains. How is this to be accomplished?

The most serious presumption about social science involvement in the human rights issue is the uncritical identification of one with the other. That is to say, an unstated commitment to the idea that clear human rights policies can and should emanate from social science information. One suspects that social science interest in human rights is not unlike past such involvements: the mandarin-like features of social scientists perceiving their interests to flow from political messages to the point where true meanings in social science are inextricably linked to political guidelines and attractive slogans. In the past, social scientists did not so much lead as follow political guidelines. Whether it be a presumed War on Poverty or a revolt against taxation, the social science community has had a strong proclivity to follow public officials rather than provide self-motivated leadership.

The human rights issue has sadly tended to follow a similar "natural history" of political ideology. This is not to deny the reality of the human rights cause. Whatever operational guidelines are employed toward maximizing human equality and fairness among citizens and governments is worthy of support: so too are motherhood and apple pie. However, the presupposition that social scientists have the capacity to extract new meanings from the human rights cause, or manufacture innovative politics, presumes that the social science community is privy to a normative structure not granted to ordinary mortals. This is clearly not the case.

At the mundane level of national policy, human rights, like the New Deal, the  Fair Deal, and the Great Society represent a historical tendency on the part of the American executive government to give distinction and individual character to each of their administrations. This seems especially true for the Democratic party which has traditionally seen the need of each administration to delineate itself in contrast to previous administrations. In part, this trend is a consequence of a breakdown of party loyalty as such in America, and the substitution of political formulas based on mass communication in its stead. Under such circumstances, it is understandable that the political system does not wait for the social science community to establish national guidelines. Rather, the large political system expects support from the relatively small social science community, and is willing to handsomely underwrite such support in the form of ongoing research grants and contracts.

What is interesting about the human rights issue, in contrast to previous executive political rallying cries, is its international dimension. In the past, most major slogans were confined to the national political system. Human rights are located in the international arena. Quite beyond the disintegration of party organization in America, is the obvious fact that the United States, like every other major power, places its best moral foot forward whenever possible.

In the 1950s, the key was modernization, a term easily enough defined as the maximization of consumer goods and human resources. In operational terms modernization was strongly equated to transportation and communication, or those areas in which the United States was a world leader. In the 1960s, with the growing apprehension that material abundance or modernization might actually be counterproductive to national goals because it leaves intact the uneven distribution and class characteristics of such consummatory impulses, the key phrase became egalitarianism—the drive toward equal distribution of world resources and goods. But by the end of the 1960s, a new dilemma became apparent: as we were urging upon others egalitarianism as an international ideology, the virtual monopoly by the United States of material conditions of abundance in the West, converted the drive for equality to a domestic rhetoric. The costs of international egalitarianism were not voluntarily borne by the richest nation on Earth. There were other problems in driving the equity stick too hard: lower innovation, higher taxation, and the huge shift in moral specifications. Above all, egalitarianism came to mean that growth itself had a higher price than many environmentalists and social ecologists were willing to pay. When the growth curve leveled off, and even began moving downward as a result of energy shortfalls and oil boycotts, the slogans of the 1960s became increasingly dubious.

The key to the 1970s, at least in explaining the turn towards human rights, has been an American policy presentation that found it more amenable to convert equity demands into liberty demands. It was the long and strong suit of the West in an era of declining American hegemony and corresponding growth in Soviet power. The human rights issue, covertly for the most part, celebrated the fact of high political and social freedom in the West—just as modernization in the 1950s celebrated the fact that America was a consumer society, and egalitarianism in the 1960s celebrated the fact that there were large numbers of people sharing in this largesse. The long and short of it is that the human rights issue like those political formulas of previous decades, provides a sharp contrast to the socialist sector with its prima facie constraints on human rights: from exacting high punishment for low crimes, to refusal to grant travel visas for immigration purposes. Human rights, whether measured by press standards, due process of law, freedom of worship, voluntary associations, multiple parties, etc., became the strong suit of the West in the 1970s. Such issues offer both a contrast to Soviet power, and provide an illustration of a certain inability of slogans of a previous decade to become transformed into reality.

*The Problem of Big-Power Priorities.* If one takes a newspaper on any given day, it becomes apparent that human rights, however potent as a normative instrument of foreign policy, are constantly tempered and even temporized by ongoing realities. Let me draw attention to one day in the life of the *Financial Times of London* (August 11, 1978) to illustrate this point: the United States, which had urged sanctions against the Soviet Union for its persecution and imprisonment of dissidents and human rights policies, generally relented on the sale of drill bit equipment and technology vital for the Soviet oil industry. Such equipment represented a considerable financial windfall for the United States, and it also meant that the Soviet Union was spared from generating new forms of research in a complex field. On the other hand, when the United States confronted a far weaker nation, such as Argentina, it held up the financial packaging to help in the sale of Boeing jet liners to Argentina because of its alleged human rights violations. As a result, on the same day that the United States sold equipment vital to the Soviet oil industry—with a pained admission that this violated human rights considerations, it denied a jet package to Argentina, on precisely the same human rights grounds.

*The Problem of Political-Economic Rivalry.* When one thinks of the human rights question in the context of international economic realities, it becomes apparent that there are limits to the implementation of any policy, especially by a weakened United States at this point in time. Vacuums are filled, economic vacuums are filled rapidly. While the United States denied certain loans to Brazil, again on the basis of presumed human rights violations, the Japanese and Italians were more than willing to fill this gap, providing for a $700 million arrangement whereby Japanese and Italian capital will help in the long-term financing of new steel projects in Brazil. In addition, three companies, Sidebras, Kawaski, and Finsider of Italy, have provided terms which assist in Brazilian capital needs on more favorable terms than United States loans in the past.

*The Problem of Indifference to Human Rights.* There are countries helping each other for which human rights are not a particulary important constraint. For example, Pakistan, one of the more overt violators of human rights for its masses, has developed close links to the Muslim countries and to Iran, with the Iranians underwriting everything in Pakistan from highway construction to wheat importation. In this situation, not only was Iran helping Pakistan, but the orchestration of this pact was done through the Eurodollars provided by none other than the American Citibank Corporation. It also helped set the rate of interest to be charged to Pakistan by Iran. These technicalities are replicated every day of the year. As a result, it is impossible to speak of the implementation of a human rights policy as if it were a geometric axiom. It might well be that the politics of boycott is the ultimate expression of a policy of human rights. But this presupposes a monopoly of goods and services, which the United States does not now possess.

*The Problem of Indirect Support for Human Rights Violators.* One serious dilemma which constantly arises is the need for diplomatic, political, and military assistance pacts between big powers, which in turn filter such aid to other nations. For example, the United States may, on strictly military grounds, be compelled to effect hardware sales to say, Egypt and Israel, and find that some of such weapons ultimately come to be employed in supporting despotic powers such as Libya. This may work in reverse of course. Egypt may decide to sell advanced Soviet MIG-23 fighters to China, the very nation that the Soviet Union would be least inclined to see such aircraft go to. What this suggests is the multilateral nature of human rights considerations, and not just a presumed bilateral character. Aid and trade can be contained only in unusual circumstances, i.e., when a threat to cancel future agreements of an urgent sort is involved. Unless a nation is prepared to monitor the circuitous routing of its entire foreign sales and aid effort, it must accept as a fact the relatively secondary status of human rights as a central foreign policy plank.

*The Problem of Which Humans, What Rights.* A special dilemma that plagues politicians interested in the centrality of human rights is a choice of persons to be preserved and rights to be guarded. In a situation such as the Cambodian dispute with Vietnam, one in which an alleged two million Cambodians were subject to genocidal liquidation and another one million Vietnamese are languishing in concentration camps, a choice between evils is often faced by appeals to larger political considerations. For example, new diplomatic recognition of the Peoples Republic of China by the United States, not only dampens criticism of China's internal human rights violations, but also leads to playing down the grotesque violations of human rights in Cambodia, a Chinese proxy state. It may also lead to heightened consciousness of human rights violations in Vietnam, as a mechanism for dealing with the Soviet Union. In short, decisions are required in the treatment of nations that have little in common other than the harsh treatment of citizens by states.

The limits of foreign policy based upon human rights are painfully revealed in a mini (or proxy) war between Cambodia, a genocidal society responsible for nearly two million deaths, and Vietnam, an incarceration society in which approximately 800,000 people languish in jails. The flagrant and clear-cut invasion of Cambodia by Vietnam in 1978-79 compelled the United States, along with a majority of states, to invoke the principle of territorial sovereignty. Considerations of policy prevailed rather than a pragmatic acceptance of incarceration as a lesser evil than genocide and hence more in keeping with the spirit of a human rights posture. This is not adduced as evidence of any foreign policy inconsistency; quite the reverse, the decision in this particular instance was entirely appropriate and had the force of international law as its precedent. But such situations, occurring with alarming frequency, do point up the inevitable disjunction between policy and principle, or more specifically, between a political requirement of statecraft and a moral requirement of world order.[2]

It is appropriate that the West, and the United States in particular, pay stricter attention to the primary and secondary forms of constraints and contradictions. The simple moralism that would deny aid to both Nicaragua and Brazil because of human rights violations, fails to account for the differential importance of the two nations in the maintenance of United States foreign policy. As a result, even if there is a basic human rights policy, implementation tends to be differentiated if it is to make any sense, or if it is not simply to be ignored as a political spoof or bluff. A central task of social science is to make clear situational realities and contradictory tendencies within a policy network. Social scientists should not simply lend moral weight to these efforts, without regard to empirical realities and world situations, but their practical weight to appropriate decision making.

The discussion concerning human rights, at least on a global perspective, has been linked to choices between political deprivation, presumably characteristic of the East (Second World), and economic exploitation, presumably characteristic of the West (First World). Aside from the reification and polarization involved, the problem is that the human rights issue is thrown back upon ideological grounds. One senses a growing apathy with human rights questions because that rhetoric has not expanded beyond the cold war or Iron Curtain countries.

A fitting and proper role of social science in the human rights issue is to move beyond such broad abstractions and seek out concrete expressions of both the exercise and abridgement of human rights. In this regard, the human rights issue can be joined to a framework larger than itself and more politically significant. It can be fused to questions about social systems, political regimes, and economic frameworks.

One contribution that social science can make at this level is the expansion of social indicators; that is, the breakout and disaggregation of the human rights question. Instead of talking abstractly about the right to work, social scientists can talk concretely about conditions of work, protection of migrant workers, occupational work and safety measures, and social services for employees. Instead of talking about the right to life and liberty, social scientists can talk specifically about protection under the law, a right to a fair and open trial, security of a person who is incarcerated, rights of individuals to deviate from official standards of behavior. If we are talking about political rights, questions should be raised about conditions of voting, levels of participation, numbers of parties permitted to contend, electoral expenses, and the role of local vis-à-vis national government. Instead of talking about citizen rights, social scientists can raise issues of the conditions of migration outside a nation, freedom of movement within a nation, rights of asylum, protection against deportation, and the character of national and ethnic affiliations. These are the sorts of distinctions that are increasingly being made by Amnesty International and by select, specialized agencies of the United Nations.[3]

There are national varieties in presenting the issue of human rights, and these cannot easily be eliminated. But at least the social scientist through a sophisticated series of social indicators, can provide some flesh, and not just flab to the human rights issue. For example, the Yugoslavs have carried questions of the right to work to include free choice of employment, conditions of employment, protection against unemployment, equal pay for equal work, the right to favorable remuneration, and even the right to form trade unions. On the other hand, the Yugoslav program does not include the right to strike. At this point in time, the need of the social science community is to achieve a stage beyond the aggregated national data of the United Nations, and develop firm internationally recognized characteristics to which all nations in the civilized world adhere, at least in terms of ideals to reach.

There will doubtless still be strong ideological components based on whether a society has an "open" or "mixed" or a "central" economic system, or whether it has a multiparty, single-party, or no-party political system. There will also be differences in terms of the character of punishment and restraint characteristic of a region or nation. But these items can themselves become an area of comparative investigation. That is to say, what nations under what circumstances are in violation of human rights when the same practices in other nations may be characterized as fully observant of such rights becomes a problem rather than a paradigm.

Another facet beyond that of social indicators is the study of social norms. What are the norms expected from a nation in the field of human rights? Here certain items can be addressed. First, that there be annual country reports on social questions, just as there are annual country reports on economic questions, and in that way focus attention on specific patterns of human rights violations or observances. Second, the encouragement of independent, nongovernmental organizations which can both monitor and pressure official reports in order to gain creditability and reliability. Third, social science is uniquely equipped to monitor unusual conditions or emergency situations, such as famine, floods, and earthquakes, and generally victims in chronic misery and distress. In this way human rights reporting will not become mechanistic and ignore flash dangers. Fourth, an area that can be examined at this normative level is whether violation of human rights is being conducted officially or unofficially by governments, or whether governments use conduits to engage in human rights violations. This distinction too will prevent the monitoring of governments from becoming mechanical, ignoring the utilization of agencies perpetuating human rights violations. Fifth, insofar as possible, human rights reporting should be made uniform and should be monitored by the social scientific community so that agencies like the International Sociological Association, or the International Political Science Association, do more than meet every four years to exchange nationalistic platitudes and develop standing committees for monitoring, evaluating, and estimating human rights gains in any period of time.

These are complex as well as ambitious tasks. But at least they provide a central role for the social scientific community beyond servicing the state as mandarins. The social science community is responsible for both the construction of a better future, and the criticism of present realities. It cannot subvert one for the other in the name of national unity; it cannot become a permanent positivist arm of state power nor a perpetual destructive critique of such power. In the dialectic of construction and criticism inheres the great strength of social science. The utilization of social science by each nation in the international community of nations will itself provide a bona fide measure of human rights. But this entails a serious recognition that the tasks of policymakers and social scientists, although intertwined, are by no means identical either in principle or in practice. Such an awareness of the durability of differences between social sectors and intellectual forces is itself a clear representation of the status of human rights in any given society.

## Notes to Chapter 9

1. This chapter was first presented at a Conference on "The Rights and Responsibilities of the Individual," at the Center for the Study of the American Experience, Annenberg School of Communications of the University of Southern California, Los Angeles, California, November 15, 1978. This revised draft completed on January 30, 1979.
2. While genocide as the ultimate crime against human rights has been a relatively well-kept secret, legislative discussion of this linkage has begun to surface. See, United States Congress, Senate Committee on Foreign Relations. *International Convention on the Prevention and Punishment of the Crime of Genocide* (94th Congress, Second Session. Executive Report 94-23). Washington, DC: U.S. Government Printing Office, 1976.
3. The most impressive application of social indicators to issues of human rights is contained in *Yearbook on Human Rights for 1973-74.* New York and Paris: United Nations, 1977. pp. 269-317.

# Chapter 10

# Personal Life and Social Structure

*Admit that I owe it to myself to protest against the ordeals You impose on man. I could drown mankind with my tears and in its blood. I could bring this farce to an end; that may even be what You want, what You are driving me to. But I shall not do it, I shall not destroy, do You hear me, I shall not kill! Had Cain spoken thus, how different history would have turned out. It would not have been the desperate adventure of two brothers, one of whom asserted himself by killing and the other by letting himself be killed, but the beautiful and pasionate, pure and purifying gesture of a noble and fervent mankind.*

Elie Wiesel, MESSENGERS OF GOD

Too often, social science resorts to the tyranny of impersonal, deterministic forces to explain major events. The burden of these final remarks is to reintroduce the person as a central factor in understanding a phonomenon such as genocide. This is not intended to mechanically reintroduce the individual back into the social order, like some sort of injection to get the deus ex machina rolling again, but simply to note that the motives of people should never have been removed from such systematic analysis to begin with. A political psychology must accompany any sound political sociology. For motives of rulers at one end, the behaviors of masses at the other, and the decision makers all along the stratification line give meaning to terms like *genocide*. We have seen how, without at least the tacit consent, if not active participation of the German people the twin Nazi drive for extermination and expansion could not have remotely been carried forth. Hence, quite beyond the distinction between life and dealth, viewing social structures in terms of personal values is of central importance.

The infusion of political psychology into such an analysis may help prompt a better understanding of why some societies generate single-party machineries, powerful secret police, and a war apparatus dedicated to geographic expansion, while others do not. We may hypothesize that the higher level of repression within a society, the greater the need for an apparatus capable of exercising maximum control. Genocidal societies, therefore, usually have either single-party or an absence of party machineries. They also reveal a striking similarity between those who have political power and those who exercise administrative and bureaucratic power. Finally, they display a police apparatus far larger than that required to simply maintain order. These mechanisms aimed at insuring obedience, are themselves exceedingly costly. They represent a chink in the armor of the genocidal society, a weakness that creates the need for greater repression at higher costs, while at the same time the potential and even necessity for more manifest resistance. It might well be that the cost factors for a genocidal-assassination society are so exorbitant in economic and human terms that those in charge of government are likely to think most carefully about going that route.

A further theoretical possibility is to develop relationships between insiders and outsiders in assassination and permissive societies. The more complete the genocidal nature of a society, the more firm the distinction of who belongs and who does not, between those who are human and those who are not. The higher the degree of tolerance, the less important is the distinction between belonging and nonbelonging, insiders and outsiders. When one considers the difference between the Jews of Italy and the Jews of Germany, it becomes painfully apparent that Italian Jews were always known as Italians, and their Jewishness was marginal, hardly understandable to most Italians. For the Germans, the difference between being a German and being a Jew was the paramount distinction at every level: biological, demographic, historical, and all the rest. The society became dedicated to making that distinction, for once made, genocide became easy, even normative. Intense nationalism, in contrast to cosmopolitanism, is itself an essential characteristic of the genocidal society. It instills not only a sense of difference between those who belong and those who do not, but also the inhumanity of those who do not belong, and thereby the rights of social order to purge itself of alien influence.

Ralf Dahrendorf offers a new beginning to solving old problems about the nature of equity. Democracy extends from "equal citizenship rights having to be generalized, to conflicts being recognized and regulated rationally, elites reflecting the color and diversity of social interests, and public virtues as the predominant value orientation of the people." He goes on to say that, strictly speaking, we need a theory of human relations as well as organizational frameworks as a precondition for a theory of democracy and social structure. What can democracy ultimately mean except respect for the lives of people and recognition that one life is as valuable as another? Life itself is a precondition for the democratic social order. It was the breakdown of this sensibility during the Nazi period, and the inculcation of what Durkheim refers to as "the myth of the state," that ultimately made impossible the practice of democracy in a world with German Nazism. Dahrendorf refers to this peculiar megalomania as a suspension of civil liberties in order to fulfill the imaginary requirements of historical retribution. Such metaphysical predispositions to correct the contours of history lead not just to government with authority, but also to an idea of the state as ultimate, irreversible, and untrammeled by individual ideas. Whether it is a matter of German character, German militarization, or German ethics becomes less important than the fact that the society conducted itself in such a way as to violate any notion of a theory of democracy.[1]

The democratic societies of the United States, Great Britain, Italy, France, Japan, and so on, have as many differences as similitudes. If we were to take systems that have been characterized in some period of their history as fascistic, such as Italy, Germany, and Spain, we would have at least as many differences as similarities. In the present period, even the socialists from the Soviet Union to China, and from the East European nations to Cuba, have as many differences as similarities. That is why the analysis of social structure in terms of the formal organization of society may be a necessary condition for explaining the system, but it is not a sufficient condition for explaining the society as a whole.

Just how important differences are between genocidal and nongenocidal societies, and certainly between punitive and permissive societies, is indicated by nations like Turkey and Japan that, almost without parallel, developed revolutions from above far in advance of other nations in the Third World. The cultural component, the belief in the military ethic, permitted the development of elites to mobilize the society toward developmental goals. Unconstrained by democratic norms, these societies were in a position to set the model for Third World development between fifty and one hundred years earlier.

The most important psychological dilemma in the study of genocide is that it may lead one to exaggerate the grim prospects for the human race. Obviously, for those who take genocide as a serious and central concern, there is already a predisposition to have a grim view toward the subject. Because genocide is so widespread, it is important to recognize the prospects for combatting it; and further, to appreciate how difficult it is to destroy an entire people. European Jews, who were a central target of twentieth-century genocidal persecution, now have a larger population in total number than they had in 1939. True, the democratic constancy was coupled with massive geographic shifts. A second example of this point are the Armenians who were the unwitting forerunner of the war against the Jews, and whose decimation at the hands of the Turks certainly rivaled the later treatment of the Jews at the hands of the Nazis. They too have survived; their numbers have increased; their culture persists. For whatever it is worth, the Armenians have maintained a distinct national identity within the framework of Soviet Russia. They exist as a minority group in Turkey. They represent a considerable element within Greek life. And many of them have made a positive impact on American culture. Another good illustration of this point is the American Indian. Here is a group that was sytematically and diabolically exterminated. Those who were not exterminated were put on tribal lands and subject to elimination through economic atrophy and political delegitimization. Tribalizing a people by placing them within the framework of a permanent compound may be viewed as slow genocide. Yet today more than a million people claim to be Indians, twice the 1960 census count. Whether it is demographic shamanism or a resurrection of self-pride, Indians exist as a people. This does not mean that one should celebrate genocide as a test of the willpower of people. I am not urging the wholesale adoption of Toynbee's world of challenge and response, testing to the maximum the stress and strain on a people. Yet it is important to emphasize that to study genocide is not simply to examine the successful liquidation of entire peoples, but also *attempts* at liquidation. It is significant to recognize the phenomenon of mass murder, for which genocide is synonym, as well as the possibilities for existence and survival.

There is a danger in broadening the concept of genocide to the point that it becomes symbolically all-embracing and hence meaningless. In raising the slogan of American genocide against Black people, or British genocide against Irish people, we risk confusing colonial dependency with physical destruction. We also falsify the actual political struggles by diminishing the resistance to genocide among many oppressed peoples and nations. For example, there are more Black people in the United States than there were in 1900, 1920, and 1940. There are more Irish people in Ireland than during the nineteenth-century famine years. We have a complex problem. At what point in this scheme of genocide are we referring to actual, physical destruction of people, and at what point are we talking about the symbolic dismemberment of a people? Is there an entity called "cultural genocide," which somehow is as horrible as physical genocide? Or are we dealing with a different phenomenon? This is not simply a matter for academic disputation; it has to do with the survival capacities of entire peoples.

If in fact we broaden our approach to include an entity called "cultural genocide," the results might be counterproductive.[2] A deflated, pessimistic, and ultimately confused concept of genocide deprives the very people who are presumably genocidal victims of the capacity to resist and retaliate. For that reason, I have come to believe that a restrictive, rather than an omnibus concept of genocide, is the most operationally valid.

Genocide means the physical dismemberment and liquidation of people on large scales; an attempt by those who rule to achieve the total elimination of a subject people. Genocide does not mean simply depriving people of their cultural heritage. It does not simply refer to a special segment of the population being deprived of opportunities for education, welfare, or health, however hideous such deprivations might be. One must avoid liberal fantasizing about people who are victimized in ways short of genocide. Broadening the concept so that everyone somehow ends up a victim of genocide only leads to a tautological reasoning. Physical genocide is tragically large enough, in raw numerical terms, not to require a vision of symbolic genocide. Literary mannerisms that add fuel to an already grotesque fire are counterproductive to practical efforts to limit or reverse genocidal patterns.

If a real danger exists in expanding a notion of genocide beyond meaningful limits, there is also a danger posed in diminishing a concept of genocide to collective suicide. Further, if one argues that genocide is merely homicide writ large, then we are dealing with a phenomenon which is more difficult to eradicate, much more difficult to describe in jurisprudential terms as requiring a separate response apart from homicide. There are all kinds of unanswered questions about the relationship of homicide to suicide. Is there a self-destructive impulse in peoples, much as there is an individual impulse to self-destruction? Are there laws of human behavior, or simply historical continuities? Are there frameworks that make collectivities perform in self-destructive ways? Or is that simply another way of using a rhetoric of blaming the system? Is there never such a tendency? Are we always dealing with people who are fighting to the last breath? And if not, when not, no less than why not? When do people fight to the bitter end? When do people submit? What are the conditions of rebellion and retaliation to genocidal patterns? What are the conditions of submission? Is resistance simply a function of raw terror or maximum use of state authority? All these questions represent a crucial theoretical issue between the psychological and the political. I am in the awkward position of answering a question with other questions. But pos ..g them in this manner moves us beyond conventional ideological postures that rest on the genocide of others and the justifiable homicide of selves. Such a one-sided position distorts, rather than clarifies, the persistence of genocide as the political primal scream of our times.

First comes the act and then comes the word. First a homicide is committed and then someone defines the conditions of murder. First genocide is committed and then a language emerges to describe the phenomenon. The Turkish assassination of the Armenians is a clear case of genocide prior to 1945. Whether such an act is recognized in war trials is a linguistic issue, not a sociological one. There is legal and historical precedent for acts of genocide. The Japanese put Americans on trial who flew the first raid over Tokyo on the same premise of random destruction of life and property, that is, on the genocidal premises that were the foundations of the Nuremberg trials. The word itself is recent. But there are more anomalies than that connected with its widespread usage. For example, American Communists were instrumental in imposing a concept of genocide on the docket of world opinion at the very time of the worst postwar Stalinist excesses. William L. Patterson, a foremost Communist Black leader, prepared the document that contained the basis of the first United Nations resolution on the treatment of Blacks in the United States. In the entire document, treatment of its national, religious, and political opponents never arose. One can see that there are more than linguistic peculiarities involved. *We Charge Genocide,* which is similar to the statement of principles of Amnesty International, was prepared by those who categorically refused to examine genocide in the Soviet Union.[3] There are powerful national myopias, sometimes called ideologies, in this area. Diplomats talk about genocide as if referring to someone else. The ability of people to develop myopic visions of their own national performance underscores and underwrites the need for social scientists to involve themselves in this field of research.

The great advantage of "bridge" disciplines such as political psychology or political sociology, is to correct the analytical shortcomings of a vulgar economism. For the most part, the question has been posed: To what degree does the structure of an economic system help explain the nature of genocide? While this is a perfectly valid line of inquiry it is no less important to ask: To what degree does the practice of genocide help to explain the nature of an economic system? What is the utility of a thing called "social system" if one cannot live to see its benefits or results? The social system is not simply a monetary exchange or a marketplace of ideas. It is a configuration of practices pertaining to life and death. All constitutions read beautifully. If one were to have a discussion about the nature of property relationships in one country vis-à-vis another, one might demonstrate how one or another system encourages a higher mix of public against private ownership. But the history of twentieth-century political practice shows such definitions often represent an intellectual snare and a delusion leading down a primrose path of self-denial and destruction. System building urges us not to worry about how many people's lives are taken, but to worry about the nature of the social system. I am arguing the reverse: that we worry less about the nature of the social system and more about how many lives are taken by each system, state, or nation. My view is a direct assault against a concept of social systems that starts with a model and ends in death. I start with a person's right to live, and if I can derive a model, so much the better. I do not consider my life consecrated to the creation of models of social order. It is infinitely more important to know what country to travel to in order to prolong one's life than to provide others with an abstract dictionary of social systems. It is not enough to argue the merits of socialism, but specifically, what brand of socialism provides the best life chances. Is it Rumania, Cuba, Yugoslavia, China, Albania, or the Soviet Union? It does little good to say that they are all socialist systems. If social science is to provide criteria about where to live and work, one needs a series of criteria, akin to a qualitative Guttman Scale, indicating the social and/or life indicators that show where one's life chances are either maximized or minimized. This is a legitimate and scientific activity of practical use to wider publics.

The basic purpose of my work on genocide is not to add another title to a growing list of horror stories exhibiting a concern over the destruction of human life, but rather to ventilate and rehabilitate the entire field of social systems analysis. I have no wish to deny the worth of class analysis or race analysis in the study of social systems; only to make it clear that populist and elitist attitudes toward life and death are an independent variable of a profound sort. It is impossible to infer from the class, race, or religious composition of a nation its attitudes toward genocide. The bonds which unite genocidal societies are as overwhelmingly potent as those which unite permissive or tolerant societies. In this sense the English tradition of political pluralism extending from Locke to Mill has as much to teach us as the continental tradition of power and class analysis.

It would be absurd to deny the importance of social structural factors in predicting national systems. But it would be equally absurd to deny the significance of cultural factors. Yet the so-called materialist interpretation of history attempts precisely this sort of reductionist one-sided analysis. And the fact that such a line of analysis came about in intellectual retaliation to the equally one-sided *Geisteswissenschaft* and *Kulturwissenschaft* analysis only means that we inherited polarized theorems that frustrate meaningful social science. Take the analysis of Japanese development: we ought not to be required to choose between a sociology which argues that the military insured bourgeois growth in relative isolation from lower-class rebellion, and a culturology which argues that the military insured a special brand of adventurism and heroism that made Japan preeminent is Asia. Surely one has a right to insist on the equal and joint validity of the economy and culture. It is about time that a multivariate, naturalistic framework replaces older dogmatic expressions of nineteenth-century metaphysics smuggled into social and political analysis. And that is what my work is definitely about.

Our social science must not become so bereft of common sense that is cannot answer the obvious, or make choices that almost any reasonable person would make without the aid of high-powered social research. Surely it is not strange, if we take the work of Luigi Barzini[4] on the Italians and Karl Jaspers[5] on the Germans seriously, that despite similitudes in economic systems and social structures during the Fascist–National Socialist period, the actual behavioral patterns of the two nations were so radically different. Likewise, if adherence to Islamic values were a unique determinant of developmental patterns, how would one explain the entirely different rates of economic growth in countries such as Turkey and Egypt? The mental structure of peoples is certainly as important as their physical structure. Heroic behavior is certainly as important as the size of an armed force. The older dualisms have outlived their intellectual usefulness, and the analysis of genocide dramatically underlines this.

My early interest in social and philosophical ideas and ideologies of war and peace, and the attendant analysis of conflict, consensus, and cooperation, was itself part of a basic commitment to a sociology which takes seriously the right to live as a determinant of other human rights and social alignments. Questions of social structures, cultural orders, and military regimes, ultimately reduce to living and dying. It is absurd to believe that transcendental rehabilitation is possible: not by Communists who perform miracles of ideology or by Christians who perform miracles of theology. A naturalistic sociology must take its stand with life and the living. The collective imposition of death by a state must be seen as a common ground at which the needs of sociology and morality interact and intersect. One cannot have a democratic ideology outside the rule of law nor a democratic sociology without the bold assertion of the right to live.

The point of these remarks is not to displace political or military factors: that would be a game of model building. My interest is not to superimpose culturology upon sociology. I am not suggesting that transhistorical concepts of spirit be substituted for historicity of all things. A cultural science would trivialize social science and return us to a condition of *Kulturwissenschaft* of Dilthey and Rickert. It has taken nearly a century to extricate ourselves from this cultural standpoint, and by no means would it be worthwhile to return to it. Cultural values, like economic interests of political systems themselves, all have a common denominator, and that is the attitude toward life within a society, and what the state does to a life, or a series of lives, to foster its own general interests. In that way the series of determinisms that plague social science can be reduced to a general theory of society: one that takes seriously not so much cultural phenomena in contrast to ecnomic phenomena, but the obligation of both to deal seriously with the fact of life and death.

We are in the midst of an enormous emotional as well as intellectual upheaval. It extends from questioning the biological meaning of life to the political taking of life. Normative and empirical standards are both being entirely overhauled. Even the most humane are now touched by the matter-of-factness of dying. A clinical view of death is a prelude to a cynical view of the tasks of social systems. In this way, the notion of a political community based on the need to live is being replaced by a vision of pluralism that is nothing more than separated, isolated interest groups tearing at each other's flesh; or at the other end of the political spectrum, demands for authority and order that eat away with equal vigor at the practice of democracy.

To presume obligations to the state is not to assert simply a theory of obedience, but rather that the state must insure the right to live without presuming the reasons for living. The management of a society may extend to commands for obedience based on the need for mutual survival, but not beyond that point. Negotiating the rights of individuals and what one does with a life, is not a matter of state power. Too much normative theorizing is a subterfuge for reintroducing a doctine of individual obligations in place of political rights. The record of the twentieth century is soiled by a juridical standpoint that asserts obligations to serve the state without any corresponding sense of right to life within a state. Michael Walzer speaks quite directly to this point: "It is surely not the case that being and feeling obligated are the same. It is not enough that a common life be felt or thought to exist; there must be a common life. I do not mean to defend all those nationalistic or ideological mystifications that lead men to believe they are living in a community when in fact they are not."[6]

One cannot conclude such an examination without at least a brief inquiry into the nature of responsibility for acts of genocide. The efforts of Falk are significant in this connection. Recognizing genocide as the most extreme offense of governments against humankind, he distinguishes between two types of models for its legal punishment: first, the indictment model "based on the plausibility of indictment and prosecution of individual perpetrators before a duly constituted court of law operating according to due process and adhering to strict rules of evidence." Second, he offers a responsiblity model that is based on the community's obligation to repudiate certain forms of government behavior and the consequent responsibility of individuals and groups to resist politics involving this behavior." While this distinction is salient, a dilemma of this legal formula is that the genocidal state is the least likely to permit such neat distinctions from being carried into practice. As Falk himself is sadly compelled to admit: "It must be acknowledged, finally, that individual acts of conscience and of resistance may be virtually impossible in a ruthless and efficient totalitarian system."[7] Thus, any efforts to move beyond genocide must again be thrown back upon the political arena, since the relief sought in international law is likely to prove chimeric.

There is a continuing need to establish an authentic sociobiology,[8] one that is grounded in the polity rather than zoology: the social world of the political system in terms of lives taken, years removed from individuals through imprisonment, damages to people through fear of speaking freely. We have moved much too far toward expanding the banality of evil as a necessary component of state existence. One can only hope that such a view of the social order will provide a methodological device for the measurement of social systems, a measurement equal in quantitative power to money for economic science. Quite beyond the methodological aspect is the ideological sense that life is not only worth living, but also that the very task of the social scientist should largely be taken up with an exploration of how to expand such worthiness in life.

One might well inquire as to the feasibility of ever understanding genocide at the empirical level, for example, whether it would not prove more efficacious to search out those aspects of state power and social order that promote equity and well-being rather than to leap to ultimate conclusions and terminations. Such an alternative approach is possible. In my typology I indicate forms of permissive and open-ended state bureaucratic behavior that discourage genocidal outcomes. Yet one is left with the strong feeling that a wider appreciation of state authority in its efforts to preserve the social order lead to a conclusion not unlike that reached by eighteenth-century utilitarians and nineteenth-century libertarians alike: that the government governs best that governs least. Instead of inventing a new radius of state activities labeled "social welfare," social scientists might well turn their attention to more fundamental issues of the optimum size for sound governance, or how much economic "waste" is worth what sorts of social "values." I am not suggesting that meliorative issues be abandoned by social research, only that basic issues of life and death not be overlooked in the process.

What conclusions can be drawn from this study? It would be superficial to say that we should bend every effort to expose and prevent any and all forms of genocide. This reflects a rather obvious and basic humanitarian persuasion, one that hardly would be defeated or voted against. Nations that have systematically practiced genocide are not only sponsors of United Nations resolutions against genocide, but have also often urged the strengthening of such resolutions, such as the Soviet desire to add to the genocide resolution a concept of any deliberate act having to do with destroying various cultural, racial, or religious beliefs. The very fact that such resolutions can be introduced by a nation that in the past has widely practiced genocide would indicate that something other than polemics is called for.

What can and should be concluded intellectually is that given the widespread practice of genocide and its virtual autonomy from both economic systems and geographical locations, one should be extremely cautious about the potential for good works of any nation-state. So much fanaticism and rampant chauvinism is generated by mindless adherence to national goals that the use of genocide as a righteous instrument of national and state policy has become highly tempting. Genocide as a technique for achieving national solidarity takes various forms as we have seen. In the United States, with respect to the Indian question, it is the absorption of "backward tribal nations" into the general nation. In the Soviet Union it has been the liquidation of bourgeois nations into a general socialist commonweal. In short, genocide is a fundamental mechanism for the unification of the national state. That is why it is so widely practiced in "advanced" and "civilized" areas, and why it is so incredibly difficult to eradicate.

The need for faith, trust, and transcendence can be presumed constant. It would be dangerous counsel to assume that nations can properly contain and channel such psychic dispositions. It would be wiser to urge faith in Providence, and trust in people. As for transcendence, an appreciation of the imminence of all existence and the transience of all nations might keep in check those proclivities of the powerful to bend, mutilate, and destroy innocent sections of the human race in order to safeguard a world of order without compassion, and ultimately of law without justice.

# Notes to Chapter 10

1. Dahrendorf, Ralf. *Society and Democracy in Germany.* Garden City, N.Y.: Doubleday & Co., 1967. pp. 205-209.
2. Fields, Rona M. *Society Under Siege: A Psychology of Northern Ireland.* Philadelphia: Temple University Press, 1977.
3. Patterson, William L. *We Charge Genocide: The Historic Petition to the United Nations for Relief from a Crime of the United States Government Against the Negro People.* New York: International Publishers, 1970 (originally published in 1951).
4. Barzini, Luigi G. *The Italians.* New York: Atheneum, 1964.
5. Jaspers, Karl. *The Future of Germany* (translated and edited by E.B. Ashton). Chicago: University of Chicago Press, 1967.
6. Walzer, Michael. *Obligations: Essays on Disobedience, War and Citizenship.* New York: Simon & Schuster, 1970. p. 98.
7. Falk, Richard A. "Ecocide, Genocide, and the Nuremberg Tradition of Individual Responsibility," in *Philosophy, Morality, and International Affairs,* edited by Virginia Held, Sidney Morgenbesser, and Thomas Nagel. New York: Oxford University Press, 1974. pp. 136-137.
8. cf. Somit, Albert. *Biology and Politics: Recent Explorations.* The Hague and Paris: Mouton, 1976. pp. 3-11.

## Chapter 11

# Genocide and Holocaust: On the Exclusivity of Collective Death

*The prime value that the Jews attached to life itself and to Jewish survival generated an activist tradition that influenced the behavior of the individual and the organized community. The pervasiveness of activism among Jews, especially in defense of their rights and their existence, derived from the exceptional responsibility that traditional Judaism places on every individual Jew. The obligations to preserve Judaism and the Jewish people have rested not on monarchs or prime ministers, nor on high priests, prophets, or rabbis, but on each Jewish man and each Jewish woman.*

Lucy S. Dawidowicz, THE WAR AGAINST THE JEWS

The subject of genocide in general and the Holocaust in particular threatens to become a growth industry of the Western cultural apparatus. Books, plays, and television dramatizations on the subject pour forth relentlessly. Sometimes they are presented soberly, other times scandalously; but all are aimed at a mass market unfortunately more amazed than disturbed by their implications. There is danger in this massification of Holocaust studies. Western culture is inclined to adopt fads; even Holocaust studies may become a moment in commercial time—interest in them may decline as well as grow, and even peak out, leaving in its wake a void. The residual debris will probably be summarized in musical comedy; we have already seen examples of this in "The

Lieutenant" (Lieutenant Calley) and "Evita" (Eva Perón) on Broadway. Peter Weiss' play, *The Investigation,* led one commentator to suggest that the major character in the play, in order to elicit shock from the audience, read lines "as if he were saying: 'Let's hear it for genocide.'"[1] This may be precursory of things to come.

One of the least attractive features of "post-Holocaust" studies is the effort of a precious few to monopolize the field, to make it the professional preserve of mourners and scholars. As a consequence, a linguistic battle looms among survivors over which exterminations even deserve the appellation "holocaust" (the total physical annihilation of a nation or people). Such a bizarre struggle over language remains a grim reminder of how easy it is for victims to challenge each other, and how difficult it is to forge common links against victimizers.[2] I do not wish to deny Jewish victims of the Nazi Holocaust the uniqueness of their experience. But there are strong elements of continuity as well as discontinuity in the process of genocide, in the evolution of life-taking as an essential dimension by which state power can be measured in the twentieth century.

Writing with compelling insight, Elie Wiesel personifies the mystic vision of the Holocaust. Those who lived through it "lack objectivity," he claims, while those who write on the subject but did not live through it must "withdraw" from the analytic challenge "without daring to enter into the heart of the matter."[3] More recently, it has been suggested that "for Jews, the Holocaust is a tragedy that cannot be shared" and "it may be unrealistic or unreasonable or inappropriate to ask Jews to share the term holocaust. But it is even more unreasonable and inappropriate not to find a new name for what has taken place in Cambodia."[4] Since what took place in both situations is a holocaust—from a demographic point of view—we need not invent new terms to explain similar barbaric processes. Those who share a holocaust, share a common experience of being victim to the state's ruthless and complete pursuit of human life-taking without regard to individual guilt or innocence. It is punishment for identification with a particular group, not for personal demeanor or performance. These are not theological, but empirical criteria. To seek exclusivity in death has bizarre implications. The special Jewish triumph is in life. All too many peoples—Jews, Cambodians,

Armenians, Paraguayans, Indians, Ugandans—have shared the fate of victims of a mindless taking of life. It is dangerously unbecoming for victims to engage in divisive squabbles about whose holocaust is real or whose genocide is worse.

Those who take an exclusive position on the Holocaust are engaging in moral bookkeeping, in which only those who suffer very large numbers of deaths qualify. Some argue that the six million deaths among European Jews is far greater than the estimated one million deaths among Armenians. However, the number of Armenian deaths as a percentage of their total population (50 percent) is not much lower than the number of Jewish deaths (60 percent). Others contend that the deaths of Ugandans or Biafrans are too few to compare to the Holocaust; yet here too, tribal deaths in percentage terms rival that European pattern of genocide. In certain instances high death rates (approximately 40 percent of all Cambodians or three million out of seven million) are indisputable; then one hears that such deaths were only random and a function of total societal disintegration. Yet it has been firmly established that such deaths were targeted against intellectuals, educators, foreign-born, and literate people—in short, the pattern was hardly random; anyone who could potentially disrupt a system of agrarian slave labor flying under communist banners was singled out and eliminated. Even making the definition a matter of percentages risks creating a morality based solely on bookkeeping.

There is a need to reaffirm the seriousness of the subject. The problem of genocide must be rescued from mass culture. It must not be returned to academic preserves, but it must be made part and parcel of a general theory of social systems and social structures. The position I oppose has been most vigorously articulated by Emil Fackenheim. I propose to subject its major premises to direct cross-examination.[5] This is no simple task; not the least because Fackenheim speaks with thunderous certitude.

Fackenheim's propositions have come to represent the main trends in the theological or rabbinic school of Holocaust studies. They carry tremendous weight among mass culture figures for whom theological sanction provides legitimation to their endeavors and respite from critics.[6] Professor Fackenheim does not remotely intend his views to become part of mass culture. Quite the contrary, his eight propositions distinguishing the Holocaust in particular from genocide in general, represent a tremendous effort to transcend journalistic platitudes, to move beyond an articulation of the banality of evil and into the evil of banility. This deep respect for Fackenheim registered, it must also be said that an alternative perspective, a social science framework, is warranted.

Fackenheim presents his eight propositions with direction and force. A general theory of genocide and state power, which accounts for the specifics of the Holocaust, can have no better base line.

> *One:* The Holocaust was not a war. Like all wars, the Roman War against the Jews was over conflicting interests—territorial, imperial, religious, other—waged between parties endowed, however unequally, with power. The victims of the Holocaust had no power. And they were a threat to the Third Reich only in the Nazi mind.

The Holocaust *was* a war; but of a modern rather than medieval variety. Earlier wars redistributed power by military means. Genocide redistributes power by technological as well as military means. Robert Lifton recently stated the issue succinctly. "The word holocaust, from Green origins, means total consumption by fire. That definition applies, with literal grotesqueness, to Auschwitz and Buchenwald, and also to Nagasaki and Hiroshima. In Old Testament usage there is the added meaning of the sacrifice, of a burnt offering. That meaning tends to be specifically retained for the deliberate, selective Nazi genocide of six million Jews—retained with both bitterness and irony (sacrifice to whom for what?). I will thus speak of the Holocaust and of holocausts—the first to convey the uniqueness of the Nazi project of genocide, the second to suggest certain general principles around the totality of destruction as it affects survivors. From that perspective, the holocaust means total disaster: the physical, social, and spiritual obliteration of a human community."[7] The precedent for this war against the Jews was the Turkish decimation of the Armenian population. Like the Nazis, the Ottoman Empire did not simply need to win a war and redistribute power; they had an overwhelming amount of power to begin with.[8] A war of annihilation is a war. To deny the warlike character of genocide is to deny its essence: the destruction of human beings for predetermined nationalist or statist goals.

The Holocaust is also modern in that it is an internal war, waged with subterfuge and deception by a majority with power against an internal minority with little power. Here too the Armenian and Jewish cases are roughly comparable. Although one can talk of genocide in relation to the bombing of Hiroshima and Nagasaki, genocidal conflict involves internal rather than external populations. But this is an ambiguous point on the nature of war rather than a denial of the warlike nature of the Holocaust per se.

The victims of the Holocaust did have a certain power: they represented a threat to the Nazi Reich. The Jew as bourgeois and the Jew as proletarian represented the forces of legitimacy and revolution in Weimar Germany. They had modest positions in universities, in labor, and industry. Regarding state power itself, where there were scarcely any Jews, they were powerless. Jews were locked out from the German bureaucratic apparatus much as the Turkish Beys locked out Armenians from the administrative apparatus, except to use them in a Quisling-like manner. The Jews posed a threatening challenge to the legitimacy of the Nazi regime.

> *Two:* The Holocaust was not part of a war, a war crime. War crimes belong intrinsically to wars, whether they are calculated to further war goals, or are the result of passions that wars unleash. The Holocaust hindered rather than furthered German war aims in World War II. And it was directed, not by passions, but rather by a plan conceived and executed with methodical care, a plan devoid of passion, indeed, unable to afford this luxury.

This argument rests on a peculiar and misanthropic rendition of the Hilberg thesis. The Holocaust did hinder the Nazi war effort in the limited sense that troop transportation took second priority to transporting Jews. But in the longer, larger perspective, there were advantages. Slave labor was itself an advantage; unpaid labor time was useful. The expropriation of goods and materials was an economic gain for the Nazi Reich. People were liquidated at marginal cost to the system. The gold taken from extracted teeth became a proprietary transfer.[9] Fackenheim questions whether war goals were furthered by the Holocaust; this is not simply answered. As a mobilizing device linking military and civil sectors of the population, war ends were enhanced by the conduct of the Holocaust. The Nazi attempt to exterminate the Jews was motivated by passion, as evidenced by the fact that troop movements to the Russian front took second priority.

Hilberg makes clear the direct collusion of the German Wehrmacht and the German Reichsbahn with respect to the systematic deportation of Jews and the front line servicing of the armed forces. The management of the German railroad illustrates how irrationality can become rationalized, how a "true system in the modern sense of the term" was employed for the unrelenting destruction of human lives. As Hilberg notes, to the extent that the technification of mass society was exemplified by the transportation network, such human engineering considerations cannot be viewed as ancillary. "It illuminates and defines the very concept of 'totalitarianism.' The Jews could not be destroyed by one Fuhrer on one order. That unprecedented event was a product of multiple initiatives, as well as lengthy negotiations and repeated adjustments among separate power structures, which differed from one another in their traditions and customs but which wre united in their unfathomable will to push the Nazi regime to the limits of its destructive potential."[10] The question of passion is a moot point at best; undoubtedly there was a collective passion undergirding the conduct of the Holocaust. It was not simply a methodical event.

Fackenheim and many other theologians overlook parallels in the pursuit of a genocidal state policy following defeat. After the Turkish defeat at the hands of Bulgaria in 1912, the most massive genocide against Armenians occurred. After the Nazi defeat of Stalingrad in 1943, the most massive destruction of Jews ensued. Whatever the vocabulary of motives—fear of discovery, of reprisal, or of judgment—the use of state-sanctioned murder to snatch victory from the jaws of defeat is evident.

The largest part of European Jewry was destroyed after Germany had in effect lost the war. When the major object of the war, defeat of the allied powers, was no longer feasible, the more proximate aim, destruction of the Jewish people, became the paramount goal. War aims have manifest and latent elements. The manifest aim was victory in the war, the latent aim was defeat of the internal "enemy," the Jews. The decimation and near-total destruction of the Jewish population might be considered the victory of the Third Reich in the face of the greater defeat they faced by the end of Stalingrad.

> *Three:* The Holocaust was not a case of racism, although, of course, the Nazis were racists. But they were racists because they were anti-Semites, not anti-Semites because they were racists. (The case of

the Japanese as honorary Aryans would suffice to bear this out.) Racism asserts that some human groups are inferior to others, destined to slavery. The Holocaust enacted the principle that the Jews are not of the human race at all but "vermin" to be "exterminated."

Here Fackenheim represents a considerable body of thought. But the Holocaust *was* a case of racism. It is not a question of which comes first, anti-Semitism or racism; that philosophical dilemma is secondary. Assignment of special conditions of life and work to Jews imples what racism is all about: the assumption of inferiority and superiority leading to different forms of egalitarian outcomes. Ultimately racism is not about institutionalizing inferiority and superiority, but about denial of the humanity of those involved. Jewish vis-à-vis Aryan physical characteristics were studied by German anthropologists to prove that there was such a thing as race involved. These stereotypes were the essence of European racism, as George Mosse has fully documented in a recent work. "Racism had taken the ideas about man and his world which we have attempted to analyze and directed them toward the final solution. Such concepts as middle-class virtue, heroic morality, honesty, truthfulness, and love of nation had become involved as over against the Jew; the organs of the efficient state helped to bring about the final solution; and science itself continued its corruption through racism. Above all, anthropology, which had been so deeply involved in the rise of racism, now used racism for its own end through the final solution. Anthropological studies were undertaken on the helpless inmates of the camps. Just as previously non-racist scientists became converted by the temptation to aid Nazi eugenic policies so others could not resist the temptation to use their power over life and death in order to further their anthropological or ethnographic ambitions."[11]

The fact that American racism has a clear-cut criterion based on skin color does not mean that the physical and emotional characteristics attributed to Jews were less a matter of racism than the characteristics attributed to American Blacks. To deny the racial character of the Holocaust is to reject the special bond that oppressed peoples share, the special unity that can bind Blacks and Armenians and Jews. To emphasize distinctions between peoples by arguing for the uniqueness of anti-Semitism is a profound mistake; it reduces any possibility of a unified political and human posture on the meaning of genocide or of the Holocaust. The triumphalism in death implicit in this kind of sectarianism comes close to defeating its own purpose.

> *Four:* The Holocaust was not a case of genocide although it was in response to this crime that the world invented the term. Genocide is a modern phenomenon; for the most part in ancient times human beings were considered valuable, and were carried off into slavery. The genocides of modern history spring from motives, human, if evil, such as greed, hatred, or simply blind xenophobic passion. This is true even when they masquerade under high-flown ideologies. The Nazi genocide of the Jewish people did not masquerade under an ideology. The ideology was genuinely believed. This was an "idealistic" genocide to which war aims were, therefore, sacrificed. The ideal was to rid the world of Jews as one rids oneself of lice. It was also, however, to "punish" the Jews for their "crime," and the crime in question was existence itself. Hitherto, such a charge had been directed only at devils. Jews had now become devils as well as vermin. And there is but one thing that devils and vermin have in common: neither is human.

Here Fackenheim has a problem of logical contradiction. First we are told the holocaust is not a case of genocide; and then we are reminded of the Nazi genocide of the Jewish people. But more significant is the contradiction within this framework, an inability to accept the common fate of the victims. Whether they are Japanese, Ugandans, Gypsies, Cambodians, Armenians, or Jews, their common humanity makes possible a common intellectual understanding. Insistence upon separatism, that the crime was *Jewish* existence, different from any other slaughter, whatever its roots, has a dangerous element of mystification. It represents a variation of the belief in chosenness, converting it from living God's commandments into chosenness for destruction. This approach is dangerously misanthropic. It misses the point that being chosen for life may be a unique Jewish mission, but being selected for death is common to many peoples and societies.

The description of Jews as devils was not the essence of Nazi anti-Semitism; it was only the rhetoric of Nazism. The Ayatollah Khomeini and other Iranian clerics constantly refer to American devils. The essence of the Jewish problem for Nazism was the Jew as a political actor, and beyond that, the Jew as a cosmopolitan, universalistic figure in contrast to fascist concepts based on nationalism, statism, and particularism. The Jewish tradition of social marginality, of reticence to participate in nationalistic celebrations, makes anti-Semitism a universal phenomenon as characteristic of France as of the Soviet Union. The special character of Jewish living cannot be easily converted into the special nature of Jewish dying. Dying is a universal property of many peoples, cultures, and nations.

> *Five:* The Holocaust was not an episode within the Third Reich, a footnote for historians. In all other societies, however brutal, people are *punished for doing.* In the Third Reich, "non-Aryans" were "punished" for being. In all other societies—in pretended or actual principle, if assuredly not always in practice—people are presumed innocent until proved guilty; the Nazi principle presumed everyone guilty until he had proved his "Aryan" innocence. Hence, anyone proving or even prepared to prove such innocence was implicated, however slightly and unwittingly, in the process which led to Auschwitz. The Holocaust is not an accidental by-product of the Reich but rather its inmost essence.

Response to this proposition must acknowledge the basic truths of the first part of this statement. The Holocaust was not merely a passing moment within the Third Reich. It did not occur in other fascist countries, like Italy, for example, where death itself was alien to the Italian culture; where not only the survival of Jews but the survival of communists was tolerated and even encouraged. Antonio Gramsci's major works were written in a prison that had been converted into a library by his jailers. The nature of national culture is a specific entity. The Italian people, the Turkish people, the German people all had a distinctive character. Social analysts do not discuss this kind of theme in public. It is not fashionable; we have become even a bit frightened of the concept of national character. Any notion of national character, as that advanced by Fackenheim, carries within itself the danger of stereotypical thought. But how else can we understand these phenomena? How can we understand the character of reaction, rebellion, and revolution in Turkey without understanding Turkish character, especially the continuity of that kind of character in the moral book-keeping of development.

Ascribing guilt through proving innocence fits the framework of the Nazi ideology. But to construct a general theory of historical guilt may have pernicious consequences; in which the sins of the fathers are bequeathed to the children and further offspring. That the Holocaust was an "inmost essence" makes it difficult to get beyond phylogenetic memories, beyond a situation in which a society might be viewed as having overcome its racism. When guilt is generalized, when it no longer is historically specific to social systems and political regimes, then a kind of irreducible psychologism takes intellectual command, and it becomes possible to stipulate conditions for moving beyond a genocidal state. The Holocaust becomes part of a rooted psychic unconsciousness hovering above the permanently contaminated society. To be sure, the Holocaust is the essence of the Third Reich. However such an observation is not necessarily the core question. Does the destruction of the Jews follow automatically upon a nation that is swallowed by the totalitarian temptation? In which forms of totalitarianism does a holocaust or genocide take place? Is anti-Semitism the essence of the Soviet Union as is now claimed? Does the existence of anti-Semitism prove a theory of totalitarian essence?

The uncomfortable fact is that genocide is the consequence of certain forms of unbridled state power. But whether anti-Semitism or other forms of racism are employed depends on the specific history of oppressor groups no less than oppressed peoples. States which demonstrate their power by exercising their capacity to take lives may be termed totalitarian. Totalitarianism is the essence of the genocidal process. This in itself provides an ample definition. If the Holocaust is unique to the Third Reich, the question of genocide loses any potential for being a general issue common to oppressive regimes. It is parochial to think that the Third Reich somehow uniquely embodied the character of the Holocaust, when we have seen since then many other societies adopt similar positions and policies toward other minorities and peoples.

> *Six:* The Holocaust is not part of German history alone. It includes such figures as the Grand Mufti of Jerusalem, Hajj Amin al-Husseini, who successfully urged the Nazi leaders to kill more Jews. It also includes all countries whose niggardly immigration policies prior to World War II cannot be explained in normal terms alone, such as the pressures of the Great Depression or a xenophobic tradition. Hitler

did not wish to export national socialism but only anti-Semitism. He was widely successful. He succeeded when the world thought that "the Jews" must have done *something* to arouse the treatment given them by a German government. He also succeeded when the world categorized Jews needing a refuge as "useless people." (In this category would have been Sigmund Freud had he still been in Germany rather than America; Martin Buber had he not already made his way to the Yishuv.) This was prior to the war. When the war had trapped the Jews of Nazi Europe, the railways to Auschwitz were not bombed. The Holocaust is not a parochial event. It is world-historical.

Curiously there is no mention of any other kind of history. Is, for example, the genocide of the Armenian people part of world history or is it simply part of Turkish history? This is a very complicated point; at the risk of sounding impervious to moral claims, one has to be history-specific if anything serious is to emerge. If one blames the whole world for what took place at Auschwitz, or if one wants to blame the whole world for what took place at Vin, one can construct such a theory. But it is more pertinent, more appropriate, more pointed to blame the Turks and not the universe, and to blame the Germans and not the whole world, including the Grand Mufti. The issue is implementation, not rhetoric. The issue is neither the Grand Mufti nor the insecurities of Ambassador Morgenthau.

Fackenheim's idea that Hitler neither exported national socialism nor wished to do so, represents a special reading of events. As Gideon Hausner reminds us,[12] as late as April 1945, when the Soviets were penetrating Berlin for the final assault and when Hitler was imprisoned in his bunker, his last will and testament concluded by enjoining "the government and the people to uphold the racial laws to the limit and to resist mercilessly the poisoner of all nations, international Jewry." Hausner makes it plain that national socialism was an international movement, whose lynch-pin was anti-Semitism. Fackenheim presumes World War II was all about anti-Semitism, but at a more prosaic level it was about conquest. There was a Nazi government in the Ukraine; there was a Nazi government in Norway; there was a Nazi government in Rumania; there was a Nazi government in Yugoslavia—all these regimes were exported. The idea that Hitler was not interested in exporting national socialism is curious. It would be more appropriate to note that wherever national socialism was exported, so too did anti-Semitism follow. However, in conditions where the Jewish population was not a factor, Nazism still sought to establish a political foothold; either with or without direct military aggression. The relation between national socialism as an ideology and anti-Semitism as a passion is one that the Nazis themselves were hard put to resolve. The linkage between the ideology and the passion which seems so close in retrospect, was far less articulated policy than felt need in the earlier stages of the Nazi regime.

Fackenheim slips in a subtle point that the Jews were "trapped" in Europe. But the Jews were not trapped in Europe. They were of Europe and had been of Europe for a thousand years. One of their dilemmas is one rendered in almost every history where those who are to be exploited or annihilated overidentify with their ruling masters. The Jews of Europe were entirely Europeanized. Only a small fragment remained outside the framework of Europeanization. The great divide of German and Russian Jews was participation in European nationalism; identification with enlightenment. Fackenheim's idea that the Jews were trapped in Europe is a clever misreading of the facts. The added horror of the Holocaust is that it happened to a people who were endemic to that part of the world.

> *Seven:* The Jews were no mere scapegoat in the Holocaust. It is true that they were used as such in the early stages of the movement. Thus Hitler was able to unite the "left" and "right" wings of his party by distinguishing, on the left, between "Marxist" (i.e., Jewish) and "national" (i.e., "Aryan") "socialism" and, on the right, between *Raffendes Kapital* (rapacious, i.e., Jewish capital) and *Schaffendes Kapital* (creative, i.e., "Aryan" capital). It is also true that, had the supply of Jewish victims given out, Hitler would have been forced (as he once remarked to Hermann Rauschning) to "invent" new "Jews." But it is not true that the Jew [was] . . . only a pretext for something else. So long as there were actual Jews, it was these actual Jews who were the systematic object of ferreting-out, torture, and murder. Once, at Sinai, Jews had been singled out for life and a task. Now, at Auschwitz, they were singled out for torment and death.

The difficulty with the exclusivist formula is that while Jews were singled out, so too were Gypsies, Poles, and Slavs. Hitler's appeal was to state power, not to unite Left and Right; not to unite bourgeoisie and proletariat, but to make sure that the bourgeoisie and the proletariat of Germany were purified of Jewish elements. If one considers the national aspects of the Third Reich rather that the mystical aspects of Jewish destruction it becomes a lot easier to fathom. German Jewish concentration points were in the bourgeoisie and proletariat; in leftist socialist politics and in high bourgeois economics. Liquidation of the Jew enabled the German bureaucratic state to manage the bourgeoisie and proletariat of Germany without opposition.[13] The destruction of socialism was attendant to the destruction of the Jews. Without socialist opposition, the German proletariat was an easy mark to Third Reich massification. The first two legislative acts of the Third Reich were bills on labor, on work, and on management. The liquidation of the Jewish population, within both the bourgeoisie and the proletariat, permitted the Nazis to consolidate state power. The Holocaust, from a Nazi standpoint, was an entirely rational process, scarcely a singular act of mystical divination. It was the essential feature of Nazi "domestic" policy in the final stages of the Third Reich.

> *Eight:* The Holocaust is not over and done with. Late in the war Goebbels (who, needless to say, knew all) said publicly and with every sign of conviction that, among the peoples of Europe, the Jews alone had neither sacrificed nor suffered in the war but only profited from it. As this was written, an American professor has written a book asserting that the Holocaust never happened, while other Nazis are preparing to march on Skokie, in an assault on Jewish survivors. Like the old Nazis, the new Nazis say two things at once. The Holocaust never happened; and it is necessary to finish the job.

On this point, Fackenheim is on sound ground. Still, the point that he does not make and that requires emphasis is that the Holocaust did happen and could happen again, but is now more likely to happen to peoples other than Jews or Armenians. It was more likely to happen to Ugandans, and it did; to Cambodians, and it did; to Paraguayans, and it did; to Biafrans, and it did. It is correct to say that the Holocaust is not over and done with. But it is not over and done with because there are other peoples victimized by the very model created by the Armenian and Nazi genocides.

It is important not to fit peoplehood into theories; theories must fit the realities of people. If the restoration of human dignity is to become a theme for social research, it becomes imperative to understand the unified character of genocide, the common characteristics of its victims, and ultimately the need for alliances of victims and potential victims to resist all kinds of genocide. To insist on universalism, triumphalism, or separatist orientations is self-defeating. If there is to be any political consequence of research into genocide, if the victim groups are to do more than pay for annual memorials and remembrances, an understanding of the unity needed to confront state oppression must be made paramount; otherwise little will have been accomplished and nothing will have changed.

Although my analysis has sharply demarcated theological from sociological viewpoints, it should be appreciated that Jewish religious thought is itself far from unanimous on the special nature of the Holocaust. Orthodox segments in particular have cautioned against an overly dramaturgical viewpoint, urging instead a position in which the Nazi Holocaust is but the latest monumental assault on the Jewish people; one that is neither to be ignored nor celebrated, but simply understood as part of the martyrdom of a people. In a recent essay, Helmreich has finely caught the spirit of this "strictly orthodox" view—which may be shared by larger numbers than either the mystifiers or the celebrationists may recognize.

He notes that this orthodox wing rejects paying special homage by singling out the victims of the Holocaust on both philosophical and practical grounds. "In their view, The Holocaust is not, in any fundamental way, a unique event in Jewish history, but simply the latest in a long chain of anti-Jewish persecutions that began with the destruction of the Temple and which also included the Crusades, the Spanish Inquisition, attacks on Jews led by Chmielnicki, and the hundreds of programs to which the Jewish community has been subjected to over the centuries. They do admit that the Holocaust was unique in scale and proportion but this is not considered a distinction justifying its elevation into a separate category."[14] Helmreich goes on to note that the ethical problem, in the view of orthodox believers, is the same if one Jew is murdered or if six million meet such a fate. Since Judaism is a *Gemeninschaft,* a community of fate, the sheer volume killed, while awesome, does not in itself transform a quantitative event into a unique qualitative phenomenon.

The significance of this minority theological report is to call attention to the fact that in the problem of the Holocaust, while there are some strong clerical/secular bifurcations, there are also cross-cutting patterns across disciplinary boundaries. For example, certain sociological lessons can be drawn from the Holocaust: the breakdown in egalitarian revolutions of the nineteenth century, the subtle abandonment of the Palestinian mandate after the Balfour Declaration, the lofty assertion followed by a total revocation of Jewish minority rights in the Soviet Union. For orthodoxy the Holocaust is more a function of the breakdown of Jewish solidarism than of any special evils of the German nation or the Nazi regime.

The sociological view attempts to transcend sectarian or parochial concerns and develop a cross-cultural paradigm that would permit placing the *Holocaust* into a larger perspective of *genocide* in the twentieth century—rather than see the former as entirely distinctive and the latter as some weaker form of mass murder, but of a different order of magnitude. For example, with the liquidation of roughly 40 percent of the Cambodian population, even the quantitative indicators of the Nazi Holocaust have been approached in at least one other situation. In the past, it has been argued that genocide of other peoples—Armenians, Ugandans, Paraguayan Indians—has been too random and sporadic to be termed a holocaust. It has also been claimed that atomic attacks on Hiroshima and Nagasaki were highly select and refined military targets, and not efforts at the total destruction of a people. Whatever the outcome of such contentions, the Cambodian case would indicate the risks in vesting too much intellectual capital on the sheer numbers involved—although it is clearly a factor to be contended with.

Having argued thusly, let me note that qualitative differences do exist which distinguish the Jewish Holocaust from any other forms of genocide. First, there is the systematic rather than random or sporadic nature of the Holocaust: the technological and organizational refinement of the tools of mass slaughter which ultimately reduced all morality to problems of human engineering such as the most effective methods for destroying and disposing of large numbers of people by the fewest cadres possible in the shortest amount of time. Second, there was an ideological fervor unmatched by any other previous variety of genocide. So intent were the Nazis on their policy of extermination of Jews that they dared contact other nations, especially axis powers and neutral countries, to repatriate Jews back to Germany to suffer the ultimate degradation. Third, genocide against the Jewish people represented and rested upon a national model of state power: the purification of the apparatus of repression by a total concentration of the means of destruction in a narrow military police stratum unencumbered by considerations of class, ethnicity, gender, or any other social factors affecting Nazi response to non-Jewish groups. The liquidation of plural sources of power and authority was made easier, indeed presupposed, the total liquidation of the Jewish population.

With all these inner disputations and disagreements accounted for, there are still those who—too guilt-ridden to face the monstrous consequences of the Holocaust against Jews in particular and victims of genocide as a whole—have chosen the path of evading reality. No longer an isolated voice like that of Arthur R. Butz[15] but now joined in a quasi-intellectual movement with all the paraphernalia of historical scholarship,[16] there is the beginning of a massive denial of a massive crime. Denials of gas chambers, rejection of photographic evidence, equation of indemnification of the victims with Zionist beneficiaries, are all linked to the rejection that the Holocaust ever occurred. The Nazi "revisionists" dare not speak of Nazism, but of national socialism; not of Germany under Hitlerism, but of a Third Reich. The Nazi epoch is even spoken of in remorseful terms: "Overwhelming British, American, and Soviet forces finally succeeded in crushing the military resistance of a Germany which they accorded not even the minimum of mercy."[17] Pity the poor victim!

Even the new Nazi "intelligentsia" does not deny mass murder, but only the numbers murdered.[18] It is not supposedly six million (then what number is it?). No matter, those massacred were Zionists, Communists, or a hyphenated variety of the two—Jewish-Bolsheviks—any euphemism for Jews other than the admission of a special assassination of Jews as a people. The need for exacting scholarship—the sort that has begun to emerge—with respect to all peoples victimized for their existence, is not simply a matter of litanies and recitations, but of the very retention of the historical memory itself. The scientific study of genocide is not a matter of morbid fascination or mystic divination, but of the need to assert the historical reality of collective crime. Only by such a confrontation can we at least locate moral responsibility for state crimes even if we cannot always prevent future genocides from taking place.

With all due weight given to the different traditions involved in the theological and sociological arguments concerning genocide, they do have a strong shared value commitment to the normative framework in which greater emphasis is placed on the protection of life than on that of economic systems or political regimes.[19] Both traditions are committed, insofar as their dogmas and doctrines permit, to the supreme place of life in the hierarchy of values. This is no small matter. Nazism witnessed the breakdown of religious and scientific institutions alike; and those that could not be broken down, were oftentimes simply corrupted—as in decadent and exotic notions of a Teutonic Church and the equally ludicrous belief in an Aryan Science. In the larger context of world history, in the wider picture of centuries-old barbarisms, we bear witness not to a warfare of science versus theology, but rather a shared collapse of any sort of normative structure in which either could function to enhance the quality or sanctity of life.

Treatment of the Holocaust as a dialogue between God and Golem, as ineffable and unspeakable, serves to return death to the antinomic and Manichean tradition of original sin versus original goodness; or as it is more fashionably called historical pessimism versus historical optimism. If social science is to make its own serious contribution to Holocaust studies it must move beyond the mystery of silence or the silence of mysteries. However limited the clinical analysis of collective death may be, we may at least be spared the repetition of some forms of genocide. To incorporate in the Jewish psyche the phrase "never again," requires an antecedent commitment to explain why genocide happened in the first place. Theologians must not presume an exclusive monopoly on meaning by insisting upon the mystery and irrationality of taking lives. The task of social science remains in this area as in all others, a rationalization of irrationality. Only in this way can victory be denied to Golem, and the struggle against evil be understood as a self-assigned task. This is far more uplifting than standing in silent awe at the tragedies that have befallen our century.

## Notes to Chapter 11

1.  John Vinocur, "In West Berlin: A New Curtain Rises on Auschwitz," *New York Times*, 7 April 1980, p. 2.
2.  Yehuda Bauer, *The Holocaust in Historical Perspective* (Seattle: University of Washington Press, 1978), pp. 30-49.
3.  Elie Wiesel, *Legends of Our Time* (New York: Holt, Rinehart, & Winston, 1968), p. 6. For an analysis of this vision, see Terrence Des Pres, "The Authority of Silence in Elie Wiesel's Art," in *Confronting The Holocaust: The Impact of Elie Wiesel*, ed. Alvin H. Rosenfeld and Irving Greenberg (Bloomington: Indiana University Press, 1978), pp. 49-57.
4.  Peter J. Donaldson, "In Cambodia, A Holocaust," *New York Times*, 22 April 1980, p. 17.
5.  Emil L. Fackenheim, "What the Holocaust Was Not," *Face to Face* (an interreligious Bulletin issued by the Anti-Defamation League of B'nai B'rith) 7 (Winter 1980): 8-9. This set of propositions is derived from Fackenheim's Foreword to Yehuda Bauer's *The Jewish Emergence from Powerlessness* (Toronto: University of Toronto Press, 1979).
6.  For a fuller vision of what has become the dominant and most widely respected Jewish viewpoint on the Holocaust, see Emil L. Fackenheim, *God's Presence in History* (New York: Harper Torchbooks/Harper & Row, 1972), pp. 70-73.
7.  Robert J. Lifton, "The Concept of the Survivor," in *Survivors, Victims, and Perpetrators: Essays on The Nazi Holocaust*, ed. Joel E. Dimsdale (Washington, D.C.: Hemisphere, 1980), pp. 113-26.
8.  Literature on the Armenian subjugation is uneven, and only now facing up to the herculean research tasks involved. An excellent compendium of available materials for 1915-23 is contained in Richard G. Hovannisian, *The Armenian Holocaust*, rev. ed. (Cambridge, Mass.: Armenian Heritage Press, 1980).
9.  Anna Pawelczynska, *Values and Violence in Auschwitz* (Berkeley and Los Angeles: University of California Press, 1979), pp. 101-5.
10. Raul Hilberg, "German Railroads/Jewish Souls," *Transaction/ SOCIETY* 14 (November-December 1976): 60-74. For a general introduction to this subject, see *Captured German and Related Records: A National Archives Conference*, ed. Robert Wolfe (Athens: Ohio University Press, 1974).
11. George L. Mosse, *Toward the Final Solution: A History of European Racism* (New York: Howard Fertig Publishers, 1978), pp. 226-27.
12. Gideon Hausner, "Six Million Accusers," in *The Jew in the Modern*

*World: A Documentary History,* ed. Paul R. Mendes-Flohr and Jehuda Reinharz (New York: Oxford University Press, 1980), pp. 521-23.

13. Irving Louis Horowitz, *Foundations of Political Sociology* (New York: Harper & Row, 1972), pp. 245-46. See in this connection D. L. Niewyk, *Socialist, Anti-Semite, and Jew: German Social Democracy Confronts the Problems of Anti-Semitism* (Baton Rouge: Louisiana State University Press, 1971).

14. For a full discussion of the orthodox (minority) viewpoint on the Holocaust in the context of Yeshiva life, see William Helmreich, "Understanding the Holocaust: The Yeshiva View," *Transaction/ SOCIETY* 18 (1980-81) (publication pending).

15. Arthur R. Butz, *The Hoax of the Twentieth Century* (Torrance, Calif.: Noontide Press, 1976).

16. See Austin J. App, "The 'Holocaust' Put in Perspective," *Journal of Historical Review* (Spring 1980): 43-58.

17. Charles E. Weber, "German History From a New Perspective," *Journal of Historical Review* (Spring 1980): 81-82.

18. The most authoritative estimate of the number of European Jews killed by the Nazis—5,978,000 out of a prewar population of 8,301,000, or 72 percent—is contained in Leon Poliakov and Josef Wulf (eds.), *Das Dritte Reich und die Juden: Dokumente und Aufsaetze* (Berlin: Arani-Verlag, 1955), p. 229.

19. For an articulate statement of legal and social issues at an individual level which have direct relevance to our discussion at the collective level, see George Z.F. Bereday, "The Right to Live and the Right to Die: Some Considerations of Law and Society in America," *Man and Medicine* 4 (no. 4, 1979): 233-56.

# Appendix I

# Demography of Life-Taking in the Soviet Union

The need for this appendix to *Taking Lives* is made clear when one considers that until publication of Iosif Dyadkin's *samizdat* monograph "The Evaluation of Unnatural Deaths in the Population of the U.S.S.R., 1927-1958" not a single demographic analysis of genocide in the Soviet Union has been made available in English.[1] Aside from broad generalizations, the Dyadkin study is the only one to scientifically identify the extent of "unnatural deaths" in the Soviet Union during the Stalinist epoch; and to indicate a certain amount of ambiguity must still obtain, barring some future empirical examination of government archives. One significant ambiguity in my text, relating to whether the Soviet state is genocidal, or at least has been, and the extent of such mass murder, is now firmly resolved.

Unnatural deaths in this period totaled between 43 and 52 million. The statistics do not draw distinctions between political deaths from Stalin's repression and war casualties (which could be called another kind of Soviet government failure). Mr. Dyadkin deduced that fighting, deprivation, and prison camps during World War II claimed 30 million Soviet lives; this is some 10 million more than the Soviet government acknowledges. He concluded that some 13 to 22 million died at other times from forced collectivization, the killing

213

of the "nonprogressive" classes, famine, floods, purges, and conditions at the Gulag, the Soviet acronym for the prison camp system.

Dyadkin devotes much of his paper to explaining his own methodology because, he says, it is very difficult to see what methods the official Soviet demographers used to derive their figures. He charges that their work is designed to mask the massive loss of lives caused by governmental repression. Official tables consistently omit data for 1929-1936, when repression in Russia was at its most lethal.

The main shortcoming in official Soviet data is to assume an average natural growth rate of 3.5 million at the end of the 1920s and then suddenly post a 2.5 million average for the 1930s. Since the net population growth is this natural birth rate minus the number of deaths, and this number has to be given with some accuracy, the government tried to hide the embarrassingly high number of deaths by lowering the figures for the birth rate. "It turns out, then," writes Mr. Dyadkin, "that the dynamics of the population cannot reflect forced collectivization, hunger, the Gulag, and executions. But the magnitude of the loss is so great that no official effort to conceal it can succeed."

Much of Dyadkin's work depends on his own guess at the normal rate of growth, and he recognizes how much his choice can change results. He gives his estimates in ranges, sometimes with a variation of up to 50, and makes a point of choosing the more conservative conclusion. For another unobtrusive measure, Dyadkin turns to the "question of the missing males." "At no time during the history of the U.S.S.R., including the present, did the percentage of men in the population reach the proportion that existed during the Czarist period, 1897-1913. In 1913, in spite of the Russo-Japanese War and Revolution of 1905, this proportion stood at 49.7." But subsequent troubles decimated the men. World War I and the Russian Civil War lowered the proportion by two full percentage points, so that in 1922 males were only 47.1 of the population.

Relative peace and Lenin's New Economic Policy (which tolerated private ownership) allowed a recovery; by 1926 males were up to 48.3. Under normal conditions, this ratio should have improved even further, but the years 1929-39 were far from normal; by 1939, the proportion of males had dropped back to 47.9. The real demographic disaster came during World War II, which pushed the male population below 44. Only by 1976 had it risen as high as 46.4.

The first period, 1929-36, is that of collectivization and "elimination of the classes," when Stalin took control with his version of Marxist economics. Though less famous than the subsequent Great Purge, this period was far more harrowing for the countryside. Kulaks, or the rich peasants, were exterminated wholesale with their families; whole regions suffered famines caused both by nature and the government. Mr. Dyadkin estimates deaths at more than 10 million men, women, and children. "I am afraid to present the upper limit," he adds, "but it is most probable that, according to the birth rate of 1937, and not the lowest of low birth rates for 1924-39, some 16 millon perished." In his second period, 1937-38, the Great Purge had reached its peak. Millions of Communist party members and bureaucrats were summarily sent to the Gulag for execution. Some 4.4 million, plus or minus 0.2 million died. In the third period, 1939-40, the purge continued to reach into the Red Army, which also suffered a less significant number of casualties from the Winter War with Finland. The total loss, says Mr. Dyadkin, was 1.8 million, plus or minus 0.2 million.

These last four years account for much of the missing males up to World War II. "In contrast to the years 1929-36, when men and women died equally, that during the repression years of 1937-40, mostly men were killed in labor camps and executions."

The period which obsesses most Russians is the unimaginably bloody struggle against Nazi Germany, the Great Patriotic War. The official casualty figure is 20 million, and it apparently derives from an off-the-cuff remark former Soviet premier Khruschev once made to the prime minister of Sweden. Western analysts have estimated 25 million; but Dyadkin derives a figure of 30 million, give or take a million. Of these deaths, some 20 million may have occurred in fighting. He says the rest, or 10 million, died through deprivation and the Gulag.

An accurate total is probably unattainable. "Only if we can get casualty figures for every important military operation on the Soviet and German sides," he writes, "will it be possible to answer the question: At what price did the Soviet Union achieve victory? . . . On the scale of the casualties depended the answer, was this really a victory?" This final period, 1950-54, is almost anticlimactic, but people were still dying in prison camps until the death of Stalin in 1953 brought about releases and rehabilitations. Dyadkin estimates the death at 450,000, plus or minus 150,000. This figure comes from his demographic deductions, and he works back from it to extrapolate an estimate of the total prison camp population. Assuming a high mortality rate in the camps, he puts the number of prisoners at 3 million; assuming a low mortality rate, he puts it at 6 million. The end result is awesome. In the absence of war and repression, the Soviet population would have reached 250 million by 1950, 20 years earlier than it actually did.

"Let us end on an optimistic note," Dyadkin concludes. "After the 20th Party Congress [in which Khrushchev revealed the crimes of Stalin] there is a coincidence of the general and natural mortality rates and their declining levels. We witness a slow decline of the birth rate. This shows that mass repression has basically ceased and the material level of life in our country has increased above that to which the population had become accustomed. The population has completely adapted to the existing governmental order. In this respect the new Soviet man has indeed been created. A small number of dissidents have ceased paying by their silence and forced ovations for the privilege of life outside of prison camps, and this leaves no trace in demographic tables. But here we also see positive movement. Now we know their number without the aid of demography; we even know their names."

Despite empirical evidence and social logic, there are those who insist upon clear distinctions between the Nazi experience under Hitler and the Soviet experience under Stalin. Usually, this distinction is urged on "structural" grounds, the presumed differences between national socialism and international communism. Such individuals have learned nothing from *Taking Lives,* and precious little from the actual events discussed in this book. The point is not the place of formal systems in the affairs of human beings, but the place of human beings in formal systems. In effect individuals are reduced to rubble as they confront totalitarian state power in the decision-making process. Yet, the vastness of Soviet genocidal practices does compel more precise accounting with respect to the Nazi holocaust.[2]

What is required is a second order distinction between systematic, concentrated, and scientifically planned state murder which characterizes the Nazi atrocities, over and against the more random, chaotic, almost Darwinian nature of Soviet genocide. Even if one can carefully plot the geographic locations and social dimensions of the *Gulag Archipelago,* it remains a fact that who lived and who died was largely a matter of raw physical strength, endurance, and just plain chance. The Nazi holocaust left little to chance; the populations targeted for destruction were pre-assigned, rank-ordered and biologically determined. If this is small comfort to those millions who perished it is nonetheless a real measure of difference between the Soviet and Nazi systems of rule.

The random character of Soviet genocide is tragically not simply a matter of history. The current demographic crisis of the Soviet Union—with its sharply declining life expectancy rates, increased infant mortality, declining standards of caloric intake, huge increases in alcoholism, and lowered portion of the national budget allocated to health care systems and clinics—is an example of a militarized state sacrificing all to preeminence in defense industry and armed might. It has been "taking lives" not simply as a function of Stalinist phobias, but as part of those very "structural" characteristics Marxists have urged everyone to take into account while studying Soviet society. In other words, just as the Soviet Union has exhibited a highly refined pattern of genocide but without the qualities of the holocaust which characterized Nazi Germany, so too this apparently less rapacious social system reveals a terrible endurance, sustaining itself through many regimes. No fall from power terminates it, as the fall of the Third Reich terminated the Nazi holocaust.[3]

We can see then from the study of Soviet demographic and mortality data that the questions posed in *Taking Lives* are indeed structural, not capriciously invoked by fanatic rulers, but enshrined in state systems that order priorities in such a way as to make the fulfillment of ideological goals more paramount than the prolongation of human life. Thus, as I approach the final words in my volume, we can observe more clearly the sociological foundations for further systematic analysis of the problem set for ourselves at the outset: the conditions under which those who rule consider taking away the lives of those who are ruled. The genocidal century has given new meaning to the classical search for the wellsprings of both domination and democracy.

# Notes

1. Dyadkin, Iosif. *Evaluation of Unnatural Deaths in the Population of the U.S.S.R.: 1927-1958.* Mimeograph translation by Ludmilla Thorne. Summarized by James Ring Adams, in "Revising Stalin's Legacy," *The Wall Street Journal,* July 23, 1980. A portion dealing with World War Two has also appeared in *Cahiers du Monde Russe et Soviétique.* This effort by Dyadkin has been incorporated in the recent monograph by Christopher Davis and Murray Feshbach, *Rising Infant Mortality in the USSR in the 1970s* (Washington, D.C.: United States Bureau of the Census, Series P-95, No. 74, September 1980).
2. The literature on Soviet genocide is vast and varied. In addition to the special Dyadkin manuscript, one should definitely turn to Nick Eberstadt, "The Health Crisis in the USSR," *The New York Review of Books* (February 19, 1981), pp. 23-31, which trenchantly summarizes a wide array of literature on this subject. Also see Ansley J. Coale, Barbara A. Anderson and Erna Harm, *Human Fertility in Russia Since the Nineteenth Century* (Princeton: Princeton University Press, 1978).
3. Robert Conquest, in *Kolyma: The Arctic Death Camps* (New York and London: Oxford University Press, 1978), confirms Alexandr Solzhenitsyn's impressions that more political prisoners died in a single Siberian camp in a single year under Stalin than in all the czar's jails in the nineteenth century. The extraordinary personal and autobiographical literature that has emanated from the Soviet Union in recent years confirms the more objective appraisals. See for instance, Olga Ivinskaya, *A Captive of the Time* (New York: Doubleday & Company, 1978); Lev Kopelev, *To Be Preserved Forever* (Philadelphia and New York: J.B. Lippincott, 1977); Andrei Sinyavsky, *A Voice from the Chorus* (New York: Farrar, Straus and Giroux, 1976).

# About The Author

Irving Louis Horowitz is distinguished professor of sociology and political science at Rutgers University, Hannah Arendt Chair, and director of Studies in Comparative International Development. He is also editor-in-chief of Transaction/SOCIETY, the leading multidisciplinary periodical in American social science. Before coming to Rutgers in 1969, Professor Horowitz was professor of Sociology at Washington University. He has held visiting professorships at the Universities of Stanford, Wisconsin, and California; and overseas at the London School of Economics, the University of Buenos Aires, the National University of Mexico, Queen's University in Canada, Hebrew University in Jerusalem, and most recently in Hosei and Tokyo Universities.

*Taking Lives* is a greatly expanded version of a monograph which initially appeared in 1976 under the title *Genocide: State Power and Mass Murder.* The work is conceived within the broad framework of political sociology and moral philosophy, and in this sense is part of an ongoing effort begun with *The Idea of War and Peace* (1957); *The War Game* (1963) and *Foundations of Political Sociology* (1972). His most recent books have emphasized the policy context of contemporary politics and international development. They include the classic text on comparative stratification, *Three Worlds of Development* (1965, 1971), and *Ideology and Utopia in the United States* (1977).

# Index

*Chapter 11 and Appendix I not indexed.*

25
4315\9